£7.99

STALINGRAD

THE VITAL 7 DAYS

STALINGRAD

THE VITAL 7 DAYS

WILL FOWLER

SPELLMOUNT

Staplehurst

British Library Cataloguing in Publication Data:
A catalogue record for this book is available
from the British Library

Copyright © Amber Books Ltd 2005

ISBN 1-86227-278-6

First published in the UK in 2005 by
SPELLMOUNT LTD
The Village Centre
Staplehurst
Kent TN12 0BJ

Tel: 01580 893730
Fax: 01580 893731
Email: enquiries@spellmount.com
Website: www.spellmount.com

Editorial and design by
Amber Books Ltd
Bradley's Close
74-77 White Lion Street
London N1 9PF
www.amberbooks.co.uk

Project Editor: Michal Spilling
Copy Editor: Stephen Chumbley
Design: Graham Curd
Picture Research: Natasha Jones

Printed in Italy

Contents

CHAPTER ONE

BARBAROSSA 1941

The German invasion of the Soviet Union at dawn on 22 June 1941 caught the border guards and forward infantry units by surprise – many were captured semi-clothed as they stumbled half-awake out of their barracks. German Army *Propagandakompanien* (PK) photographers caught the dazed look on their shocked faces in the watery spring light.

THE INVASION PLANS HAD BEEN DRAFTED as early as 6 December 1940 with the code-name *Fall Fritz* – Plan Fritz, but on 18 December Hitler changed the name. It now would be *Unternehmen Barbarossa* – Operation Barbarossa – after the emperor known as 'Red Beard', the hero of the Holy Roman Empire who led the Third Crusade and died en route in Asia Minor. In discussion Hitler assured his generals that 'When Barbarossa begins the World will hold its breath and say nothing'.

In June 1941 German troops, with their Romanian, Finnish, Hungarian and Italian allies, began to turn these ideas into reality, as they punched eastwards deep into the Soviet Union. The attack was split between three army groups. Army Group North, under Field Marshal Ritter von Leeb, consisted of seven divisions and three panzer divisions; Army Group Centre, under Field Marshal Fedor von Bock, 42 divisions and nine panzer divisions; and Army Group South, under Field Marshal Gerd von Rundstedt, 52 divisions of which 15 were Romanian, two Hungarian, two Italian plus five panzer divisions.

Left: A German 3.7cm Pak 36 anti-tank gun covers a crossroads on the southern sector of the Eastern Front. The Pak 36 was ruefully named the 'door knocker' by its crews because of its inability to penetrate the thick armour of the KV1 and T-34.

The army groups were supported by nine line of communications divisions and over 3000 aircraft. The Soviet forces opposite them were grouped in three army groups known as fronts – the Northwest, West and the Southwest Fronts, consisting of 158 divisions with 54 tank brigades.

However, they also had huge reserves and within six months 300 new divisions had been mobilized. In the first few days of the offensive, the *Luftwaffe* destroyed 3000 Soviet aircraft in the air and on the ground, nearly half the VVD, or Red Air Force. The tactical bombers attacked road and rail communications, destroyed headquarters and could even hit small targets like bunkers and trench lines.

Though the opening months of the war in the East were a disaster for the USSR and Stalin, geography favoured the Soviet Union. Whereas in the West the German panzer divisions were able to advance on metalled roads, and the distances between objectives like ports, airfields and cities were measured in tens or hundreds of miles, in the USSR roads that were dirt tracks linked cities that were vast distances apart.

Dust, impassable mud and snow and later extreme cold would take a toll of men and machines. Photographs showed the dusty German *Landser* – 'Squaddies' or 'Grunts', slogging through dust with their Kar 98k rifles slung over their shoulders, the dust that coated their sweat-stained tunics later turning to mud in the autumn and finally being covered in snow in the winter.

INITIAL SUCCESS

On 3 July Stalin broadcast to the people of the Soviet Union and at this low point in its fortunes assured his listeners 'History shows us that there are no invincible armies'. Since British forces were severely stretched and the United States was not a yet belligerent in World War II, Churchill

Below: PzKpfw III tanks of Panzergruppe Kleist *grind through a Russian village. The poor roads slowed down the German advance in the late summer of 1941 – later, the dust would turn into thick mud with the autumn rains.*

BLITZKRIEG

The tactics of *Blitzkrieg* served the German forces superbly in the first three years of World War II. In essence they involved launching diversionary spoiling attacks on the enemy front line as strong armoured forces – tanks and mechanized infantry – were committed to an attack on a narrow front supported by dive-bombers working like flying artillery. This was the *Schwerpunkt* (The Heavy Punch), and here a brutal assault would lead to a breakthrough that would allow these forces to stream into the vulnerable rear of the paralyzed enemy formations. Reconnaissance troops would push ahead to seize bridges and choke-points ahead of the tanks, and high-value targets would be captured by airborne forces. Tactical air support would attack enemy HQs and reinforcements or counter-attacking forces. It was a tactical concept that had been studied in Britain, France and Germany in the 1920s and 1930s, but it was the Germans in 1939 who had demonstrated its effectiveness in a speedy campaign in Poland. In France in 1940 the *Schwerpunkt* had been at Sedan and the French high command had been unable to comprehend how quickly German forces were advancing westwards to the Channel before it was too late. The tactics had been very effective in densely populated Western Europe where space could not be traded for time and where in 1939 and 1940 the concept of defence in depth had not been fully comprehended.

To describe what appeared to be a new style of warfare that contrasted dramatically with the grim struggles of World War I, the journalist Eugene Hadamovsky coined a new word. Writing in 1940 about operations in Poland in 1939 he described it as a *Blitzmarsch nach Warschau* (Lightning March to Warsaw) and from this came *Blitzkrieg* (Lightning War). The Nazi propagandists were quick to use the word and it has now passed into everyday use as a synonym for intense air attacks.

welcomed the new Communist ally in the war against Nazi Germany.

The German Army would also not be well served by Hitler who would increasingly interfere, reducing tactical flexibility and as a result causing needless casualties. Even before the operation was launched there was a conflict of views. The first plan drafted by General Marcks, chief of staff of the Eighteenth Army, envisaged a twin thrust at Moscow and Kiev, in which a huge encircling battle could be fought as the Moscow thrust swung south to link up with the Kiev axis at Kharkov.

General Halder, chief of the OKW (*Oberkommando der Wehrmacht*, the Armed Forces High Command), proposed an attack that spread the weight more equally between the north, centre and south but made Moscow the main objective. But Hitler proposed that Leningrad, 'the cradle of the Bolshevik revolution', should be the main objective and Moscow should be taken subsequently.

Optimistic German planners envisaged holding a line from Archangel in the north to Astrakhan in the south, the 'A–A line', by the onset of winter in 1941. Optimism and ignorance also featured in the assessment of the severity of

Right: German infantry rest by a road to allow a convoy of trucks to pass. Much of Operation Barbarossa was conducted at the speed of marching men and horse-drawn guns and wagons; this allowed some Soviet forces to evade complete encirclement.

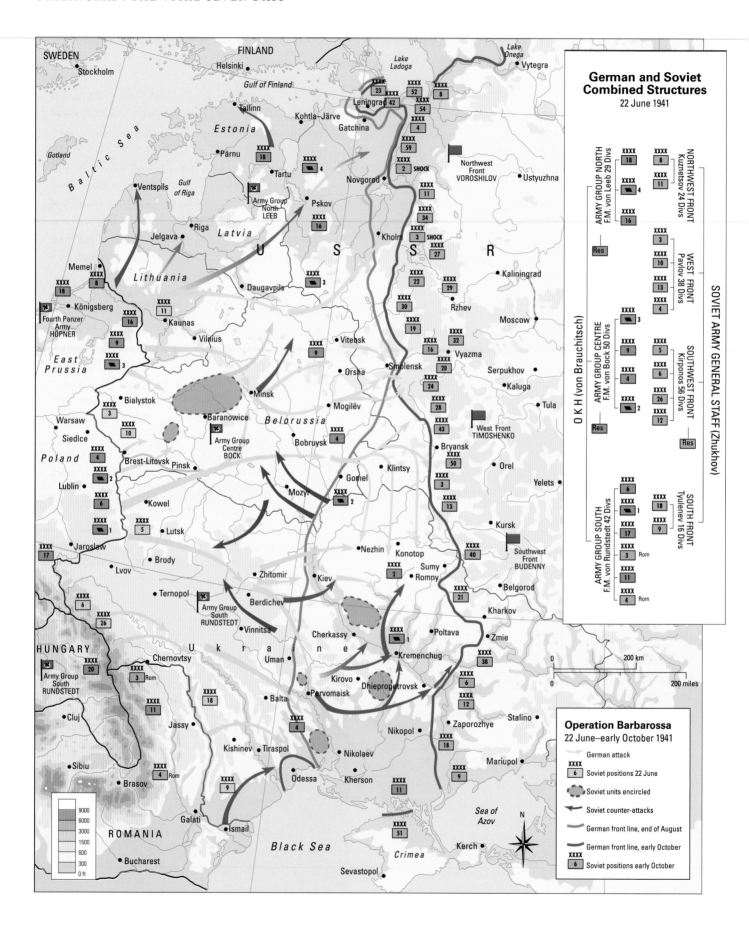

German and Soviet Combined Structures
22 June 1941

SWEDEN
Stockholm
FINLAND
Helsinki
Gulf of Finland
Lake Ladoga
Lake Onega
Vytegra
Tallinn
Estonia
Kohtla-Järve
Gatchina
Leningrad
Ustyuzha
Northwest Front VOROSHILOV
Pärnu
Tartu
Novgorod
Army Group North LEEB
Pskov
Kholm
Baltic Sea
Ventspils
Gulf of Riga
Gotland
Riga
Latvia
Daugavpils
Kaliningrad
Rzhev
Moscow
Jelgava
U S S R
Memel
Lithuania
Kaunas
Vilnius
Vitebsk
Smolensk
Serpukhov
Kaluga
Tula
East Prussia
Königsberg
Fourth Panzer Army HOPNER
Orsha
Mogilëv
Vyazma
Warsaw
Bialystok
Baranowice
Belorussia
Minsk
Bobruysk
Bryansk
Orel
Yelets
Siedlce
Army Group Centre BOCK
Gomel
Poland
Brest-Litovsk
Pinsk
Mozyr
Klintsy
Lublin
Kowel
Kursk
Jaroslaw
Lutsk
Nezhin
Konotop
Sumy
Romny
Belgorod
Lvov
Brody
Zhitomir
Kiev
Kharkov
Ternopol
Berdichev
Cherkassy
Poltava
Zmie
Army Group South RUNDSTEDT
Vinnitsa
Kremenchug
HUNGARY
Chernovtsy
Army Group South RUNDSTEDT
Uman
Kirovo
Pervomaisk
Dhiepropetrovsk
Stalino
Cluj
Jassy
Balta
Nikopol
Zaporozhye
Sibiu
Brasov
Kishinev
Tiraspol
Nikolaev
Mariupol
Romania
Odessa
Kherson
Sea of Azov
Galati
Ismail
Black Sea
Crimea
Kerch
Bucharest
Sevastopol

ARMY GROUP NORTH
F.M. von Leeb 29 Divs

NORTHWEST FRONT
Kuznetsov 24 Divs

O K H (von Brauchitsch)

SOVIET ARMY GENERAL STAFF (Zhukhov)

WEST FRONT
Pavlov 38 Divs

ARMY GROUP CENTRE
F.M. von Bock 50 Divs

SOUTHWEST FRONT
Kirponos 56 Divs

West Front TIMOSHENKO

SOUTH FRONT
Tyulenev 16 Divs

ARMY GROUP SOUTH
F.M. von Rundstedt 42 Divs

Southwest Front BUDENNY

Operation Barbarossa
22 June–early October 1941

→ German attack

Soviet positions 22 June

Soviet units encircled

← Soviet counter-attacks

German front line, end of August

German front line, early October

Soviet positions early October

9000
6000
3000
1500
600
300
0 ft

0   200 km
0   200 miles

10

ENIGMA and LUCY

The Enigma was a highly sophisticated mechanical encryption device that had a keyboard and looked superficially like a typewriter. The German engineer Arthur Scherbius developed it in 1923 from a design by Dutchman H.A. Koch; the German Army and Navy saw its potential and bought it in 1929, and later the *Luftwaffe* became enthusiastic users. The Germans firmly believed that it was completely secure. It seemed ideal for units operating in North Africa and Soviet Russia where communications relied on radio. In its simplest form, for every letter it sent there were hundreds of millions of possible solutions. However, the Germans forgot how few letters there are in the alphabet; that no letter could stand for itself; and that the machine had no number keys so that figures had to be spelled out. The Poles began deciphering signals in 1932, the French in 1938 and the British in February 1940. For the British the secrecy of the project was at such a high level that they classified it as 'Ultra Secret', and so it became ULTRA.

When Germany invaded the Soviet Union it was decided that ULTRA intelligence would be passed to the USSR via a spy ring run by the GRU (Soviet Military Intelligence) based in Switzerland with the code-name 'Lucy'. In this way it was hoped that Moscow would not realize what an invaluable intelligence resource was available to the West.

For the British Chiefs of Staff in London, following the fighting at Stalingrad and in the Caucasus, there was particular concern because of the threat that a German victory there would pose for Iran and Iraq and Western oil supplies. The intelligence came partly from *Luftwaffe* Enigma decrypts and partly from what the British military mission in Moscow could glean. Stalin assured Churchill that the Soviet Caucasus front would hold until the onset of winter. The Chiefs of Staff knew from a decrypt of a Japanese message that the Germans were greatly exaggerating the casualties that they reported they were inflicting on the Soviets.

On 7 September 1942 British intelligence read an Enigma message that confirmed that the main German effort would now be focused on Stalingrad. It became clearer with every day that passed that the outcome of the battle on the whole Soviet southern front hinged on the outcome of the fighting at Stalingrad. By 14 September the Chiefs of Staff expected the city to fall at any moment, but a week later they were confident that the Soviets would hold. By the end of the month there was real optimism throughout Whitehall with the realization that the Germans now faced a second winter in Russia on a greatly extended line against a Soviet Army that would still be capable of tying down large enemy forces.

---

the Russian winter. Men were woefully ill-equipped and in the first winter received no cold-weather uniforms while the lubricants in engines and grease in their weapons thickened and froze. In the winter of 1941–42 the German Army suffered 133,620 frostbite casualties.

German tanks and mechanized infantry in fast-moving panzer divisions outmanoeuvred the Soviet armies, cut them off and surrounded them in huge pockets, or *Kessels* (cauldrons). By 9 July 1941 the Axis advance had crossed the old 1939 Russo-Polish border, swallowed up Latvia, Lithuania and most of Estonia on the Baltic and captured Minsk where 300,000 Soviet soldiers were trapped. By 7 August von Bock's Army Group Centre had captured 850,000 prisoners. By the end of September the German

Opposite: The opening moves of Barbarossa looked like a rerun of the German victories in Western Europe. However, the huge distances, poor roads and the dogged determination of some of the Soviet defenders slowed down the onslaught and soon bad weather would bog the advance down completely.

armies had surrounded Leningrad, Odessa on the Black Sea and Sevastopol in the Crimea and held a line that ran almost due south from Lake Ladoga to the Sea of Azov. On 7 October the trap closed on 650,000 Soviet soldiers at Vyazma near Moscow. By the end of the year 12 pockets, large and small, had been encircled and neutralized in western Russia and the Ukraine.

The war against Russia will be such that it cannot be conducted in a knightly fashion. The struggle is one of ideologies and racial differences and will have to be conducted with unprecedented, unmerciful and unrelenting harshness ... The commissars are the bearers of ideologies directly opposed to [Nazism]. Therefore the commissars will be liquidated. German soldiers guilty of breaking international law ... will be excused.

Adolf Hitler

Above: A wounded Soviet soldier is moved to the rear by a German armed with an MP38 on 24 June 1941. The Germans were amazed by the huge numbers of prisoners they captured and also by the ability of the Soviet forces to sustain these losses.

By December 1941 the German forces had taken 3,350,639 prisoners in addition to the huge casualties they had inflicted on the Soviet Army. The pages of newspapers in Germany were filled with pictures of burning or wrecked vehicles and columns of tired, scruffy, starving prisoners plodding westwards. They were the *Untermenschen* (subhumans); the brutal racist name was coined by the Nazis.

Now all that remained for the German forces was a final push to capture Moscow and, in Hitler's words at the beginning of Barbarossa, to watch as 'the whole rotten structure [comes] crashing down'. The thrust that finally came to an exhausted halt on 5 December was in places actually to the east of Moscow. The tanks of General Guderian's Second *Panzerarmee* were at Mikhaylov, about 150km (93.2 miles) south and 30km (18.6 miles) east of the Soviet capital. To the north of the city the tanks of General Erich Hoepner's *Panzergruppe* IV had reached the tram stops for the outer suburbs of Moscow before they were halted by the Twentieth and Thirty-Third Armies of the Soviet West Front. On 8 December, as winter set in, the German commanders realized that they must go onto the defensive.

COUNTER-ATTACK

On 6 December the Red Army under General Georgi Zhukhov, who had already galvanized the defences of Leningrad, launched the counter-attack around Moscow. The Soviet counter-attack was ambitious, with attacks along a wide front by the Northwest Front, Kalinin Front, West Front and Southwest Front forces between 18 and 22 January. There was even an airborne landing by the 21st Parachute Brigade and 250th Airborne Regiment to the rear of the forces of German Army Group Centre facing Moscow.

The fighting lasted from December to March and in that time the German forces pulled back in some sectors as much as 500km (310.6 miles). Hitler sacked Field Marshal von Brauchitsch, the army commander-in-chief, took personal command of the army and ordered it to stand and fight. Two pockets to the north at Demyansk and Kholm held out, were kept supplied by air and were later relieved by the Sixteenth Army.

On 19 December 1941, Hitler had issued a General Order that included the words 'Every man must fight where he

MARSHAL GEORGI ZHUKHOV (1896–1974)

Georgi Zhukhov, who would become one of the finest leaders of the Soviet Army, had modest beginnings. Born near Moscow of peasant stock like many of Stalin's cronies, he had been a cavalry NCO in the Imperial Russian Army, which he entered at the age of 15. He joined the Communist Party in 1919. Unlike generals from this background like Voroshilov and Budenny, he was tough and highly competent. His nicknames with the *frontoviks* (the front-line soldiers) were 'Vinegar Face' or 'Cropped-Head'.

In September 1939 the then little-known General Zhukhov inflicted a sharp defeat on the Japanese Kwantung Army on the Halha River at Khalkin-Gol in Outer Mongolia. His skilful handling of five armoured brigades expelled the Japanese from the positions that they had captured on the Mongolian–Manchurian border. The Japanese commander, who had disobeyed orders and invaded Soviet territory, had air superiority and had assembled three infantry divisions, 180 tanks, 500 guns and 450 aircraft. The Soviets had 100,000 infantry with 498 tanks, strong artillery and 580 outclassed aircraft. Zhukhov used his infantry to hold the Japanese front and then launched his armour in a pincer attack. The Soviet losses were about 10,000 but the shaken Japanese withdrew after suffering losses of about 18,000.

For this Zhukhov received the Order of Lenin. At Leningrad he was seen as halting the German attack and so Stalin moved him to Moscow. Here poor weather, fatigue and stiffening Soviet resistance halted the attack and, using reinforcements from the Far East, Zhukhov attacked in December and remained on the offensive until March 1942. At Stalingrad he would mastermind Operation Uranus, the counter-attack that was followed by Operation Saturn that forced the Germans back to the Donets River. In January 1943 he was promoted to the rank of marshal.

At Kursk Soviet forces under his overall command halted the German attacks and then rolled onto an unstoppable offensive. In Operation Bagration in June and July 1944 he

Above: Zhukhov was one of the outstanding commanders of World War II. Unlike British or US commanders, he was less inhibited about incurring losses but was also under often under intense pressure from Stalin to deliver victory.

destroyed Army Group Centre, finally leading the First Belorussian Front to victory in Berlin in 1945.

Resentful of his popularity, Stalin banished him to command a remote military district after the war. However, following Stalin's death, Zhukhov would rise to be minister of defence in the USSR in 1953.

T-34/76 TANK

The T-34/76 had been developed secretly from the pre-war BT series of fast tanks that used the American-designed Christie suspension. It came as a shock to the Germans, who believed that Soviet tank design was crude and unsophisticated. The range of the T-34 could be further extended by topping up from two or four spare fuel drums carried on the rear decking. In the attack, infantry would ride on the rear deck, deploying from the moving tanks when they hit German positions.

Early T-34s had a two-man hexagonal all-welded turret which was cramped and lacked a radio and vision devices for the commander. The short-barrelled 76.2mm (3in) gun was soon replaced by one with a longer barrel and better anti-armour performance. It required a larger turret and this was fitted with a cupola for the commander. Though the T-34 was an excellent design, it had the added advantage that it could be mass-produced and upgraded with radio equipment and in 1944 the more powerful 85mm (3.34in) gun.

The T-34/76 had a crew of four and a 76.2mm (3in) gun plus two 7.62mm (0.3in) machine guns. Its armour ranged from 18 to 60mm (0.71 to 2.36in). It weighed 26,000kg (25.59 tons), the hull was 5.92m (19ft 5in) long, 3m (9ft 10in) wide and 2.44m (8ft) high. It was powered by a V-2-34 12-cylinder diesel engine developing 500hp that gave a road speed of 54km/h (33.5mph) and range of 300km (186.3 miles) cross-country.

From June to September 1942, the Stalingrad Tractor Factory was the main supplier of T-34s. The Kharkov Locomotive Factory was moved to the *Uralmashzavod* (Ural

Above: The T-34 was a unique tank that combined the principles of mobility, firepower and protection. Here T-34s from a unit commanded by an officer named Yakunin move through Izyum near Kharkov in January 1942.

Machine Building Plant), or URALMASH, in the Urals and merged with the Nishni Tagil auto factory. During 1942 the Ural Heavy Machinery Company in Sverdlovsk started to produce T-34s. The Ural-Kirov Tank Factory in Chelyabinsk was set up by the People's Commissariat for the Tank Industry to produce T-34s. It was later known as 'Tankograd'. There were a total of nine large tank factories: six factories produced hulls and turrets, and three produced engines.

Red Army troops called the tank '*Prinadlezhit-Chetverki*', which means '34'.

stands. No falling back where there are no prepared positions in the rear.'

The successful defence of these small pockets and the 'stand and fight' order that actually prevented the collapse of Army Group Centre would be seen by Hitler as a panacea in battles of encirclement, notably for the Sixth Army at Stalingrad a year later.

With the onset of the spring mud, the front finally stabilized. German soldiers who survived this grim period received the *Ostmedaille* – Eastern Medal. In the *Landsers'* grim slang the campaign medal was known as the *Gefrierfleischorden* – the Cold Meat Medal – or, more kindly,

the Frost Medal. The Russian writer and propagandist Ilya Ehrenburg, writing in the army newspaper *Red Star*, commented dryly on the German Army's experience of the winter of 1941–42 'The Russian winter was a surprise for the Prussian tourists'.

Opposite: Although German forces got to within 30 km (18.6 miles) of the Kremlin, they were halted by a concerted Soviet counter-offensive over the winter of 1941–42. Fresh Siberian rifle divisions were brought to the front to provide impetus for the attack. The Germans were so hard pressed that it was as much as they could do to avoid being routed.

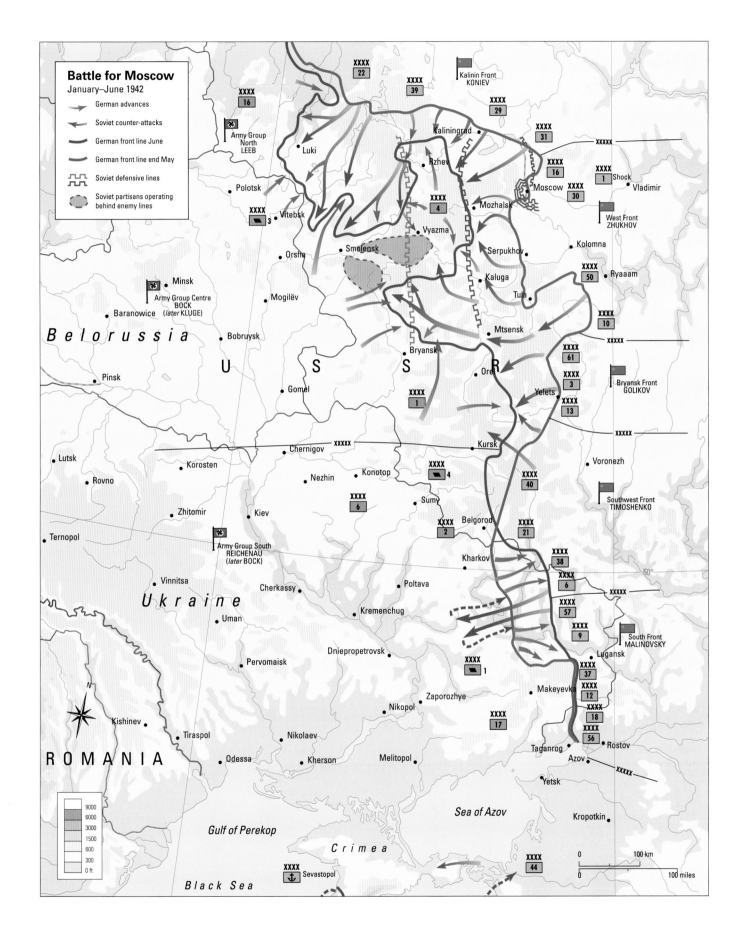

Battle for Moscow
January–June 1942

→ German advances

→ Soviet counter-attacks

German front line June

German front line end May

Soviet defensive lines

Soviet partisans operating behind enemy lines

XXXX 22

XXXX 39

Kalinin Front
KONIEV

XXXX 16

XXXX 29

XXXX 31

Kaliningrad

XXXX 16

XXXX 1 Shock

Army Group North
LEEB

Luki

Rzhev

Moscow

XXXX 30

Vladimir

Polotsk

Mozhalsk

XXXX 4

West Front
ZHUKHOV

XXXX 3 Vitebsk

Vyazma

Orsha

Smolensk

Serpukhov

Kolomna

Minsk

Army Group Centre
BOCK
(*later* KLUGE)

Mogilëv

Kaluga

Tula

XXXX 50 Ryaaam

Baranowice

Bobruysk

Mtsensk

XXXX 10

B e l o r u s s i a

XXXX 61

Pinsk

U   S   S   R

Gomel

Orel

XXXX 3

Bryansk Front
GOLIKOV

Bryansk

Yelets

XXXX 1

XXXX 13

Lutsk

Chernigov

Kursk

Voronezh

Korosten

Rovno

Nezhin

Konotop

XXXX 4

XXXX 40

Zhitomir

Kiev

XXXX 6

Sumy

Southwest Front
TIMOSHENKO

Ternopol

Belgorod

XXXX 2

XXXX 21

Army Group South
REICHENAU
(*later* BOCK)

Kharkov

XXXX 38

Vinnitsa

Cherkassy

Poltava

XXXX 6

U k r a i n e

XXXX 57

Uman

Kremenchug

XXXX 9

South Front
MALINOVSKY

Pervomaisk

Dniepropetrovsk

Lugansk

XXXX 1

XXXX 37

Zaporozhye

Makeyevka

XXXX 12

Kishinev

Nikopol

XXXX 17

XXXX 18

Tiraspol

Nikolaev

XXXX 56 Rostov

R O M A N I A

Odessa

Kherson

Melitopol

Taganrog

Azov

Yetsk

Sea of Azov

Kropotkin

Gulf of Perekop

C r i m e a

0   100 km

XXXX 44

0   100 miles

Sevastopol

Black Sea

9000
6000
3000
1500
600
300
0 ft

15

CHAPTER TWO

OPERATION BLUE 1942

Moscow had been saved. The Soviet counter-attack that pushed back Army Group Centre in 1941–42 finally ground to a halt in the mud of early spring. However, it had saved the city and made General Zhukhov, who had commanded the West Theatre, a national hero. However, the ability of the German Army to recover and re-form after defeats or withdrawals would amaze both the Soviets and the Western Allies.

IN APRIL 1942, HITLER ISSUED WAR DIRECTIVE 41, which detailed his plan for the Russian Front for summer 1942, code-named *Unternehmen Blau* – Operation Blue. The plan was to concentrate all available forces in the southern flank of the long front, destroy the front-line Soviet forces there, and then advance in two directions to the primary and secondary objectives, which were the two most important remaining industrial centres in south Russia:

1. Advance far southeast, through the mountainous Caucasus region, to capture the rich oil fields on the Caspian Sea.
2. Advance east, to Stalingrad, a major industrial and transportation centre on the west bank of the wide Volga river, the main waterway of inner Russia, which runs all the way from north of Moscow to the Caspian Sea in the south.

Significantly Hitler's directive did not order the occupation of the city of Stalingrad. The directive was 'to reach

Left: An MG34 machine gunner jumps a shallow stream as a collective farm blazes in the background. The retreating Soviet forces ruthlessly applied the principles of 'scorched earth', destroying anything that might be of value to the Germans.

Above: The spring of 1942 offered the German commanders in the East a chance to regain the initiative. Here, an infantry MG34 machine gun troop slogs past a Russian Orthodox church in the first moves of Operation Blue.

Stalingrad itself, <u>or</u> at least to cover it with heavy artillery, so that it will no longer be an industrial or transportation centre'.

FIRST BATTLE OF KHARKOV

On 8 May 1942 the re-equipped German forces launched Operation Blue. In savage fighting at Kharkov between 12 and 28 May they defeated a Soviet offensive by General Malinovsky's South Front, part of Marshal Timoshenko's Southwest Theatre, and then launched *Unternehmen Fredericus 1* against the Izyum salient and rolled eastwards. The action at Kharkov cost the Germans 20,000 men, but the Soviet losses were staggering – 214,000 men, 1200 tanks and 2000 guns were captured in a huge pocket.

On 1 June Hitler flew to the HQ of Army Group South at Poltava to discuss attacks to the south and east; he decided to split Army Group South into Groups A and B. In Berlin Dr Joseph Goebbels, the *Reichsminister für Volkserklärung und Propaganda* (Reich Minister for Public Enlightenment and Propaganda), hinted to the foreign press that Moscow would be the objective for a summer offensive.

This worked so well that when on 19 June copies of the plans for the attack on the Caucasus fell into Soviet hands they believed them authentic but were still convinced that the main attack would be on Moscow. A staff officer of the 23rd Panzer Division had been carrying the plans in a Fieseler Storch liaison aircraft and had been shot down and captured. Hitler was enraged and the commander of XL Corps, General Georg Stumme, and his chief of staff were immediately sacked and arrested. Stumme was later released, transferred to the *Afrika Korps* and died of a heart attack in October at the Second Battle of El Alamein in North Africa.

After a long siege by the Eleventh Army under General Erich von Manstein, the Black Sea naval base of Sevastopol fell on 3 July. It had been a hard fight in which Manstein had been forced to bring in reinforcements from the Seventeenth Army. It had cost the German and Romanian forces 24,000 casualties but they had taken 90,000 prisoners. Survivors of the action were awarded the 'Krim Shield', a metal sleeve shield showing a map of the Crimea. Hitler was impressed by the performance of the forces under Manstein and ordered him north to undertake the siege of Leningrad, but this prevented him crossing the Kerch Strait into the Caucasus.

For the final heave on the Eastern Front Hitler transferred to a forward headquarters in the Ukraine, code-named 'Werewolf', at Vinnitsa. At 08:15 on 16 July his entire staff flew in 16 planes to the new site. A secretary wrote soon after: 'The airfield was an imposing sight – with the great aircraft lined up ready to take off, their engines turning over, and the air filled with the deep roar of vibrating wings and wires until one after another they rolled down the runway and lifted into the air.' Three hours later they touched down at Vinnitsa. Staff cars carried them along rustic lanes to the three-cornered copse concealing Werewolf – a summer camp of log cabins and wooden huts. Here Hitler's guard commander feared only an attack by Soviet paratroopers, perhaps disguised in German uniforms, so the *Führer* found none of the concrete bunkers characterising the Wolf's Lair at Rastenburg. But the cabins were damp, the climate was humid, and the site swarmed with malaria-carrying mosquitoes.

On 17 July the Sixth Army issued a communiqué that stated 'Our units have gained ground in the east according to plan'. One PK photographer with the army wrote 'We have no more maps and can only follow the compass needle to the East…!'

ROSTOV FALLS

Following fierce street fighting, in which artillery was used at point-blank ranges, Rostov-on-Don fell on 23 July. On that day Hitler issued Directive 45 for *Unternehmen Brunswick*, the assault on the Caucasus and the oil fields of the Caspian Sea. He also instructed Army Group North to prepare for the capture of Leningrad by the beginning of September. The operation was originally code-named *Feuerzauber* – Fire Magic, and then renamed *Nordlicht* – Northern Light. Despite a series of massive assaults the city held.

Right: General Erich von Manstein studies the detail of an upcoming operation with his staff. German and Romanian forces of the Eleventh Army under Manstein captured Sevastopol on 3 July 1942.

In Moscow Stalin was enraged at the loss of Rostov. The city of the Cossacks had initially been lost to Army Group A, then commanded by Field Marshal von Rundstedt, in a direct attack by the tanks and infantry of General von Kleist's First *Panzerarmee* in November 1941. However a quick counter-attack by the Soviet Ninth and Thirty-Seventh Armies under General Timoshenko had ousted the exhausted and overstretched German forces. Von Rundstedt was ordered not to withdraw by Hitler and tendered his resignation. The action in the south had helped divert Hitler's attention from the key objective of Moscow.

For many Ukrainians and Don Cossacks the German forces entering the area in the summer of 1942 were seen as liberators from the repressive government of Stalin. They were greeted with the traditional offerings of bread and salt, while children offered flowers and women stood by the roads holding icons and crucifixes blessing the columns as they marched or drove by. All this was filmed and photographed by the Germans, making superb propaganda images.

ORDER 227

The Order of the National Commissar for the Defence of the Soviet Union.

28 July 1942, Moscow.

The enemy throws new forces to the front without regard to heavy losses and penetrates deep into the Soviet Union, seizing new regions, destroying our cities and villages, and violating, plundering and killing the Soviet population. Combat goes on in region Voronezh, near Don, in the south, and at the gates of the Northern Caucasus. The German invaders penetrate toward Stalingrad, to Volga and want at any cost to trap Kuban and the Northern Caucasus, with their oil and grain. The enemy already has captured Voroshilovgrad, Starobelsk, Rossosh, Kupyansk, Valuyki, Novochercassk, Rostov-on-Don, half Voronezh. Part of the troops of the Southern front, following the panic-mongers, have left Rostov and Novochercassk without severe resistance and without orders from Moscow, covering their banners with shame. The population of our country, who love and respect the Red Army, start to be discouraged in her, and lose faith in the Red Army, and many curse the Red Army for leaving our people under the yoke of the German oppressors, and itself running east. Some stupid people at the front calm themselves with talk that we can retreat further to the east, as we have a lot of territory, a lot of ground, a lot of population and that there will always be much bread for us. They want to justify the infamous behaviour at the front. But such talk is falsehood, helpful only to our enemies.

Each commander, Red Army soldier and political commissar should understand that our means are not limitless. The territory of the Soviet state is not a desert, but people – workers, peasants, intelligentsia, our fathers, mothers, wives, brothers, children. The territory of the USSR which the enemy has captured and aims to capture is bread and other products for the army, metal and fuel for industry, factories, plants supplying the army with arms and ammunition, railroads. After the loss of Ukraine, Belorussia, Baltic republics, Donets, and other areas we have much less territory, much less people, bread, metal, plants and factories. We have lost more than 70 million people, more than 800 million pounds of bread annually and more than 10 million tons of metal annually. Now we do not have predominance over the Germans in human reserves, in reserves of bread. To retreat further means to waste ourselves and to waste at the same time our Motherland. Therefore it is necessary to eliminate talk that we have the capability endlessly to retreat, that we have a lot of territory, that our country is great and rich, that there is a large population, and that bread always will be abundant. Such talk is false and parasitic, it weakens us and benefits the enemy, if we do not stop retreating we will be without bread, without fuel, without metal, without raw material, without factories and plants, without railroads. This leads to the conclusion, it is time to finish retreating. Not one step back! Such should now be our main slogan. It is necessary to defend each position, each meter of our territory, up to the last drop of blood, to cling for each plot of Soviet land and to defend it as long as possible. Our Motherland is experiencing hard days. We must stop, and then to throw back and smash the enemy regardless of cost.

The Germans are not so strong, as it seems to the panic-mongers. They strain their last forces. To withstand their impact now, means to ensure our victory in some months. Can we withstand the impact, and then throw back the enemy to the west? Yes we can, because our factories and plants in the rear are fine and our army receives ever more and more aircraft, tanks, artillery and mortars. What do we lack? There is no order and discipline in companies, battalions, regiments, in tank units and air squadrons. This is our main deficiency. We should establish in our army the most stringent order and solid discipline, if we want to salvage the situation, and to keep our Motherland. It is impossible to tolerate commanders and commissars permitting units to leave their positions. It is impossible to tolerate commanders and commissars who admit that some panic-mongers determined the situation on the field of combat and carried away in departure other soldiers and opened the front to the enemy. The panic-mongers and cowards should be exterminated in place. Henceforth the solid law of discipline for each commander, Red Army soldier, and commissar should be the requirement – not a single step back without order from higher command. Company, battalion, regiment and division commanders and appropriate commissars, who retreat without orders from higher commanders, are betrayers of the Motherland. These are the orders of our Motherland. To execute this order means to defend our lands, to save the Motherland, to exterminate and to conquer the hated enemy. After the winter retreat under pressure of the Red Army, when in German troops discipline became loose, the Germans for recovery of discipline imposed severe measures which resulted in quite good outcomes. They formed 100 penal companies from soldiers who were guilty of breaches of discipline because of cowardice or bewilderment, put them at dangerous sections of the front and commanded them to redeem their sins by blood. They have also formed approximately ten penal battalions from commanders guilty of breaches of discipline through cowardice or bewilderment, deprived them of their decorations, transferred them to even more dangerous sections of the front and commanded them to redeem their sins. Finally, they have formed special squads and put them behind unstable divisions and ordered them to shoot panic-mongers in case of unauthorised retreats or attempted surrender. As we know, these measures were effective, and now German troops fight better than they fought in the winter. And here is the situation, that the German troops have good discipline, though they do not have the high purpose of protection of the Motherland, and have only one extortionate purpose – to subdue another's country, and our troops have the higher purpose of protecting the abused Motherland, and do not have such discipline and so suffer defeat. Is it necessary for us to learn from our enemies, as our grandparents studied their enemies in the past and achieved victory? I think it is necessary.

***Stavka* commands:**

1. Military councils of the fronts and first of all front commanders should:

a) Unconditionally eliminate retreat moods in the troops and with a firm hand bar propaganda that we can and should retreat further east, and that such retreat will cause no harm;

b) Unconditionally remove from their posts and send to the High Command for court martial those army commanders who have allowed unauthorized troop withdrawals from occupied positions, without the order of the Front command;

c) Form within each Front from one up to three (depending on the situation) penal battalions (800 persons) where commanders and high commanders and appropriate commissars of all service arms who have been guilty of a breach of discipline due to cowardice or bewilderment will be sent, and put them on more difficult sectors of the front to give them an opportunity to redeem by blood their crimes against the Motherland.

2. Military councils of armies and first of all army commanders should:

a) Unconditionally remove from their offices corps and army commanders and commissars who have accepted troop withdrawals from occupied positions without the order of the army command, and route them to the military councils of the fronts for court martial;

b) Form within the limits of each army 3 to 5 well-armed defensive squads (up to 200 persons in each), and put them directly behind unstable divisions and require them in case of panic and scattered withdrawals of elements of the divisions to shoot in place panic-mongers and cowards and thus help the honest soldiers of the division execute their duty to the Motherland;

c) Form within the limits of each army up to ten (depending on the situation) penal companies (from 150 to 200 persons in each) where ordinary soldiers and low ranking commanders who have been guilty of a breach of discipline due to cowardice or bewilderment will be routed, and put them at difficult sectors of the army to give them an opportunity to redeem by blood their crimes against the Motherland.

3. Commanders and commissars of corps and divisions should:

a) Unconditionally remove from their posts commanders and commissars of regiments and battalions who have accepted unwarranted withdrawal of their troops without the order of the corps or division commander, take from them their orders and medals and route them to military councils of fronts for court martial;

b) Render all help and support to the defensive squads of the army in their business of strengthening order and discipline in the units.

This order is to be read in all companies, cavalry squadrons, batteries, squadrons, commands and headquarters.

The National Commissar for Defence
J. Stalin

Above: In a classic image of tank and infantry co-operation, German grenadiers hunch close to a PzKpfw III. While the tank can use its armament to engage long-range targets and enemy armour, the infantry can root out enemy infantry and anti-tank teams. Such tactics were to prove less effective in the built-up confines of Stalingrad.

On 25 July, Sixth Army, part of Army Group B under Field Marshal Fedor von Bock, commanded by the 52-year-old General Friedrich Paulus, attempted to cross the Don just west of Stalingrad, but the Soviet forces blocked these attacks. The Sixth Army commander decided to wait until the Fourth *Panzerarmee* under General Hermann Hoth was in position to drive south to assist.

On the same day William Hoffman, a German soldier with the 267th Regiment of the Sixth Army's 94th Division, noted in a diary that would eventually fall into Soviet hands:

'Today, after we'd had a bath, the company commander told us that if our future operations are as successful, we'll soon reach the Volga, take Stalingrad and then the war will inevitably soon be over. Perhaps we'll be home by Christmas.

'29 July 1942.... The company commander says the Russian troops are completely broken, and cannot hold out any longer. To reach the Volga and take Stalingrad is not so difficult for us. The *Führer* knows where the Russians' weak point is. Victory is not far away....'

His diary is a remarkable record that begins with almost arrogant optimism and descends through anger and disbelief to despair:

'2 August.... What great spaces the Soviets occupy, what rich fields there are to be had here after the war's over! Only let's get it over with quickly. I believe that the *Führer* will carry the thing through to a successful end!

'10 August.... The *Führer's* orders were read out to us. He expects victory of us. We are all convinced that they can't stop us.'

On the same day that Hoffman wrote his diary Army Group A, supported by the bombers of General Wolfram von Richthofen's *Luftflotte* IV, crossed the Don and reconnaissance units reached the outer defences of the industrial city of Stalingrad.

FIELD MARSHAL FRIEDRICH VON PAULUS (1890–1957)

Friedrich von Paulus was born in Breitenau, Melsungen District, on 23 September 1890. His family was not aristocratic and the title 'von' was only given to him by Allied propaganda. A career soldier, he served in World War I as adjutant of an infantry battalion. In 1915 he was assigned to the staff of the 2nd Prussian Regiment and two years later to the operations staff of the Alpine Corps. During the war he served on both the Eastern Front and the Western Front. Paulus remained in the army after the war and was appointed adjutant to the 14th Infantry Regiment at Konstanz. In 1922, he was given general staff training and the following year joined Army Group 2 at Kassel. From 1924 to 1927, he was a General Staff officer with *Wehrkreis* V at Stuttgart. One senior officer commented that Paulus was 'A typical Staff officer of the old school. Tall, and in outward appearance painstakingly well-groomed. Modest, perhaps too modest, amiable, with extremely courteous manners, and a good comrade, anxious not to offend anyone. Exceptionally talented and interested in military matters, and a meticulous desk worker, with a passion for war-games and formulating plans on the map-board or sand-table. At this he displays considerable talent, considering every decision at length and with careful deliberation before giving the appropriate orders.' Paulus had a strange fixation for a soldier. He despised dirt, bathing and changing uniforms several times a day, even on the rare occasions he ventured into the field.

He continued to be promoted and in 1930 he became a tactics instructor with the 5th Infantry Division. In 1934, Paulus was promoted to the rank of lieutenant-colonel and appointed commander of Motor Transport Section 3. In September 1935, he succeeded Heinz Guderian as chief of staff to the commander of Germany's Mechanized Forces. Considered to be an expert on motorized warfare, Paulus was promoted to major-general and became director of training for Germany's four light divisions in 1939. This included two motorized infantry regiments, a reconnaissance regiment and a motorized artillery regiment.

Just before the outbreak of World War II, Paulus became chief of staff of the Tenth Army. Serving under General Walther von Reichenau, Paulus took part in the invasion of Poland in September 1939. This was followed by the Western Offensive in Belgium and France. He was given command of the Sixth Army in 1942 and tasked with the capture of Stalingrad.

After the Sixth Army had been encircled he was promoted to field marshal on 31 January 1943 but surrendered with the remnants of the Sixth Army in February. On the night of 12/13 June 1943 at Krasnoyarsk near Moscow the *Nationalkomitee Freies Deutschland* (National Committee for a Free Germany), an anti-Nazi group composed of captured senior officers headed by Paulus, was set up under the control of the GRU, the Soviet Military Intelligence Service. It included German Communists like Walter Ulbricht who would play a major part in the establishment of the German Democratic Republic (DDR; Communist East Germany) after the war. The League of German Officers (BDO) contained many veterans of the Sixth Army and along with the *Nationalkomitee Freies Deutschland* worked to foment disaffection in front-line troops and officers. Paulus never saw his wife, a woman of the Romanian nobility, Elena Rosetti-Solescu, again. She was imprisoned by the Nazis and released by US forces at the end of the war. Paulus was released in 1953 and died in Dresden in East Germany after a long illness in 1957.

Above: Field Marshal Paulus is one of the classic examples of a man promoted beyond his ability. An able and diligent staff officer he lacked the confidence to disobey Hitler and save the Sixth Army from destruction in November 1942.

Above: A Russian girl welds steel girders to construct a 'Czech hedgehog' anti-tank obstacle. The Soviet Union mobilized not only women but even boys who were too young for military service to work in the munitions factories.

THE CITY OF STALINGRAD

Stalingrad had been built as a 'model' city in the 1920s and 1930s and included parkland and solid public buildings. It was as young as the Soviet epoch, having been rebuilt almost entirely after the Civil War on the site of a sixteenth-century fortress and trading post named Tsaritsyn, built to defend the southern border of the Russian Empire. This name (in Tartar) was given to the town because it is situated where the river Tsaritsa meets the river Volga. The city was renamed Stalingrad in 1925 because of Stalin's leadership in 1918 during the Civil War, which was supposed to have been decisive in the fighting with White Guard forces. The new name was a typical example of how Stalin was retrospectively given a much larger role in the Revolution than he had actually played. The city was renamed Volgograd in 1961 as part of Nikita Khrushchev's attempt to liberalize the Soviet Union after Stalin's death.

In the 1920s and 1930s 7000 *Komsomols* – members of the Communist Union of Youth – did much of the physical labour at Stalingrad that raised the enormous *Stalingradsky* Tractor Factory (STZ), one of the largest tractor plants west of the Urals, which produced heavy tracked tractors for the new collective farms of the Ukraine. Other newly built factories in Stalingrad and several new trade schools attracted young people from all over the USSR.

The 500,000 citizens of Stalingrad were young in their ideas as well as their Communist ideals. Scores of American engineers and architects were brought in to advise on the construction of the industrial complexes. Young women, who dressed and laboured like men within the factories, made regular visits to beauty parlours for manicures and perms. Trucks fitted out as mobile soda fountains toured the city, and at dances Russian couples performed a step known as the Boston. Everything in Stalingrad worked astonishingly well, even the various Five Year Plans. Workers' apartments were erected on schedule.

Machine shops, steel plants, textile mills, shipyards on the Volga and great collective farms in the surrounding country-side poured high-quality products into the Soviet economy. Yet the citizens of Stalingrad had time for musical and the-atrical events at a giant opera house, and for civic-minded volunteer work.

The city stretched along the west bank of the Volga and consisted of two distinct districts. To the north were workers' apartments and the *Stalingradsky* (or Dzerzhinsky), *Barrikady* and *Krasny Oktyabr* Tractor Factories. The Lazur

Below: Soviet infantry with the most basic equipment – Mosin Nagant rifle, rolled greatcoat and pilotka *side hat – take cover behind the smoking remains of farm buildings. At some stages in the fighting in Stalingrad soldiers went into action with no rifles – they were told to pick up weapons from fallen comrades.*

chemical plant was in the centre of a circular railway layout that was nicknamed 'the Tennis Racket' by German aircrews. Each factory had its own schools, parks and housing devel-opment and shops. The railway links ran along the east shore of the Volga through Station No 1 and No 2 in the south of the city. Close to Station No 2 were the towering concrete cylinders of the Grain Elevator.

In the centre the city was dominated by a 103m (334.6ft) high hill that had been a Tartar burial ground and was a popular haunt for courting couples before the war and which divided the southern district from the north. On Soviet military maps it was simply designated as Hill 103. The feature known as the Mamayev Kurgan (literally the Hill of Mamay), named after a medieval commander of the Tartar Golden Horde, commanded a view of central Stalingrad and the surrounding steppe. To the south was the

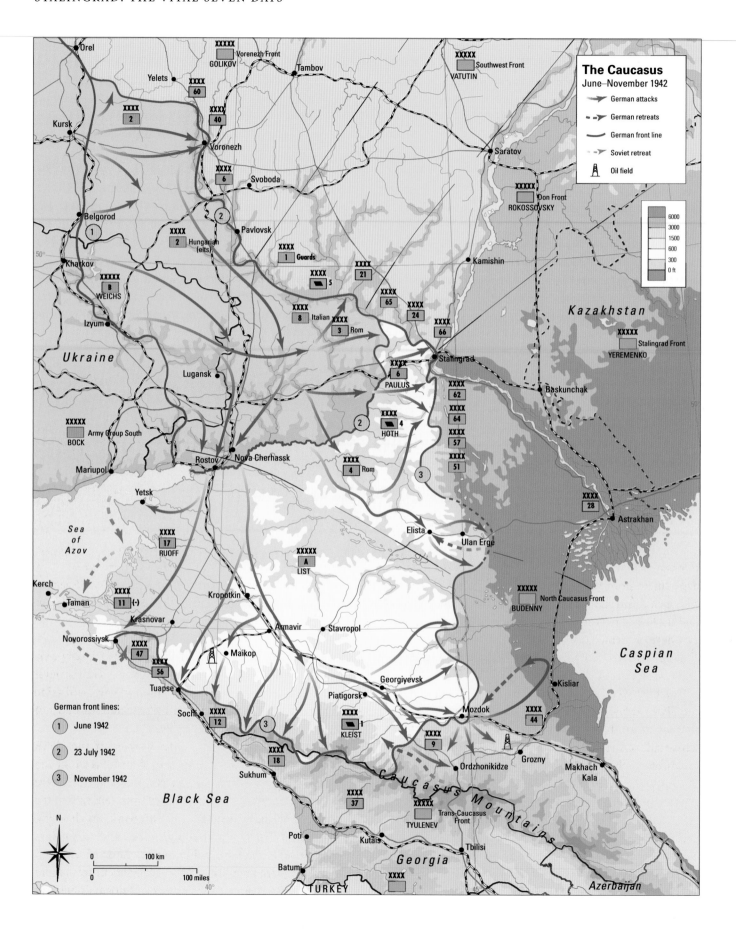

The Caucasus
June–November 1942

→ German attacks

--→ German retreats

— German front line

--→ Soviet retreat

⛏ Oil field

6000
3000
1500
600
300
0 ft

German front lines:

① June 1942

② 23 July 1942

③ November 1942

Orel
Yelets
XXXXX GOLIKOV Vorenezh Front
XXXX 60
Tambov
XXXXX VATUTIN Southwest Front
XXXX 2
Kursk
XXXX 40
Voronezh
Saratov
Belgorod
XXXX 6
Svoboda
② 2
Pavlovsk
XXXXX ROKOSSOVSKY Don Front
Kharkov
① 1
XXXX 2 Hungarian (elts)
Kamishin
XXXXX WEICHS B
XXXX 1 Guards
XXXX 21
Izyum
XXXX 8 Italian
XXXX 5
XXXX 3 Rom
XXXX 65
XXXX 24
Kazakhstan
XXXX 66
Ukraine
Lugansk
Stalingrad
XXXXX YEREMENKO Stalingrad Front
XXXX 6 PAULUS
XXXX 62
Baskunchak
XXXX 64
② 2
XXXX 4 HOTH
XXXX 57
XXXXX BOCK Army Group South
XXXX 51
Rostov
Nova Cherhassk
XXXX 4 Rom
③ 3
Mariupol
XXXX 28
Yetsk
Astrakhan
Sea of Azov
XXXX 17 RUOFF
Elista
Ulan Erge
Kerch
XXXXX LIST A
Taman
XXXX 11 (-)
Krasnovar
Kropotkin
XXXXX BUDENNY North Caucasus Front
Novorossiysk
Armavir
Stavropol
Caspian Sea
XXXX 47
Maikop
XXXX 56
Georgiyevsk
Kisliar
Tuapse
Piatigorsk
Mozdok
XXXX 44
Sochi
XXXX 12
③ 3
XXXX 1 KLEIST
Grozny
XXXX 18
Ordzhonikidze
Makhach Kala
Sukhum
XXXX 9
Black Sea
XXXX 37
XXXXX TYULENEV Trans-Caucasus Front
Caucasus Mountains
N
Poti
Kutais
Tbilisi
0 100 km
0 100 miles
Batumi
Georgia
Azerbaijan
TURKEY
XXXX

city centre that included the towering pillared *Univermag* department store, the Gorky theatre and the formal gardens, wide paths and statues of the Square of the Fallen Fighters that the Germans would name Red Square. Across the river a new development, Krasnaya Sloboda, was connected by ferries that delivered workers to landing stages along the shore in the southern part of the city.

The river Volga, which would prove an effective barrier to the Sixth Army, was fed by a number of small tributary streams around Stalingrad. They had cut deep into the steppe soil and underlying sandstone and formed gullies, or *balkas*, of which the Tsaritsa and Krutoy in the southern part of the city would prove invaluable access points for Soviet reinforcements and stores that were landed from ferries. The

Opposite: At the high point in November 1942, the outer limits of the Nazi empire reached as far as the oil wells of Maikop and the highest peaks of the Caucasus. However, in attempting to capture Stalingrad and the oil fields the Germans had overreached themselves.

Above: The snow-covered mountains of the Caucasus provide a dramatic backdrop to a German tank crew from Army Group South. In the propaganda magazines published in Occupied Europe these pictures made German forces look invincible.

Soviet logistics system at Stalingrad would be brutally simple. The priorities were men and ammunition, since survival rates in the fighting could be measured in days, and aside from vodka and tobacco, rations, which included carcasses of sheep and dry goods, took third place.

Movement westwards from the interior of the USSR started by train, escorted by anti-aircraft armoured trains to provide cover against *Luftwaffe* attacks. Men and stores were then offloaded into trucks, or marched from railheads to the suburbs of Krasnaya Sloboda on the left bank, which were a holding area. Then, mostly at night, men and stores were moved down to the ferry points and transported across to the landing stage near Station No 1. Movement from there was along the *balkas* or via the sewers and storm drains that emptied into the Volga. The sewers would also be used for concentrating troops for local counter-attacks.

THE BATTLE BEGINS

On 12 August 1942 the British Prime Minister Winston Churchill flew in to Moscow for four days of talks with Stalin. Churchill outlined the plans for Operation Torch, the Allied landings in North Africa, and longer-term plans for a second front in Europe. However, with German forces driving towards the southern oil fields and Stalingrad, Stalin demanded more immediate intervention.

His fears seemed justified, for on 24 August Sixth Army, part of Army Group A under List, reached Stalingrad on the Volga. To the south the summer offensive would have extended to its furthest limits by 18 November. Army Group A reached the burning or demolished oil wells of Maikop on 9 August and then was into the Caucasus and within 140km (86.9 miles) of Grozny. The Germans set to work rebuilding the refineries. Though they lacked oil exploration equipment like drills, 40 experts were sent to Maikop to resolve the problems. They were housed in a large barrack block with German guards, but in a night attack Soviet partisans broke in and cut the throats of the sleeping technicians. When the drilling equipment was finally ready, it was held up in the overtaxed railway system and failed to reach Maikop before Soviet forces recaptured the town. A city that had been producing two million tons of oil annually only generated 70 barrels a day for the Germans. The German forces were conquering territory, but were no longer rounding up huge numbers of prisoners. Photographs showed German tank crews with the snow-clad Caucasus on the horizon. They reached the foothills of the mountains on 15 August. Eight days later a *Gebirgsjäger* expedition led by *Leutnant* Spindler, a Knight's Cross holder, accompanied by PK photographer Kintscher and a film crew, even climbed the 5641m (18,510ft) high Mount El'brus in the Caucasus, and planted the Swastika flag on the highest mountain in Europe.

In 1942 the map of Europe and North Africa was coloured red to denote either an ally or a conquest of the Third Reich, with the only exceptions being Sweden, Spain, Portugal, Switzerland, and of course Britain. It was a powerful and beguiling image, but it was soon to change. The day the Swastika flew over the Caucasus was almost the high-water mark of German conquests. This would be reached on 2 November, when the tanks of von Kleist's First *Panzearmee* halted 8km (5 miles) west of Ordzhonikidze in the Caucasus Mountains.

WAR OF ANNIHILATION

In June 1942 *SS-Reichsführer* Heinrich Himmler, talking to *SS* leaders, had explained that this was a 'war of annihilation [*Vernichtungskampf*]'. Two 'races and peoples' were locked in 'unconditional' combat; on the one side 'this brute matter, this mass, these primeval men, or better these subhumans [*Untermenschen*], led by Commissars'; on the other, 'we Germans'. Despite this brutal approach and the loss of tens of thousands of men and vast areas of the USSR, the pressure on the Soviet Union was so severe that secret contacts had even been made with Germany to explore the possibility of calling a cease-fire to be followed by peace negotiations.

OCCUPIED UKRAINE

The German-occupied Ukraine was split into three sectors of which the bulk (the *Reichskommissariat Ukraine*) came under the administration of *Gauleiter* Erich Koch. Koch, a fanatical Nazi and a crude individual, described himself as a 'brutal dog'. His task was, he said 'to suck from Ukraine all the goods we can get hold of, without consideration for the feelings or the property of the Ukrainians'. Koch declared 'if I find a Ukrainian who is worthy of sitting at the same table with me, I must have him shot'. He closed schools on the grounds that Russians did not need education and deported many thousands to Western Europe as slave labourers.

Koch, with his toothbrush moustache and brown uniform with red armband, was the most extreme example of the *Goldfasan*, the 'Golden Pheasants', as front-line soldiers nicknamed the party administrators in the East. His brutality was so extreme that it even provoked opposition from the *Waffen-SS*.

The Ukraine suffered particularly harshly in World War II. For every village like Oradour in France or Lidice in Czechoslovakia that was destroyed, some 250 villages with their inhabitants suffered a similar fate in the Ukraine. Over 16,000 industrial plants and 28,000 collective farms were destroyed and direct material damage constituted over 40 per cent of the USSR's wartime losses.

By the end of the war, starvation, executions and death in combat had killed over seven million Ukrainians.

Stalin was on record as saying 'In war I would deal with the Devil and his grandmother.'

Progress had been slow as the Sixth Army under Paulus advanced toward Stalingrad with 250,000 men, 500 tanks, 7000 guns and mortars, and 25,000 horses because fuel was rationed and Army Group A was given priority. At the end of July 1942, a lack of fuel brought Paulus to a halt at Kalach. It was not until 7 August that he had received the supplies needed to continue with his advance.

Over the next few weeks his troops killed or captured 50,000 Soviet troops but on 18 August, Paulus, now only 56km (35 miles) from Stalingrad, ran out of fuel again. Paulus began to attack the outer defences of Stalingrad on 19 August, but Hoth had still not joined him as his forces were held north of Tinguta. Advancing German tanks fired at an anti-aircraft battery crewed by young female volunteers. These girls had recently graduated from colleges and

Above: With Soviet prisoners huddled behind them, German infantry take cover in a ditch. Prisoners were often used to carry boxes of machine gun ammunition and later many were incorporated into the German Army as volunteer helpers, or 'Hiwis'.

institutes and had no practice in firing guns and no one had trained them to engage ground targets. Though there was an acute shortage of shells the girls put up a fierce defence. They furiously turned the wheels to depress the barrels to take aim at the tanks. But the German tank crews quickly overcame their surprise and launched attacks. Some time later the resistance put up by the young artillerists was suppressed.

The battery commander, Captain Sarkisyan, watched the unequal battle in agony. Every time the crews stopped firing he exclaimed 'Everything is finished, none of them are alive! They have been wiped off the face of the earth!' But after a short break they again and again returned fire. Writer Vasily

HERMANN HOTH (1891–1971)

Hermann Hoth, the son of an army medical officer, was born in Neuruppen, Germany, on 12 April 1891. He joined the German Army and served throughout World War I. Hoth remained in the army and in 1935 was given command of Germany's 18th Division at Liegnitz. Promoted to lieutenant-general he was appointed head of XV Motorized Corps on 10 November 1938, and the following year took part in the invasion of Poland.

During the Western Offensive Hoth drove through the Ardennes to the Channel before entering Normandy and Brittany. His success resulted in him being promoted to general on 19 July 1940.

Hoth was head of *Panzergruppe* III during Operation Barbarossa. He captured Minsk and Vitebsk before heading for Moscow. In October 1941, Hoth was sent to command the Seventeenth Army in the Ukraine. The Red Army counter-attacked in January 1942, and Hoth was driven back.

In June 1942, Hoth succeeded Erich Hoepner as head of the Fourth *Panzerarmee* and was involved in the siege of Stalingrad. He also took part in the battle of Kursk in July 1943, but was forced to withdraw to better defensive positions. Adolf Hitler recalled Hoth to Germany in November 1943 and for the rest of the war he joined the reserve.

After the war Hoth was arrested and charged with war crimes at Nuremberg. Found guilty, he was sentenced on 27 October 1948 to 15 years in prison. Released after six years he retired and wrote books about military history. He died in 1971.

Opposite: In a lethal game of hide and seek, a German MG34 machine gun crew move cautiously through a field of sun flowers under the shadow of the Caucasus Mountains. The NCO in the background, in command of the gun team, holds an MP38/40 submachine gun.

Grossman later wrote 'This was the first page of the chronicle of the Stalingrad battle'.

A day later, thousands of kilometres to the west, Operation Jubilee, an amphibious raid by the Canadian 2nd Division on the French port of Dieppe, would have implications for the battle for Stalingrad that at the time no one could foresee. The raid was a disaster, the Canadians suffering heavy losses, but it made the OKW nervous. Fearing more ambitious attacks, the Germans retained troops in France that could have been deployed in Russia – crucially in the winter attacks of 1942.

We are advancing toward Stalingrad along the railway line. Yesterday Russian 'katyushi' [multiple rocket launchers] and then tanks halted our regiment. 'The Russians are throwing in their last forces,' Captain Werner explained to me. Large-scale help is coming up for us, and the Russians will be beaten. This morning outstanding soldiers were presented with decorations.... Will I really go back to Elsa without a decoration? I believe that for Stalingrad the *Führer* will decorate even me.

William Hoffmann, 12 August 1942

On 22 August, however, all was going well for the Germans as the XIV Panzer Corps broke through the outer defences of the Soviet Sixty-Second Army around Stalingrad. The terrain was ideal for armoured warfare with little cover and good visibility but in the factories and sewers of Stalingrad this advantage would disappear. The Sixth Army would lose the advantage of mobility and firepower and become bogged down in grinding street fighting. In the city territorial gains that had been measured in hundreds of kilometres would be reduced to streets, buildings and even rooms. But the Sixth Army would persist since capture of Stalingrad would give the Germans control of the Volga River, access to Astrakhan and the supply of petroleum from the south.

Right: If well led, Romanian infantry were formidable combatants as they had demonstrated at Sevastopol. However, their equipment was poor and leadership often terrible; under the pressure of Soviet attacks they would crumble in November 1942.

CHAPTER THREE

THE ASSAULT BEGINS

On 23 August 1942 the spearhead of the Sixth Army reached the Volga just north of Stalingrad and captured an 8km (5 mile) wide strip along the river bank, and the German tanks and artillery began to fire on shipping. On the same day, other units of the Sixth Army reached the outskirts of Stalingrad, and at 18:00 hundreds of bombers and dive-bombers of *Luftflotte* IV began heavy attacks on the city; the attacks would continue daily for weeks, destroying or damaging every building in Stalingrad.

MARSHAL A. YEREMENKO, COMMANDER-IN-CHIEF of the Stalingrad Front, remembered that opening day: 'We'd been through a lot in the war up to that time, but what we saw in Stalingrad on 23 August was like a nightmare. Bombs were exploding all round us and the sky was filled with columns of fiery smoke. Near the oil-storage tanks [they were situated on the banks of the Volga, north of the town centre], huge sheets of flame stabbed the sky, deluging the ground with a sea of fire and acrid fumes. Torrents of burning oil and petrol flowed on the Volga till its surface was a river of fire. Boats in the river were ablaze, asphalt on the streets emitted choking fumes and telegraph poles flared up like matches. The earth of Stalingrad was crumpled and blackened. The city seemed to have been struck by a terrible hurricane, which whirled it into the air, showering the streets and squares with rubble. The air was hot, stifling and filled with acrid fumes which made breathing difficult.'

Left: Smoke rises from the burning fuel tanks close to the Volga as a German machine gun team approach through the Stalingrad suburbs. Workers' flats that would be defended as strong points stand out among the single-storey wooden houses.

GENERAL WOLFRAM FREIHERR VON RICHTHOFEN (1895–1945)

Born on 10 October 1895 Wolfram von Richthofen was a cousin of Manfred von Richthofen, the World War I fighter ace known as the 'Red Baron' who commanded the 'Flying Circus' of which Wolfram was a junior member. After the war he studied engineering, but returned to the Army in 1923. In 1936 he served as chief of staff to *General* Hugo Sperrle and

Above: The tough opinionated General von Richthofen whose Stukas would support the Sixth Army. He would be a harsh critic of Paulus and the tactics he employed in the street fighting at Stalingrad.

Generallmajor Helmuth Volkmann, the commanders of the Condor Legion in Spain. As an *Oberst*, von Richthofen was the final commander of the Condor Legion in 1938. In the campaign in Poland, Junkers Ju 87 Stuka dive-bombers under his command demonstrated their effectiveness in ground attack operations. In the campaigns in France, the Balkans and USSR von Richthofen commanded the VIII *Fliegerkorps* that became 'flying artillery', providing very efficient close support for the armoured formations. It consisted of three squadrons of Stukas and reconnaissance aircraft. During the Battle of Britain, the *Fliegerkorps* established its HQ at Deauville, but suffered heavy casualties over Britain. In June 1942 von Richthofen became commander of *Luftflotte* IV on the Eastern Front where he worked very effectively with von Manstein in the attack on the fortified Soviet naval base at Sevastopol. In 1943 he took command of *Luftflotte* II in Italy.

Richthofen routinely circled over battlefields at low altitude, monitoring progress on the ground and sending radio instructions back to his headquarters. Sometimes Richthofen was very lucky to survive these daring flights; Soviet flak gunners filled his plane with red-hot shrapnel. He was the target not only of Soviet gunners, but, with distressing frequency, also of German gunners.

For instance, while inspecting Axis positions on the Eastern Front on 25 June 1942, troops of the German 387th Infantry Division mistakenly opened fire on his little aircraft, wounding his co-pilot, puncturing the fuel tank and filling his plane with holes. After making an emergency landing, he sent the commander of the division involved a sarcastic letter 'thanking' his men for their efforts. His diary entry for that day was far more blunt. Well aware that he'd escaped death by the closest shave, he angrily scrawled: 'Damned dogs! They don't fire at the Russians, but at our Storch!'

A brain tumour ended his military career in October 1944 and he died at Lüneburg on 12 July 1945.

During the afternoon Hube's Sixth Army panzers started driving into the city from the north. Simultaneously, another force from Fourth *Panzerarmee* drove in from the south. Hube's tanks overran the Soviet defences with their usual speed and efficiency. Yeremenko received reports of the German attacks. His defence was built around the Sixty-Second and Fourth Tank Armies – though the latter had no tanks. Yeremenko alerted his reserve, the 10th NKVD

Division. By 08:00 the following day Panzers were clearly heading for the city, with heavy fighting at Malaya Rossoshka. Russian pilots reported everything on the ground was burning, and two columns each of 100 German tanks, followed by motorized infantry, were heading for Stalingrad with massive close air support.

Yeremenko scrambled all his fighters at once and ordered his light bombers to harass Hube's column. While he was

> Stalingrad was drowned by the misty flames, surrounded by smoke and soot. The entire city was burning. Huge clouds of smoke and fire rose up above the factories. The oil reservoirs appeared to be volcanoes throwing up their lava. Hundreds of thousands of peaceable inhabitants perished. One's heart got caught in one's throat in compassion for the innocent victims of the fascists.
>
> *Marshal A. Yeremenko, Commander-in-Chief of the Stalingrad Front*

grappling with this changing situation Yeremenko's *zampolit* (political officer), Nikita Khrushchev, phoned from his quarters:

'What's new?'

'Not specially pleasant news.'

'I'll come to HQ at once.'

Breakfast arrived but was ignored. German tanks were so close to Stalingrad's anti-aircraft gun batteries that the sound-locator operators could hear the squeal of their tracks. Yeremenko ordered the weakened remnants of two

tank corps to block the German advance. Between them the two corps had 50 T-70 light tanks.

The 10th NKVD Division and the two tank corps dug in around the Tractor Factory, using the ruins to good advantage. German tanks and armoured vehicles could not manoeuvre through rubble-filled streets, bomb craters and ruined buildings. The fighting increased in intensity amid the destruction. Hube's tanks tore through improvised defences and AA guns, some manned by female workers of the *Barrikady* Factory. By 11:00 Khrushchev had mobilized Stalingrad's Communist Party organizations for the defence. Yeremenko, who still had not eaten, remained calm. Major-General Korshunov telephoned to say that a trainload of ammunition, food, and reinforcements had been shot up by the Germans.

'Enemy tanks are moving on Stalingrad. What are we to do?' Korshunov pleaded.

Below: PzKpfw IV tanks drive along a street of burned-out buildings. The German tanks are stacked with fuel containers to reduce the dependency on the sometimes erratic logistic chain following behind.

'Your duty. Stop panicking,' Yeremenko snapped back.

The Fourth *Panzerarmee* captured Tinguta station by noon and the siding at the 74-kilometre marker. They surrounded 38th Rifle Division, but elsewhere the German attacks were beaten off. Yeremenko scraped up the 56th Tank Brigade to counter-attack. Orderlies produced lunch, but Yeremenko had no time to eat. Bad news continued. German troops of Sixth Army annihilated a regiment of the 87th Rifle Division north of Malaya Rossoshka. Yeremenko started to dig into his reserves, which included T-34 tanks being built at the Tractor Factory that rolled out into action unpainted from the production lines. In August, as the Tractor Factory came under fire, the workers continued to build tanks, producing 400 up to September. After that they concentrated on repairing battle-damaged vehicles and even organized an independent 'Repair Brigade' that scoured the battlefield for parts that could be cannibalized from wrecked vehicles. The brigade was later incorporated into the Sixty-Second Army.

By now, however, the defenders at the Tractor Factory could see the approaching enemy force of 2000 men backed by 30 tanks.

Major-General Feklenko called Yeremenko to report 'I have decided to defend the factory.'

'A correct decision,' Yeremenko said. 'I appoint you sector commander.'

Yeremenko sent Feklenko a tank brigade and an infantry brigade. Amid the battle there appeared to be good news for the Russians – the pontoon bridge across the Volga, 3.2km (2 miles) long, had been completed in 10 days instead of 12. Yeremenko signalled 'Thank the men who built it and the officers who supervised them. As for the bridge, I order it to be destroyed.' The Germans were now too close to it. By late afternoon, the Germans were being slowed down or brought to a halt. Hube's tanks had run into heavy anti-tank fire on the Sukhaya Mechetka *balka*, 800m (0.5 miles) north of the Tractor Factory. After hours of hard fighting, Hube's battered tanks withdrew, while the Soviets brought up reinforcements. The Germans had split the Stalingrad Front in two and wrecked Soviet communications, but the Soviet forces were undeterred. At 18:00 Yeremenko received reports that the German offensive had been stopped and so sat down for his first meal of the day.

That evening *Luftflotte* IV attacked the city in strength. Richthofen committed every aircraft available, even Ju 52 tri-motor transports, in the heaviest bombardment by the *Luftwaffe* since 22 June 1941. Pilots flew three missions per day, and so 2000 sorties hammered Stalingrad with high explosive and incendiaries, shredding the wooden workers' settlements that surrounded the factories. The raid went on into the night, and people could read newspapers by the light of the resulting blaze 64km (40 miles) away.

Hoffman wrote: '23 August. Splendid news north of Stalingrad, our troops have reached the Volga and captured part of the city. The Russians have two alternatives, either to flee across the Volga or to give themselves up. Our company's interpreter has interrogated a captured Russian officer. He was wounded, but asserted that the Russians would fight for

Opposite: Men of a Soviet workers' militia take Luftwaffe *aircraft under massed fire with their Mosin Nagant rifles. Hits by single 7.62mm (0.3in) rounds might not be lethal, but multiple hits could damage controls or even wound or kill pilots.*

ANDREI I. YEREMENKO (1892–1970)

Andrei Yeremenko (Eremenko) first saw action as a cavalry NCO in the Imperial Russian Army in World War I. He joined the Red Army in 1918. In 1939 he commanded the 6th Cossack Division that was part of the Soviet forces that invaded eastern Poland. Between 1940 and 1941 he served in the Far East commanding the 1st Special Red Banner Division and then transferred to the Bryansk Front in August 1941 following the German invasion. Along with Koniev he was criticized by Zhukhov for failing to hold a common front during the drive by Army Group Centre on Moscow in October. During this period Yeremenko was wounded and relieved of active command for a year. In August 1942 he was appointed to command the Southeast Front that was renamed the Stalingrad Front. While Rokossovsky was given the honour of destroying the Sixth Army, Yeremenko was tasked with keeping Manstein at bay. In May 1944, commanding the Independent (Black Sea) Maritime Front, he recaptured Sevastopol, taking 67,000 prisoners. He subsequently commanded the 2nd Baltic Front and captured Dvinsk in Latvia. He was assigned to the Carpathian Front where his forces destroyed the German Army Group Centre in 1945. He was promoted marshal in 1955, two years after Stalin's death. The rank of Marshal of the Soviet Union was created in 1935 and abolished in 1991. A total of 41 people held the rank.

T-70 LIGHT TANK

The T-70 entered service in January 1942. It had a crew of two and was armed with a Model 38 45mm (1.7in) gun with 94 rounds and a 7.62mm (0.3in) DT machine gun. The tank was made at *Zavod* Nr 38 and GAZ plants and was powered by two GAZ-202 engines that gave a maximum road speed of 45kph (27.9mph) and a range of 360km (223.6 miles). When production ceased in 1943, 8226 vehicles had been built. Despite its narrow tracks, its weight of 9960kg (9.8 tons) meant that drivers were able to steer it across firm snow. Its major design defects were the slab-sided one-man turret with its low-calibre main armament.

Stalingrad to the last round. Something incomprehensible is, in fact, going on. In the north our troops capture a part of Stalingrad and reach the Volga, but in the south the doomed divisions are continuing to resist bitterly. Fanaticism.'

A POLITICAL GESTURE

A day later Stalin ordered that Stalingrad should be held. Its defence was initially a political gesture rather than a decision taken as part of a military strategy. For Stalin a city that bore his name could not be given up without a fight, while for Hitler too the name of the industrial city had a special appeal. However, thousands of houses and blocks of flats had been destroyed in the heavy bombing, and consequently the civilian population suffered heavy casualties. Approximately 40,000 people died and more than 150,000 were wounded in the air attacks on 24 August. They took shelter in the gullies and in the basements of houses. By the end of August the population had been reduced to 400,000. To avoid further loss of life the City Defence Committee organized the evacuation of the civilian population together with valuable property belonging to the state. From 24 August to 14 September some 300,000 people and a large amount of industrial equipment were taken across the Volga under continuous enemy fire.

Right: The little Soviet T-70 Light Tank was not powerful enough to take on tanks like the PzKpfw III or IV, but dug in behind the protection and cam-ouflage of rubble it was very effective in defence.

Opposite: The German break-in towards Stalingrad in August was delayed by a breakdown in fuel supplies. If Hoth had been able to join Paulus in a fast attack, together they might have caught the defenders off balance and captured the city.

The Sixth Army attempted to take Stalingrad from the west, sending 25 tanks and an infantry division across the Don south of Rubezhnoye. They advanced on central Stalingrad and hit a tank brigade and an infantry division. The Soviets counter-attacked to relieve the partially encircled 87th Rifle Division. Thirty-three Siberian soldiers from the division held out for two days against a force of 70 German tanks that had surrounded them, destroying 27, making good use of 'a bottle with an inflammable mixture'. Yeremenko sent the Sixty-Third Army to counter-attack, but his artillery support was not co-ordinated with the assault.

Under heavy air attack the drive failed to gain ground, but the counter-attacks threw the Germans off-balance. As the Germans moved into the city, their plans began to disintegrate. Their mechanized and armoured forces were restricted by Stalingrad's maze of ruined buildings, factories and ravines. The Soviets, knowing the terrain, were well dug in, and kept up a high volume of small-arms and mortar fire. Heavy artillery was dug in on the opposite bank of the Volga.

Hoffman noted on 27 August 'A continuous cannonade on all sides. We are slowly advancing. Less than twenty miles to go to Stalingrad. In the daytime we can see the smoke of fires, at night time the bright glow. They say that the city is on fire; on the *Führer*'s orders our *Luftwaffe* has sent it up in flames. That's what the Russians need, to stop them from resisting.'

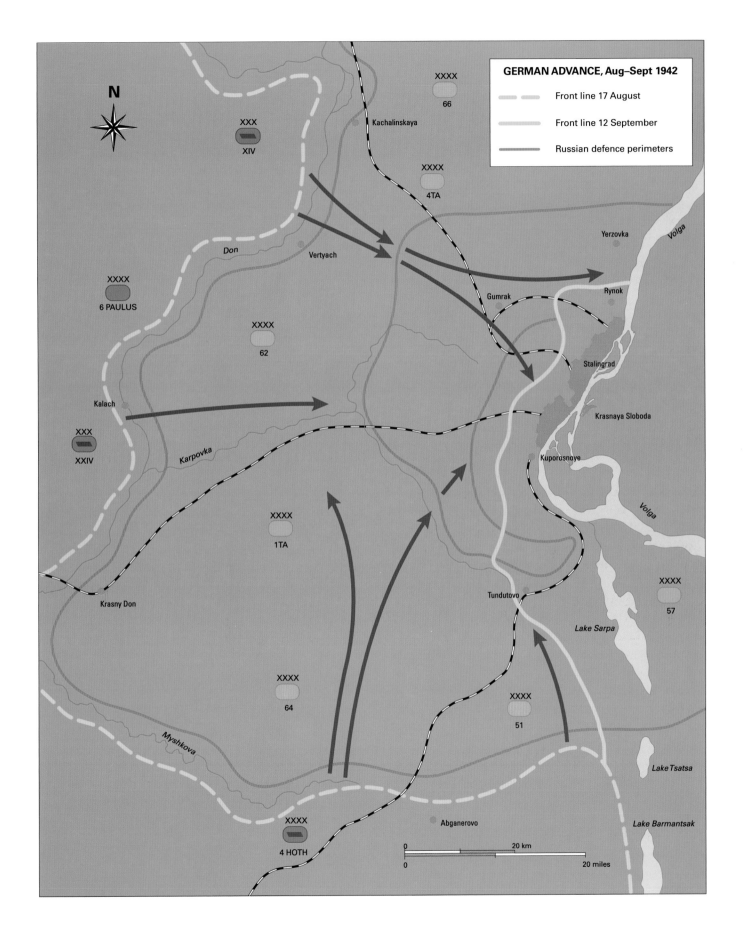

GERMAN ADVANCE, Aug–Sept 1942

Front line 17 August

Front line 12 September

Russian defence perimeters

N

XXXX
66

Kachalinskaya

XXX
XIV

XXXX
4TA

Don

Vertyach

Yerzovka

Volga

XXXX
6 PAULUS

Gumrak

Rynok

XXXX
62

Stalingrad

Kalach

Krasnaya Sloboda

XXX
XXIV

Karpovka

Kuporosnoye

Volga

XXXX
1TA

XXXX
57

Krasny Don

Tundutovo

Lake Sarpa

XXXX
64

Lake Tsatsa

Myshkova

XXXX
51

Lake Barmantsak

XXXX
4 HOTH

Abganerovo

0   20 km

0   20 miles

Opposite: Officers and men of the Volga Naval Flotilla, some of whom fought in the city; most, though, carried out the vital task of ferrying troops and supplies across the Volga under constant and brutal air and artillery attack.

ZHUKHOV ARRIVES

On the same day that Hoffman was writing about the bombardment, General Georgi Konstantinovich Zhukhov flew in to Stalingrad with orders from Stalin: save Stalingrad. The plan would be that while Yeremenko held the city, Zhukhov would prepare a counter-attack. At Yeremenko's HQ, the two generals studied maps.

Zhukhov believed that the German attackers were greatly overextended, despite air superiority and their advantage in tanks. The long German left flank was held by Romanian, Italian and Hungarian troops, with the Italians deployed between the Romanians and Hungarians to keep these bitter rivals apart. Zhukhov recognized the opportunity to cut through the weakly defended sides of the salient and isolate German forces at Stalingrad in a giant pincer movement. But to do so, the Germans had to be defeated and tied down at Stalingrad. Zhukhov flew back to Moscow to make his plans. Meanwhile the battle of Stalingrad raged on.

The Fourth Panzer Army attacked from the south of the city while Yeremenko handled the threat to the north. The Fourth Panzers aimed to drive a wedge into Sixty-Fourth Army, hook to the right and cut the enemy off. Backed by Stukas the tanks blasted their way through the defences and it suddenly seemed possible to cut off the right wing of Sixty-Fourth Army and the whole of the Sixty-Second as well, if Fourth Panzer Army kept driving north and Sixth Army pushing south.

At noon Army Group B drafted orders to adopt these tactics, telling Paulus to concentrate 'strongest forces possible … to destroy the enemy force west of Stalingrad'. Paulus, however, did not move, because he believed that if he detached his mobile forces, his northern front might collapse under the weight of a Soviet counter-attack.

THE VOLGA NAVAL FLOTILLA

The city of Stalingrad has always been a major port on the Volga River. In July 1941, a month after the Nazi invasion, a special Soviet Army detachment was formed on the Volga River under command of Rear-Admiral Rogachev to train the rank-and-file servicemen for the Volga fighting fleet. The ferries that would transport troops and stores were mostly small cutters and barges. At the time that Rogachev received his mission he feared that he might 'miss the war'. In October, his command was transformed into the Volga Naval Flotilla. At that time it comprised seven gunboats, 15 armoured boats, more than 20 minesweepers and two floating artillery batteries.

As the battlefront drew closer to the Volga River in 1942, the strategic role of the major inland waterway became greater and more vital to both sides. The *Luftwaffe* started laying mines in the riverbed to halt all shipping along the Volga. In a relatively short period of time, the bombers had laid up to 350 mines. The Soviet Army did not have enough special equipment, sweeps in particular, to neutralize them. To make up for this, several wooden river ships and barges were turned into minesweepers. Then, the *Luftwaffe* started to attack vessels in port and *en route*. Cargo ships had to be formed into convoys, which were protected by anti-aircraft vessels. Armoured boats were also used as escort vessels for such convoys. But the Volga Naval Flotilla kept on carrying troops, war equipment and supplies. Its personnel displayed courage and heroism, which equalled that of the defenders of the city. It is no exaggeration to say that 60 years ago the fate of the city depended on the uninterrupted supply of everything the Stalingrad Front needed. All in all, the Volga Naval Flotilla undertook more than 35,000 runs across the river. What was more, wherever it could, the Volga Naval Flotilla also supported the Soviet land forces with gunfire. The enemy kept the river under fire, forcing the flotilla to take advantage of the night hours, but still its ships were not always able to reach the city undetected. The Germans fired flares to illuminate Soviet ships and then called in artillery fire and air attacks. More than 50 vessels were lost as a result of the heavy *Luftwaffe* bombing and about 20 vessels struck mines.

The Soviet side constantly devised measures to make the Volga shipping safer. The armoured boats were equipped with T-34 tank turrets, and it was in the battle of Stalingrad that the boats first employed rocket launchers. In September and October 1942 the men and women of the shipyards on the river at Krasnoarmeisk repaired the battered ships of the flotilla largely by hand because the local power station had been destroyed. They also overhauled and repaired weapons and tanks – some of these AFVs were used to tow ships on or off the slipways.

Left: Stalingrad seen from the south – the Grain Elevator that would become a fortress can be seen on the horizon, with the Volga to the right. In the foreground is an abandoned panje *wagon, the useful little Russian farm vehicle.*

On 28 August a situation report presented to Hitler read 'Colonel General Baron von Richthofen has ... personally examined the situation at Stalingrad and as a result of these observations, and also from consultations with the Commanders of the Fourth Panzer Army and of the Sixth Army, he has established that there is no question of further strong enemy resistance ... The General's overall impression was that the enemy lacked a unified command ...'

On the last day of August Army Group B ordered Paulus to head south and cut off the Russian defenders at Stalingrad. Paulus did not move because Soviet pressure on his north was too great. Soviet 76mm (2.9in) guns, across the Volga, hammered his men. Yeremenko was able to withdraw the Sixty-Second Army out of the closing gap, while the Sixty-Fourth pushed to a small bridgehead on the Volga. Ferryboats evacuated some of the civilian population to the east bank of the river, while carrying guns, ammunition and troops the other way.

Hoffmann asked almost plaintively in his diary 'Are the Russians really going to fight on the very bank of the Volga? It's madness.'

STREET FIGHTING

On 1 September units of the Sixth Army reached the suburbs of Stalingrad following fierce fighting, and three days later the *Luftwaffe* renewed its heavy attacks on the city, causing massive damage and many civilian casualties in the wooden houses clustered on the western fringes. A day later at Vinnitsa, Hitler announced 'upon penetration into the city [of Stalingrad], the entire male population be eliminated, since Stalingrad with its one million uniformly Communist

> Their [the Germans'] morale would not stand it. They did not have the spirit to look an armed Soviet soldier in the eyes. You could locate an enemy soldier in a forward post from a long way off, especially by night; he would constantly, every five to ten minutes, give a burst on his tommy-gun, obviously to boost his morale. Our soldiers could find such 'warriors', creep up and polish them off with bullet or bayonet.
>
> *Lieutenant-General V.I. Chuikov*

Above: On the outskirts of Stalingrad, infantry cluster around a German StuG III assault gun that will provide direct fire support for their attack. Though assault guns did not have a turret and so very limited traverse, they had a low silhouette.

inhabitants is extremely dangerous'. The fate of the women and children was not specified.

At Stalingrad on 2 September the Soviet Sixty-Second Army evaded the closing trap. The Germans pushed on, fighting for one building at a time backed by direct fire from self-propelled guns. Stalin sent a signal to Zhukhov at Ivanovka, where the general was planning the counter-offensive: 'The situation at Stalingrad is getting worse. The enemy is two miles from Stalingrad. Stalingrad may be taken today or tomorrow if the northern group of forces does not give immediate help. Require the commanders of the forces deployed north and northwest of Stalingrad to strike at the enemy at once, and go to help the Stalingraders. No procrastination is permitted. Procrastination now equals crime. Throw all aviation in to help Stalingrad. In Stalingrad there are very few aircraft left. Report receipt and

measures taken without delay.' Three days later Zhukhov committed the Twenty-Fourth and Sixty-Sixth Armies, neither fully trained and both containing older reservists, into action.

Hoth finally linked up with Paulus near the airfield at Pitomnik and on Thursday 3 September the German forces attempted break into the city from the west but were halted by local counter-attacks. In Berlin the Reich Press Chief was in upbeat mood when he announced to journalists 'Due to the successful course of our operations against Stalingrad, it is recommended that our newspapers now keep on hand material on the enormous economic and military importance of this bastion of Communism and centre of Soviet industry'.

CHUIKOV APPOINTED

It was a day that would be very significant for Stalingrad. General Alexander Lopatin, commanding Sixty-Second Army, reported to Yeremenko that the Sixty-Second could not hold. Yeremenko promptly sacked him and replaced him with Vasily Ivanovich Chuikov, the son of a peasant, who until recently had been a military advisor to the Nationalist Chinese leader Chiang Kai-Shek and was subsequently the Sixty-Fourth Army's chief of staff. Chuikov had been scheduled to take over an army in July, but on the way to the front, his drunken driver crashed the car, putting Chuikov in hospital for a week. He seemed dogged with bad luck, for a few weeks later, Chuikov's light plane was forced to crash by enemy aircraft. On hitting the ground it split in two, throwing Chuikov out. Fortunately he suffered nothing more than a bump on the head.

Chuikov would prove to be a master of improvisation and surprise. Ordered to hold Stalingrad, he saluted and headed into the city to find the Germans 3.2km (2 miles) from the river, and the city unrecognizable. To reach Sixty-Second Army HQ he had to cross the Volga by boat, take a nightmare vehicle ride to the left bank to report to Khrushchev and Yeremenko at front HQ, then back on the ferry, and into the burning city.

He wrote 'The streets of the city are dead. There is not a single green twig left on the streets; everything has perished in the flames. All that is left of the wooden houses is a pile of ashes and a stove chimney sticking up out of them …' Only the concrete and iron structures of factories and stone buildings in the city's centre remained standing above ground – roofless, interior walls crushed away.

Chuikov admired how the Germans used combined arms in battle, but considered them sluggish and irresolute. Their combined forces were powerful, he said, but the elements themselves were not of outstanding quality. He noted that the Panzers did not attack until the *Luftwaffe* was over Soviet positions, and until the tanks reached their objectives, infantry would not go in. The key therefore was to break the German chain, by whatever means. Chuikov also noted that the German infantry shunned close combat, preferring to use firepower at long range. Chuikov's solution would be to fight battles at as close a range as possible, so that the *Luftwaffe* could not attack without putting their own forces in danger. The chain would be broken at its first link, and the

CRISIS OF COMMAND

In September 1942 Hitler sent *Generaloberst* Alfred Jodl, chief of the *Oberkommando der Wehrmacht* (OKW – the German Armed Forces High Command), to Field Marshal Siegmund List, commanding Army Group A. He was to establish why Army Group A was making such slow progress in the capture of Batumi, which would deny the Soviet Black Sea Fleet its last base in the area.

The reason was simply that Army Group A lacked the resources for the mission since these were going to the Sixth Army at Stalingrad. Jodl discussed the problem with List and returned on 7 September to brief Hitler, reporting that 'List had acted exactly in conformity with the *Führer*'s orders, but the Russian resistance was strong everywhere, supported by a most difficult terrain.' The *Führer*'s reaction was to rage at Jodl, but to Hitler's surprise the normally quiet Jodl vehemently defended List. Jodl then wrote out his resignation and requested a posting to a front-line command. However, he was persuaded by his father-in-law, Field Marshal Wilhelm Keitel, the head of the OKW, to remain in his post.

Hitler was shaken by the show of opposition, refusing to shake hands with Keitel and Jodl for months, and stopped eating his meals with the HQ staff, preferring to dine alone. All contacts were now filtered through a small group of aides, including the bullish, omnipresent and sinister *Reichsleiter* Martin Bormann. Hitler said that Jodl would be replaced by Friedrich Paulus and the news was passed on to Paulus at the Stalingrad front, along with an urgent demand to capture the city. Paulus replied that he was running short on men and ammunition, the Soviet resistance was heavy and the Sixth Army was exhausted.

Hitler had already sacked two Panzer Corps commanders, von Wietersheim of XIV Panzer Corps and von Schwedler of IV Panzer Corps. Wietersheim was sacked for using his tanks to hold open the Rynok corridor from the Don to the Volga, a task better suited to infantry, and von Schwedler for the 'defeatist' suggestion that the concentration of such strong forces at the tip of a salient with vulnerable flanks at Stalingrad was dangerous for the Sixth Army. After these two generals were sacked, Hitler fired his Chief of the General Staff at Army High Command (OKH), *Generaloberst* Franz Halder. The new OKH head was *Generaloberst* Kurt Zeitzler, a logistics specialist. The last to get the axe was Field Marshal List.

Lorryloads of infantry and tanks tore through the city. The Germans obviously thought that the fate of the town had been settled, and they all rushed to the centre and the Volga as soon as possible and grabbed souvenirs for themselves ... we saw drunken Germans jumping down from their lorries, playing mouth organs, shouting like madmen and dancing on the pavements.

Lieutenant-General V.I. Chuikov

German infantry would be forced fight in their least favourable tactical environment. Chuikov explained it to his troops later 'Every German soldier must be made to feel he lives under the muzzle of a Russian gun.... It occurred to us, therefore, that we should reduce the no-man's land as much as possible close enough to the throw of a grenade ...'

A ruthless commander, Chuikov took the calculated decision that the civilians in Stalingrad would no longer be evacuated because he asserted that Soviet soldiers would fight harder for a 'living city'.

On 4 September, the OKW announced 'In the fortress zone at Stalingrad, German panzer troops have broken through strongly defended enemy positions and captured the heights overlooking the city just west of Stalingrad in hard fighting. During the night we bombed the city zone and Soviet airfields east of the Volga.'

The Germans attacked again at Stalingrad, splitting Sixty-Fourth Army and driving to the Volga at Krasnoarmeisk. The city had been under continuous bombardment for 24 hours. 'Anyone without experience of war would think that in the blazing city there is no longer anywhere left to live, that everything has been destroyed and burned out ... But I know that on the other side of the river a battle is being fought, a titanic struggle is taking place.'

The pressure on the Sixty-Second Army was becoming intense and on 11 September the XLVIII Panzer Corps

Below: The defenders of Stalingrad included men who until recently had been working in the huge factories in the city. Though some fought hard, others, after suffering heavy losses, attempted to surrender to the Sixth Army.

LIEUTENANT-GENERAL VASILY IVANOVICH CHUIKOV (1900–1982)

Born at Serebryannye Prudy near Moscow on 12 February 1900, Vasily Chuikov was the son of peasants, and worked as an apprentice mechanic from the age of 12. There were 12 children in the family, and all survived to adulthood. His father – Ivan – was the village's famous wrestler, and his mother – Elizaveta – an exemplary parishioner of a local Orthodox church. At the age of 20, Vasily commanded a troop, and during the Civil War received two Orders of the Red Banner.

By a strange historic twist his first experience of combat in the Civil War was in 1918 at Tsaritsyn, the city that became Stalingrad and is now Volgograd. By the following year he was a member of the Communist Party and a regimental commander. He served against Kolchak in the Russo-Polish war of 1920.

Chuikov graduated from the M.V. Frunze Military Academy in 1925, took part in the Soviet invasion of Poland (1939) and in the Russo-Finnish War (1939–40), and had just finished serving as military attaché in China when he was called to Stalingrad to command the Sixty-Second Army. At Stalingrad Chuikov allegedly declared 'We shall hold the city or die here'. Commenting on German firepower he urged his soldiers 'We should get as close to the enemy as possible, so that his air force cannot bomb our forward units or trenches'.

He subsequently led his forces, redesignated the Eighth Guards Army, into the Donets Basin and then into the Crimea and north to Belorussia before spearheading the Soviet drive to Berlin. Chuikov personally accepted the German surrender of Berlin on 1 May 1945.

After the war he served with the Soviet occupation forces in Germany from 1945 to 1953. He died in 1982.

Above: Following the victory at Stalingrad a relaxed and confident General Chuikov talks to soldiers of the 39th Guards Rifle Division. During the fighting he smoked heavily and developed stress-related skin disorders.

reached the Volga, and in the Rynok and Spartanovka suburbs they held 8km (5 miles) of the bank from where they were able to engage shipping on the river.

On 5 September the Russian Twenty-Fourth and Sixty-Sixth Armies had attacked but failed to gain ground at Stalingrad, but they took the pressure off Sixty-Second and Sixty-Fourth Armies, giving them time to lay barbed wire, dig trenches, plant mines, and receive reinforcements. The 87th Division was down to 180 men, 112th had 150, and 99th Tank Brigade had 120 men and no tanks.

Paulus was planning another assault on the blasted city. He was suffering from dysentery, and was tired and listless, but he began each morning with a fresh cotton collar for the shirt inside his tunic and with highly polished boots. As the battle developed he became increasingly depressed by the heavy casualties.

Paulus planned to concentrate two assault groups against the southern half of the town, to grab the 'Central landing stage' opposite Krasnaya Sloboda. Three divisions would assault from Gumrak railway station while another force, including the 29th Motorized Division, would attack from the northeast.

By 12 September the Soviet perimeter around Stalingrad had been reduced to a length of just 48km (30 miles). Chuikov was now in overall command of the troops in and around the city.

CENTRAL STATION

By 14 September German attacks had forced the Soviet Sixty-Second Army back into the industrial areas of Stalingrad along the west bank of the Volga. However, casualties had reduced the strength of the Sixth Army and it was only able to attack on narrow frontages that reduced progress.

The diary of Sixty-Second Army, describing the intensity of fighting for the Central Station in Stalingrad, which changed hands 15 times in three days, reads: '08:00 [Central] Station in enemy hands. 08:40 Station recaptured. 09:40 Station retaken by enemy. 10:40 Enemy ... 600m [457 yards] from Army command post ... 13:20 Station in our hands.'

'At the Central Station, a battalion of Soviet Guardsmen dug in behind smashed railroad cars and platforms. Bombed and shelled, 'the station buildings were on fire, the walls burst apart, the iron buckled'. The survivors moved to a nearby ruin where, tormented by thirst, they fired at drainpipes to see if any water would drip out. During the night, German sappers blew up the wall separating the room holding the Russians from the German-held part of the building and threw in grenades. An attack cut the battalion in two and the headquarters staff was trapped inside the *Univermag* department store where the battalion commander was killed in hand-to-hand fighting. The last 40 men of the battalion pulled back to a building on the banks of the Volga. They set up a heavy machine gun in the basement and broke down the walls at the top of the building to prepare lumps of stone and wood to hurl at the Germans. They had no water and only a few pounds of scorched grain to eat. After five days, a survivor wrote 'the basement was full of wounded; only twelve men were still able to fight'.

The battalion nurse was dying of a chest wound. A German tank ground forward and a Russian slipped out with the last anti-tank rifle rounds to deal with it. He was captured by German machine gunners. Apparently, he persuaded his captors that the Russians had run out of ammunition, because the Germans 'came impudently out of

Opposite: Infantry manhandle a 75mm (2.95in) leichte Infantriegeschutz 18 – light infantry gun, during fighting in the Stalingrad suburbs. An experienced crew could fire between four and six shells a minute.

Right: German infantry advance towards Soviet positions, led by an NCO carrying a stick grenade. The grenade had a hollow handle and a screw cap at the base. When this was removed the friction cord fell free and was pulled to set off the time delay.

their shelter, standing up and shouting'. The last belt of machine-gun ammunition was fired into them and 'an hour later they led our anti-tank rifleman on to a heap of ruins and shot him in front of our eyes'. More squat German tanks appeared and reduced the building to ruins with point-blank fire. At night, six survivors of the battalion freed themselves from the rubble and struggled to the Volga.

Hoffman recorded the fighting:

'4 September. We are being sent northward along the front toward Stalingrad. We marched all night and by dawn had reached Voroponovo Station. We can already see the smoking town. It's a happy thought that the end of the war is getting nearer. That's what everyone is saying. If only the days and nights would pass more quickly. ...

'5 September. Our regiment has been ordered to attack Sadovaya station – that's nearly in Stalingrad. Are the Russians really thinking of holding out in the city itself? We had no peace all night from the Russian artillery and aeroplanes. Lots of wounded are being brought by. God protect me. ...

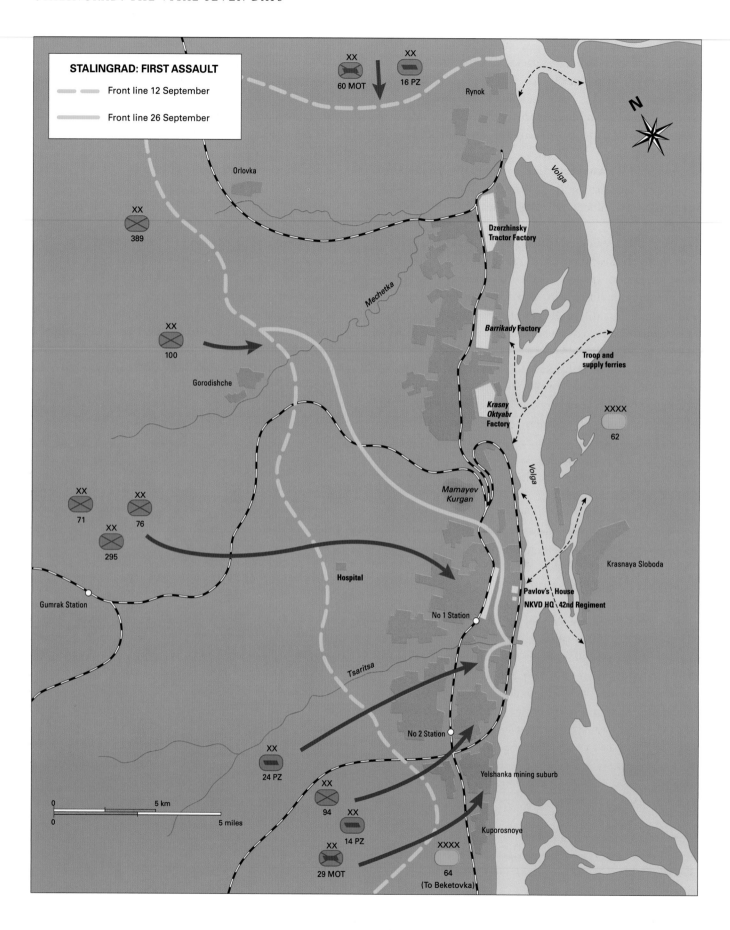

STALINGRAD: FIRST ASSAULT

- - - Front line 12 September

——— Front line 26 September

XX
60 MOT

XX
16 PZ

Rynok

Volga

Orlovka

XX
389

Mechetka

Dzerzhinsky
Tractor Factory

Barrikady Factory

XX
100

Gorodishche

Troop and
supply ferries

*Krasny
Oktyabr
Factory*

XXXX
62

Volga

XX
71

XX
76

*Mamayev
Kurgan*

XX
295

Krasnaya Sloboda

Hospital

Gumrak Station

No 1 Station

Pavlov's House
NKVD HQ 42nd Regiment

Tsaritsa

No 2 Station

0   5 km

0   5 miles

XX
24 PZ

Yelshanka mining suburb

XX
94

XX
14 PZ

Kuporosnoye

XX
29 MOT

XXXX
64

(To Beketovka)

'8 September. Two days of non-stop fighting. The Russians are defending themselves with insane stubbornness. Our regiment has lost many men from the "katyushi", which belch out terrible fire. I have been sent to work at battalion H.Q. It must be mother's prayers that have taken me away from the company's trenches. …

'11 September. Our battalion is fighting in the suburbs of Stalingrad. We can already see the Volga; firing is going on all the time. Wherever you look is fire and flames. … Russian cannon and machine-guns are firing out of the burning city. Fanatics. …

'13 September. An unlucky number. This morning "katyushi" attacks caused the company heavy losses: twenty-seven dead and fifty wounded. The Russians are fighting desperately like wild beasts, don't give themselves up, but come up close and then throw grenades. Lieutenant Kraus was killed yesterday, and there is no company commander.'

THE MAMAYEV KURGAN

On 13 September the Germans made a final concentrated effort to drive the defenders of Stalingrad into the Volga. Their objective was the Mamayev Kurgan. Meanwhile Chuikov, new commander of the Sixty-Second Army, planned a counter-attack, but he found the army weak and dispirited from the pounding it had received. However, he knew that help was on the way: 10 infantry divisions and two armoured corps that would be ferried across the river in two weeks.

The capture of the Mamayev Kurgan by the German 295th Infantry Division gave them a commanding view of the city. To defend it, the Soviets had built strong defensive lines on the slopes of the hill, including trenches, barbed wire and minefields. The Germans had pushed forward against the hill, taking heavy casualties. When they finally captured it, they started taking the city centre under fire, as well as the Stalingrad-1 railway station beneath the hill. They captured the railway station on 14 September.

Chuikov's counter-attack in Stalingrad was forestalled at 06:30 by a two-pronged attack by the German LI Corps. Two panzer divisions and one motorized division overran the forward defences, the Tractor Factory Station, and the housing estate. Chuikov's HQ at Mamayev Kurgan came under heavy artillery fire and its communications were

Opposite: By late September large parts of southern Stalingrad were in German hands and some of the ferry routes were under fire. The factories to the north would be defended with courage verging on fanaticism and prove to be virtual fortresses.

We shall never surrender the city of our birth to the depredations of the German invader. Each single one of us must apply himself to the task of defending our beloved town, our homes and our families. Let us barricade every street; transform every district, every block, every house into an impregnable fortress.

Stalingrad Regional Party Committee, 25 August 1942

knocked out. He moved his HQ to a bunker in the Tsaritsa gully, and ordered his troops to fight to the last man. The most vicious fighting of the entire war was taking place.

The only available reinforcements entered the fighting, General Alexander Rodimtsev's 13th Guards Division. Rodimtsev was a veteran of street fighting from the Spanish Civil War. His division moved across the river at dusk, to reinforce a line held by a mere 15 tanks. The 13th arrived straight from a gruelling forced march. One thousand of its men had no rifles, and the rest were short of ammunition. Chuikov, however, sent it straight into the battle. The division was inexperienced, and lacked both maps and knowledge of Stalingrad's blitzed terrain. Even so, the division stemmed the German attack, aided by Chuikov's headquarters company and staff officers. Thirty per cent of the 10,000 soldiers of the 13th Division were killed in the first 24 hours of their arrival, and only 320 survived the battle of Stalingrad, a grim 97 per cent casualty rate, but they saved Stalingrad in the most critical moment.

RODIMTSEV'S GUARDSMEN

One of Rodimtsev's junior officers was hand-picked by the commander of the Sixty-Second Army himself to carry out a vital, but near-suicidal mission – to hold the railway station. Lieutenant Anton Kuzmich Dragan received these orders from Vasily Chuikov in person. Gathering a platoon of less than 50 men, Dragan and his soldiers proceeded to frustrate the Germans in an epic room-by-room struggle for control of the depot for nearly three weeks. Breaking through walls, crawling over the rafters and burrowing under the floorboards, the Russians would yield a portion of the building to the Germans only to emerge elsewhere and start the struggle all over again.

Exchanging gunfire down hallways, lobbing grenades back and forth between rooms, Dragan's men inflicted as many casualties as possible on the enemy. In spite of this heroic resistance, Dragan's force was eventually reduced to a handful of men. They were running out of ammunition,

Above: Military tourists – a German officer peers cautiously through the ruins of one of the major buildings in Stalingrad. His lack of helmet, weapon and personal equipment indicates that he is not a front-line soldier, but an observer of some kind.

their rations gone; one of his soldiers took out a bayonet and carved on the wall 'Rodimtsev's Guardsmen fought and died for their country here.' Under cover of darkness, Dragan and five of his soldiers slipped out of the building, made their way through enemy lines, and later rejoined the fight. After the war a formal stone memorial was erected to the memory of the division. It reads: 'The Guardsmen of Rodimtsev held their ground here to the last man.'

In his memoirs Rodimtsev has left a vivid description of the tension of street fighting: 'Night combat in a building is the most difficult form of combat. Here such terms as forward line, front rear and flanks do not apply. The enemy may be everywhere: on the floor above you, below you and around you. You hear a rustle. Who is that breathing in pitch

darkness? Who's there? Friend? Foe? How can you identify him? By challenging? What if he responds with a burst of submachine gun fire? You have to decide and be quick about it. You may have only a moment to make your decision, maybe only a fraction of a second separates you from a silently thrown grenade or a knife thrust.'

However, Chuikov was running out of troops. He assigned 1500 armed police, firefighters, factory workers and men from an NKVD division to defend the larger buildings in the city. Despite these measures, the Germans continued to advance. The 71st Infantry Division held front-line positions within 500m (547 yards) of Chuikov's HQ where the staff could hear the small-arms fire. By now all 15 Soviet tanks had been knocked out. Chuikov ordered the immobilized survivors to fight on as darkness descended. The 13th Guards

Opposite: A PzKpfw IV Ausf F2 noses forward across a filled-in stretch of an anti-tank ditch. The ditch offers temporary cover for the German infantry who are preparing to advance with the tank's support.

'We would spend the whole day clearing a street, from one end to the other, establish blocks and fire-points at the western end, and prepare for another slice of the salami the next day. But at dawn the Russians would start up firing from their old positions at the far end! It took us some time to discover their trick; they had knocked communicating holes through between the garrets and attics and during the night they would run back like rats in the rafters, and set their machine guns up behind some topmost window or broken chimney,' wrote a German soldier. The Mamayev Kurgan battle went on all day, as Rodimtsev's men died in place, fending off the 22nd Panzer Division. The Germans finally took the high ground. At Chuikov's HQ the general himself led the local defence, but exhausted headquarters troops had begun making excuses to come into the shelter of the bunker on 'urgent business'. To address the possible onset of combat fatigue Chuikov set up a secondary HQ on the opposite bank of the Volga to allow staff to be rotated. The 42nd Soviet Regiment crossed over the river and dug in.

On 16 September the regiment attacked Mamayev Kurgan and the railway station, taking heavy losses. By the following day, almost all of them were dead. The Soviets kept reinforcing their units in the city as fast as they could. The Germans assaulted up to 12 times a day, and the Soviets would respond with fierce counter-attacks. At dawn in Stalingrad, the 42nd Regiment attacked through heavy mortar fire pushing for the summit of the Mamayev Kurgan. A short and vicious hand-to-hand battle settled the issue and Soviet troops recaptured the feature. In the lead platoon, out of 30 men six survived to secure the summit. As soon as they had begun to dig in, the Germans counter-attacked, but the Soviet forces held on.

At Stalingrad-1 railway station, the 24th Panzer Division had encountered elements of the 13th Guards. Twenty tanks had forced the Soviet forces out of the buildings, but they counter-attacked and recovered the station. The Germans counter-attacked in turn and regained it. Eventually the station changed hands four times that day. At dusk, it was

Above: Luftwaffe ground and air crew check the equipment of a Stuka pilot prior to a sortie over Stalingrad in September 1942. When there was no coherent defence either in the air or on the ground the Ju 87 could deliver attacks of almost pin-point accuracy against enemy positions.

Division was nearly wiped out, but its sacrifice held off the Germans. The battle raged on into the night and into the early hours of the morning of 15 September. German machine gunners were now raking the Soviet landing stages.

surrounded by hundreds of burned bodies and burnt-out tanks, but the Soviets still held the station.

The Sixth Army communiqué for 16 September read 'The southern flank of the Sixth Army has made good progress. On the *Führer*'s orders, the battle for Stalingrad will be placed under the unified command of the Sixth Army … Attacks were hampered by sandstorms.'

Hoffman's diary records the grim reality with his notes on the battle for the Grain Elevator on the southern edge of the Stalingrad sector:

'16 September. Our battalion, plus tanks, is attacking the [grain storage] elevator, from which smoke is pouring – the grain in it is burning, the Russians seem to have set light to it themselves. Barbarism. The battalion is suffering heavy losses. There are not more than 60 men left in each company. The elevator is occupied not by men but by devils that no flames or bullets can destroy.

'18 September. Fighting is going on inside the elevator. The Russians inside are condemned men; the battalion commander says: "The commissars have ordered those men to die in the elevator."

'If all the buildings of Stalingrad are defended like this then none of our soldiers will get back to Germany. I had a letter from Elsa today. She's expecting me home when victory's won.

'20 September. The battle for the elevator is still going on. The Russians are firing on all sides. We stay in our cellar; you can't go out into the street. Sergeant-Major Nuschke was killed today running across a street. Poor fellow, he's got three children.

'22 September. Russian resistance in the grain elevator has been broken. Our troops are advancing towards the Volga. We found about 40 Russians dead in the elevator building. Half of them were wearing naval uniform – sea devils. One prisoner was captured, seriously wounded, who can't speak, or is shamming. … Our soldiers have never experienced such bitter fighting before.'

On 19 September, with Sixty-Second Army under pressure, Yeremenko mounted an attack to link up with the battered army. Three divisions and a tank brigade attacked

---

Stalingrad is hell on earth. It is Verdun, bloody Verdun, with new weapons. We attack every day. If we capture 20 yards in the morning the Russians throw us back again in the evening.

German NCO, Stalingrad, September 1942

THE NEWS – OFFICIAL AND UNOFFICIAL

'The struggle for Stalingrad is nearing a successful conclusion. Today or tomorrow we may expect to receive important OKW announcements about the success achieved. The German Press will have to prepare an impressive tribute to celebrate the victorious outcome of this all-important battle for the city of Stalingrad.'

Daily Keynote from Reich Press Chief
Tuesday 15 September 1942

In Berlin the official *Wehrmacht* accounts of the battle gave rise to mock communiqués:

'Our troops captured a two-roomed flat with kitchen, toilet and bathroom, and managed to retain two-thirds of it despite hard-fought counterattacks by the enemy.'

---

the Mamayev Kurgan, but were defeated by German anti-tank guns. Chuikov and Yeremenko would later blame each other for the failure in their memoirs. Both the Soviet forces and the Germans were modifying their tactics to cope with Stalingrad's distinctive terrain. The Germans moved in specialist troops, some of them police battalions, engineers, and even *Luftwaffe* ground forces skilled in street fighting and demolition work. The Soviets formed 'Storm Groups' and developed 'killing zones', heavily mined squares and streets that were covered by small arms and anti-tank guns into which the German attacks were channelled.

HEAVY CASUALTIES

Paulus requested more reinforcements on 20 September and explained that he had been obliged to halt attacks due to increased casualties. In order to sustain attacks he had been obliged to bring in German forces from his flanks and here Axis allies now held the line. Paulus and General von Weichs of Army Group B both warned the OKW that the flanks were now increasingly vulnerable. But Hitler insisted that the attacks against Stalingrad should be continued. By 21 September most of southern Stalingrad was in German hands, except for the Grain Elevator. The fighting was brutal, as the Soviet troops were low on food, water, and ammunition. In the centre of the city, German troops tried to break through to the left bank of the Tsaritsa River, but were slowed by heavy Soviet artillery fire.

THE BATTLE FOR THE GRAIN ELEVATOR

Andrey Khozyaynov, a sailor serving in the Naval Infantry Brigade, who was the only survivor of the battle for the Grain Elevator, lived to write an account of the battle fought by 30 Guards and 18 sailors:

'I remember on the night of the 17th, I was called to the battalion command post and given the order to take a platoon of machine-gunners to the grain elevator and … to hold it come what may. We arrived that night and presented ourselves to the garrison commander. At that time the elevator was being defended by a battalion of not more than 30 to 35 guardsmen. Eighteen well-armed men had now arrived from our platoon.

At dawn … enemy tanks and infantry, approximately ten times our numbers, launched an attack from the south and west. After the first attack was beaten back, a second began, then a third, while a reconnaissance "pilot" plane circled over us. It corrected the fire and reported our position. In all, ten attacks were beaten off on 18 September.

In the elevator, the grain was on fire, the water in the machine-guns evaporated, the wounded were thirsty, but there was no water. This is how we defended ourselves 24 hours a day for three days. Heat, smoke, and thirst – all our lips were cracked. During the day many of us climbed up to the highest points in the elevator and from there fired on the Germans; at night we came down and made a defensive ring round the building. We had no contact with other units.

20 September arrived. At noon 12 enemy tanks came up from the south and west. We had already run out of ammunition for our anti-tank rifles, and we had no grenades left. The tanks approached the elevator from two sides and began to fire at our garrison at point-blank range. But no one flinched. Our machine-guns and tommy-guns continued to fire at the enemy's infantry, preventing them from entering the elevator. Then a Maxim, together with the gunner, was blown up by a shell, and the casing of the second Maxim was hit by shrapnel … We were left with one light machine-gun.

At dawn a German tank carrying a white flag approached from the south. We wondered what could have happened. Two men emerged from the tank, a Nazi officer and an interpreter. Through the interpreter the officer tried to persuade us to surrender to "the heroic German army", as defence was useless and we would not be able to hold our position any longer. "Better to surrender the elevator," affirmed the German officer. "If you refuse you will be dealt with without mercy. In an hour's time we will bomb you out of existence."

"What impudence," we thought, and gave the Nazi lieutenant a brief answer: "Tell all your Nazis to go to hell! You can go back, but only on foot." The German tank tried to beat a retreat, but a salvo from our two anti-tank rifles stopped it. The Germans made 10 attacks on the elevator, all failed. As the grain burns, the water in the machine-guns evaporated, leaving all, especially the wounded, thirsty. The explosions were shattering the concrete; the grain was in flames. We could not see one another for dust and smoke, but we cheered one another with shouts. German tommy-gunners appeared from behind the tanks. There were about 200 of them. They attacked very cautiously, throwing grenades in front of them. We were able to catch some of the grenades and throw them back. On the west side of the elevator, the Germans managed to enter the building, but we immediately turned our guns on the parts they occupied. Fighting flared up inside the building. We sensed and heard the enemy soldiers' breath and footsteps, but we could not see them in the smoke. We fired at the sound.

At night, during a short lull, we counted our ammunition. There did not seem to be much left. … We decided to break out … To begin [with] all went well. We passed through a gully and crossed a railroad line, then stumbled on an enemy mortar battery. The Germans scattered, leaving behind their weapons, but also bread and water. "Something to drink!" was all we could think about. We drank our fill in the darkness. We then ate the bread … and went on.

But alas, what happened to my comrades I don't know, because the next thing I remembered was waking in a dark, damp cellar. A door opened, and in the bright sunlight I could see a tommy-gunner in a black uniform. On his left sleeve was a skull. I had fallen into the hands of the enemy.'

The Grain Elevator finally fell on 22 September and so the southern suburbs of Stalingrad were in German hands. The whole of Sixty-Second Army's rear was vulnerable to German artillery fire. The Soviet forces could only use the landing stages in the north of the city and then only at night. General Batyuk's Siberian division was sent in to push the Germans away from the central landing stage. Batyuk did not have much combat experience so Chuikov sent for him and began a long lecture on street fighting, but Batyuk interrupted his superior and explained that he had actually studied the battle, and was aware of the situation. 'I've come to fight, not parade. My regiments have Siberians in them.' Chuikov released Batyuk to carry out his orders and the Siberians crossed the river.

Political control of all the Soviet armed forces was exercised through the *politicheskii rukovoditel* (*politruk*) or *kommissar* (commissar). One of the commissars on the Stalingrad Front was Nikita Khrushchev, the future leader of the post-war Soviet Union. On the east bank of the Volga the commissars attempted to reassure the reinforcements that were being marched to the ferries: 'From this side it looks as

though everything is on fire and there's nowhere to set down your feet. But whole regiments and divisions are living there, and fighting well. They need help. They are waiting for you.' However, on 10 October 1942 the Presidium of the Supreme Soviet issued a decree establishing a single command and abolishing political commissars in the army. The commissars had gained military experience and their former status had become superfluous. The decree was issued to free responsible military commanders from any hindrances in carrying out their duties and to add to their ranks. Stalingrad's defenders were informed that NKVD guards were covering all crossing points on the Volga, and anyone crossing the river to the east bank without permission would be shot on the spot. In addition, a stream of fresh reinforcements, including elite units, began to arrive and cross the Volga under German fire into Stalingrad. Most were killed, but they enabled Chuikov to keep hold of at least part of Stalingrad despite the tremendous German pressure. The

Below: A 10.5cm (4.134in) leFH howitzer fires over open sights against Soviet positions near the Grain Elevator in southern Stalingrad. The howitzer, developed in the 1920s, fired a 15kg (33lb) shell to a maximum range of 10,675m (11,674 yards).

average life expectancy of a reinforcement soldier in Stalingrad was as low as 24 hours. Whole units were sacrificed in Stalingrad's desperate defence.

A BATTLE OF ATTRITION

At 10:00 on 23 September Batyuk's Siberian division attacked in the northwest of Stalingrad but it met fierce German resistance and the Germans could not be dislodged, but it stalled Paulus's offensive and bought time for the Sixty-Second Army.

On the same day an officer from the OKH visited the German 295th and 71st Infantry Divisions in the centre of the town on a fact-finding mission. He noted that the Soviet troops remained as physically close to the Germans as possible to reduce the effectiveness of the latter's firepower. The Soviet troops were ever alert and whenever they thought they spotted a German weakness, they immediately counter-attacked. They were particularly tough now that there was little room left to retreat. The officer observed that after the heavy artillery bombardment, troops quickly emerged from their cellar-holes ready to fire. In spite of German counter-measures, the Soviets continued to move supplies across the Volga at night.

The two German divisions he visited were old, battle-tested formations that had been considerably weakened by infantry casualties. He observed that their combat power was dropping daily and the average strength of an infantry company was 10 to 15 men. Losses were particularly high among officers and NCOs. Although replacements had arrived, they were insufficient in number and considerably lacking in experience, training, and soldierly bearing. When an officer fell, the men drifted back to their starting point. To get them moving forward again, a higher-ranking officer had to intervene and lead them. The soldiers were particularly dependent on the divisional *Sturmgeschutze* (self-propelled

Left: The 8 cm (3.1in) Schwere Granatwerfer *34 was a well-designed medium mortar. It could be packed as a three-man load and was an ideal weapon in the confines of Stalingrad.*

assault guns) whose 7.5cm (2.95in) gun was designed to take out point targets for the infantry. The small bands of infantry did not want to attack without a *Sturmgeschutz*, and viewed it as a failure in leadership if one was not provided for them. This German officer concluded that attacking through the ruins had exhausted the infantry, and that they were too dulled. With so few troops, there was no rest because every soldier had to be deployed. There were no reserves.

It was especially hard to get necessary supplies forward to the combat infantry. Their diet suffered considerably. The surviving infantry expressed bitterness toward the perceived luxury of the *Luftwaffe*. They had also become resentful towards the special food bonuses that the armoured units received. The officers maintained that it was pointless to offer the infantry propaganda, since none of the promises could be kept. Out in the steppes of southern Russia, all supplies had to be brought from Germany. Besides food, the infantry's major requirement was ammunition for the 8cm (3.1in) mortar, one of the few weapons that could hit the enemy's holes in cellars and gully cliffs.

Senior officers noted that they had managed to get into a battle of attrition with the Russians and although their

Opposite: A Flammenwerfer 35 crew advance against an enemy strongpoint. The man stooped behind the operator may be adjusting the pressure on the flame-thrower, which had a range of 25–30m (27.3–32.8 yards) and duration of 10 seconds.

FLAME-THROWER

The Germans had pioneered the use flame-throwers in World War I at Verdun. The models deployed in the early days of World War I had in fact been developed at the turn of the twentieth century. The German Army tested two models of *Flammenwerfer* in the early 1900s, one large and one small, both developed by Richard Fiedler. They used several types in World War II. The *Flammenwerfer* 35 flame-thrower weighed 35.8kg (78.9lbs), had a range of 25–30m (27.3–32.8 yards) and duration of fire of 10 seconds. It had a single trigger that operated the pressurized nitrogen tank and ignited the 11.8 litres (2.6 gallons) of petrol in the fuel container. It was superseded by the *Flammenwerfer* 40 and 41. The first was a cylindrical 'lifebuoy-type' flame-thrower that weighed only 21.32kg (47lbs). It had a similar range to the *Flammenwerfer* 35 but about half the fuel capacity. The *Flammenwerfer 41* weighed about 20kg (44lbs) and used an ignition system of hydrogen that passed over a heated element that in turn set the fuel alight. Five blasts could be fired producing a flame of about 700° to 800° C (1292° to 1472° F).

Below: A Flammenwerfer *41 had two cylinders in the horizontal position, the lower one for fuel and the upper for nitrogen. It could fire five blasts of flame at heats of between 700° and 800° C (1292°–1472° F).*

THE MOLOTOV COCKTAIL

Named in the West after the Soviet foreign minister Vyacheslav Molotov, this weapon is now more widely known as a petrol bomb. It consisted of a thin-walled 1 litre (2.1 pint) or 0.75 litre (1.58 pint) bottle containing about 0.5 litre (1 pint) of petrol with a rag stuffed into the open neck. The petrol could be thickened with one part oil or raw rubber. Immediately before throwing, the bottle was tipped up so that the rag was soaked with petrol and it was then lit. When the bottle hit the target and shattered, flaming petrol would splash over an area of about 2–3 square metres (6.5–9.8 square feet), burning for up to five minutes. The aim was to pitch the bottle so that it landed on the rear deck of a tank and the burning petrol entered the engine space. Soviet soldiers would sometimes follow up an attack with bottles filled with petrol to stoke the fire started by the Molotov Cocktail. It could look spectacular when it burst, but the lethality varied.

The first soldiers to use these petrol bombs were the Republican troops during the Spanish Civil War as early as 1936. Burning petrol penetrated the fighting compartment and caused ammunition detonation; when hitting the transmission section, petrol easily set the engine on fire.

Later this primitive ignition mechanism was improved through use of an igniting chemical agent, which was a modified Kibalchich fuse for hand grenades. The only difference was that Molotov Cocktails used petrol instead of a solid inflammable substance. The Red Army received two types of petrol bombs: ones with self-igniting mixture KS (a mixture of phosphorus and sulphur, which had a very low melting temperature) and ones with inflammable mixtures Number 1 and Number 3. These mixtures were made of ordinary petrol, thickened by OP-1 hardening powder into a type of napalm.

KS mixture was normally bottled in 0.5–0.75 litre (1–1.5 pint) containers sealed with rubber corks, which were attached to the bottleneck with wire and wrapped in adhesive tape. Once ignited, the liquid burned with a bright flame for some 1.5–3 minutes, at temperatures of up to 1000° C (1832° F).

Petrol bombs with inflammable liquids Numbers 1 and 3 were sealed with conventional corks. Ampoules with chemical agents were used for ignition. The liquid ignited when contacting the chemical agent in the ampoules – this occurred as both the bottle and the ampoule broke when hitting a tank. The ampoules were attached to the bottle with a rubber band or were inserted in the bottles. Another ignition mechanism used matches, attached to the bottle with rubber bands. These fuse-matches were sticks fully covered with igniting agent. They were set on fire before the bottle was thrown using a friction strip or a regular matchbox. The contents burned for 40–50 seconds at up to 800° C (1472° F) when the bottle hit the tank. When fuse-matches were unavailable, the recommendation was to throw a bottle with KS liquid followed by one or two containing Number 1 or Number 3 solution.

The tactics employed by an infantryman armed with a Molotov Cocktail were very simple. He had to let a tank come as close as 15–20m (50ft) and throw a bottle at it, targeting the engine compartment or the area between the turret and the hull. This all sounds easy in theory, but not in the real engagement when the armoured assault is accompanied by an artillery barrage and the enemy infantry follows the tanks. Quite often, when a soldier got up to throw a bottle at the tank, a bullet or a shell fragment hit the bottle, and a soldier would instantly become a living torch.

One man to whom this happened was Naval Infantryman Mikhail Panikakha. Panikakha prepared to throw a bottle at a German tank in Stalingrad, but a bullet hit the bottle, and the infantryman burst into flames. However, he managed to grab another bottle, ran to the tank and smashed the second bottle against the tank's armour. He was posthumously awarded the Golden Star of the Hero of the Soviet Union, albeit in 1990, 45 years after the war.

casualties were very high, those inflicted on the Russians were much greater. As soon as the city was captured, however, the divisions would have to be rested and reorganized. They also stated that it was critical to secure sufficient fodder and straw for the horses.

In his diary for 26 September Hoffman noted grimly: 'Our regiment is involved in constant, heavy fighting. After the elevator was taken the Russians continued to defend themselves just as stubbornly. You don't see them at all, they have established themselves in houses and cellars and are firing on all sides, including from our rear – barbarians, they use gangster methods.

'In the blocks captured two days ago Russian troops appeared from somewhere or other and fighting has flared up with fresh vigour. Our men are being killed not only in the firing line, but in the rear, in buildings we have already occupied.

Above: A squad of Soviet infantrymen inch forward in a bomb and shell shattered building. They are all armed with the PPSh-41 7.62mm (0.3in) submachine gun with 71-round drum magazine. The SMG shared the same calibre as the Tokarev automatic pistol.

'The Russians have stopped surrendering at all. If we take any prisoners it's because they are hopelessly wounded, and can't move by themselves. Stalingrad is hell. Those who are merely wounded are lucky; they will doubtless be at home and celebrate victory with their families. …'

On 25 September the Sixth Army again attacked in Stalingrad. German troops, worn by battle, were alternating between optimistic frenzy and depression. Some green German troops yelled across streets goading Soviet troops 'Russ! Tomorrow bang-bang!'

'The days were shortening again, you could definitely sense it,' wrote a German officer. 'And in the mornings, the air was quite cool. Were we really going to have to fight through another of those dreadful winters? I think that was behind our efforts. Many of us felt that it was worth anything, at any price, if we could get it over before the winter.' Gains and losses were now being measured in metres, and sniper rifles, SMGs, and hand grenades were the weapons of choice along with crowbars, picks, and explosives. The Sixty-Second Army had become a highly competent force of street fighters, reinforced by General Smekhotvorov's 193rd Infantry Division.

The German attack on 25 September was launched by three infantry and two panzer divisions. While the Germans attacked by day, the Soviets counter-attacked at night.

On 26 September Chuikov reminded his officers in Army Order No 166 'I again caution all unit and formation commanders not to execute combat operations with entire units such as companies and battalions. The offensive should be organised mainly on a small-group basis, with automatic weapons, hand grenades, bottles of inflammable mixture and anti-tank rifles.'

Chuikov was finally receiving help from the Soviet Air Force's Eighth Air Army, whose 1400 aircraft included the new Yak-9 and La-5 fighters, far superior to the earlier I-16s and Lagg-3s. The Soviet pilots had trained extensively in night flying and experimented with radio communication to concentrate units for attacks.

On 27 September the Sixth Army captured the Communist Party headquarters, and unfurled the Swastika from the building in front of a PK camera crew. The event also attracted Soviet mortar fire. Hitler marked the Sixth Army's latest triumph by flying from Vinnitsa to Berlin, to prepare his big speech announcing the capture of Stalingrad.

Above: A Yakovlev Yak-1 fighter flown by B.N. Yevemen that bears the slogan, 'To the pilot of Stalingrad Front Guards Major Comrade Yevemen. From the Collective Farm workers of the Collective Farm Stakhanov'.

Back in the city, the Russians attacked at 06:00 but were halted two hours later by Stuka attacks. The Germans launched their own attack on the Mamayev Kurgan and *Krasny Oktyabr* factory housing estate. The 24th Panzer, 100th Infantry and 389th Infantry Divisions attacked. The 100th was fresh and the 389th had recently been brought up to strength with replacements. The *Luftwaffe* hit the Sixty-Second Army's bridgehead with bombs and the Soviet 95th Division's strongpoints on the Mamayev Kurgan were almost obliterated by high explosive.

MIXED FORTUNES

The Germans breached the minefields and penetrated the *Barrikady* Factory housing estate. They also drove the Soviets off the Mamayev Kurgan, nearly destroying the 95th

---

YAKOVLEV YAK-9

The Yak-9 was a single-engined single-seat low-level fighter and ground attack aircraft that made its debut at Stalingrad. It was powered by a 1360hp Klimov VK-105PF-3 engine that produced a maximum speed at 2000m (6560ft) of 602km/h (374mph) and a range of 1410km (876 miles). It weighed 2770kg (6107lb) empty and 3080kg (6790lb) loaded. Its wing span was 9.74m (32ft 11in), its length 8.55m (28ft) and its height 3m (9ft 10in). One version of the Yak-9, the Yak-9DK, which had a dedicated anti-tank role, mounted a single

45mm (1.7in) NS-P-45 cannon in the nose. Normal armament was one 20mm (0.78in) ShVAK cannon firing through the propeller hub and one 12.7mm (0.5in) Berezin machine gun in the upper cowling. In the Korean War of 1950–53 the Chinese and North Korean Air Forces used the Yak-9 in action against USAF bombers. The Yak-9 showed that it had a tough and versatile airframe, and the huge Factory No 153 in the Urals began to build it in quantity. By the close of the war it had built 15,000 of the 30,000 Yak-9s.

Division. 'One more battle like that,' Chuikov said, 'And we'll be in the Volga.' The hill changed hands several times. By 27 September the Germans had again captured half of the Mamayev Kurgan. The Soviets held their own positions on the slopes of the hill, as the 284th Rifle Division desperately defended the key stronghold. The defenders held out until 26 January 1943, when the Soviet winter offensive relieved them, trapping and destroying the German forces inside Stalingrad.

When the battle ended, the blood-soaked soil on the hill was cratered and full of shrapnel: between 500 and 1250 splinters of metal were found per square metre. The earth on

STALINGRAD, A TRIUMPH OF MORALE

It is, indeed, something more than material conditions, something that transcends the pure mechanics of war, that is involved at Stalingrad. It is the great imponderable morale that has turned a defensive with so many handicaps, a defensive, moreover, that seemed spent, into this astounding episode that is clearly baffling the German Command.

The Daily Telegraph, September 1942

the hill had remained black in the winter, as the snow kept melting in the fires and explosions. The following spring the hill would remain black, as no grass grew on its scorched soil. The hill's formerly steep slopes had been flattened by months of intense shelling and aerial bombardment.

After the war, the Mamayev Kurgan memorial complex was built. On top of the hill a huge allegorical statue of Mother Russia was erected. The statue is 52m (137ft) high and is made of 5588 tonnes (5500 tons) of concrete and 2438 tonnes (2400 tons) of metal. The sword is stainless steel and is 29m (79ft 6in) long, weighing 14.3 tonnes (14 tons). The hanging part of the scarf weighs 254 tonnes (250 tons). It dominates the skyline of the city of Stalingrad, later renamed Volgograd.

The Soviet troops had discipline imposed by the *Narodnyy Kommissariat Vnutrennikh Del* – the NKVD or 'People's Commissariat for Internal Affairs'. The secret police units had been ruthless in keeping them in the front line.

At dusk, Chuikov received a call from Khrushchev, Yeremenko's political officer. 'What help do you need?' Khrushchev asked Chuikov. 'I'm not complaining about

Left: The vertiginous dive of a Ju 87 over Stalingrad. The howl of the dive bombers' sirens induced fear in people on the ground by making them think that the attack was aimed directly at them. This made the Stuka a formidable psychological weapon.

the air force, which is putting up a heroic fight, but the enemy has mastery of the air. The *Luftwaffe* is his trump card in attack. Therefore I ask for more help in this field – air cover for only a few hours a day,' he replied. Khrushchev promised help.

That night Chuikov sent his officers and *zampoliti* (political officers) to exhort the Sixty-Second Army to their highest pitch of resolve. Two regiments of infantry were ferried across to hold the *Krasny Oktyabr* housing estate. Soviet guns shelled the Mamayev Kurgan to prevent the Germans from digging in.

Chuikov's instructions to his troops is a model of low-level tactics: 'Get close to the enemy's positions: move on all fours, making use of craters and ruins; dig your trenches by night, camouflage them by day; make your build-up for the attack stealthily, without any noise; carry your tommy-gun on your shoulder; take 10 to 12 grenades. Timing and surprise will then be on your side ...

'Two of you get into the house together – you, and a grenade; both be lightly dressed – you without a knapsack and the grenade bare; go in grenade first, you after; go through the whole house, again always with a grenade first and you fire....

'There is one strict rule now – give yourself elbow room! At every step danger lurks. No matter – a grenade in every

Below: Surrounded by the brick chimneys – the only remains of the wooden homes that clustered around the western fringes of the city – a stray horse grazes on the meagre grass. It would soon become horsemeat for the Sixth Army.

NKVD (*NARODNYY KOMMISSARIAT VNUTRENNIKH DEL*)

In 1934, the Government Political Administration (GPU) became known as the People's Commissariat for Internal Affairs (NKVD). Later that year the new head of the NKVD, Genrikh Yagoda, arrested Lev Kamenev, Gregory Zinoviev, Ivan Smirnov and 13 others and accused them of being involved with Leon Trotsky in a plot to murder Stalin and other party leaders. All of these men were found guilty and were executed on 25 August 1936.

After Yagoda's failure to obtain enough evidence to convict Nikolai Bukharin, he was sacked and Stalin appointed Nikolai Yezhov as head of the NKVD. Yezhov quickly arranged the arrest of all the leading political figures in the Soviet Union who were critical of Stalin.

The NKVD broke prisoners down by intense interrogation. This included the threat to arrest and execute members of a prisoner's family if they did not confess. The interrogation went on for several days and nights and eventually prisoners became so exhausted and disoriented that they signed confessions agreeing that they had been attempting to overthrow the government.

In 1936 Bukharin, Alexei Rykov, Genrikh Yagoda, Nikolai Krestinsky and Christian Rakovsky were arrested and accused of being involved with Leon Trotsky in a plot against Stalin. They were all found guilty and were eventually executed.

In August 1936 Alexander Orlov was appointed by the Soviet Politburo as advisor to the Popular Front government in Spain. Orlov was given considerable authority by the Republican administration during the Spanish Civil War. Orlov supervised a large-scale guerrilla operation behind Nationalist lines. He later claimed that around 14,000 people had been trained for this work by 1938. Orlov also used NKVD agents to deal with left-wing opponents of the Communist Party (PCE) in Republican-held areas. This included the arrest and execution of leaders of the Workers' Party (POUM), *Confederación Nacional del Trabajo* (CNT) and the *Federación Anarquista Ibérica* (FAI). In July 1938 Orlov was ordered back to the Soviet Union by Stalin. Aware of the Great Purge that was going on, Orlov fled to France with his family before making his way to the United States.

The Soviet purges continued, and with the murder of Leon Trotsky in Mexico on 20 August 1940, all the leading figures involved in the Russian Revolution were dead except for Stalin. Of the 15 members of the original Bolshevik government, 10 had been executed and four had died (sometimes in mysterious circumstances). Of the 1966 delegates who had attended the Communist Party Congress in 1934, 1108 were arrested over the next five years. Only 70 people were tried in public. The rest were tried in secret before being executed. Official figures suggest that between January 1935 and June 1941, 19.8 million people were arrested by the NKVD of whom an estimated seven million were executed. The armed forces also suffered at the hands of the NKVD. It has been estimated that between 1936 and 1941 a third of all officers were arrested. Three out of five marshals and 14 out of 16 army commanders were executed. Members of the NKVD were also purged by Stalin. The first three heads of the NKVD were all executed: Genrikh Yagoda (1934–36), Nikolai Yezhov (1936–39) and Lavrenti Beria (1939–53).

After World War II, the Communist secret police was renamed the Committee for State Security (KGB).

corner of the room, then forward! A burst from your tommy-gun around what's left; a bit further – a grenade, then on again! Another room – a grenade! A turning – another grenade! Rake it with your tommy-gun! And get a move on!'

IMPROVISATION

At dawn on 28 September the *Luftwaffe* attacked, dropping everything they had. *Luftwaffe* supply officers were running out of bombs so ground crews loaded their Junkers 88 bomb bays with pieces of scrap metal, agricultural equipment, tractor wheels and empty cans, to use as shrapnel. At the time it was thought that the *Luftwaffe* was dropping this metal junk as a way of demoralizing Soviet forces. The *Luftwaffe* hammered everything in sight and knocked out five of the six cargo ferries.

Flames from burning oil tanks spread to the Military Council's dugout, and Chuikov's personal cook, Glinka, was injured in the shell hole that doubled as his kitchen. Despite the hammering, Chuikov still had hope. The German attacks were becoming less well co-ordinated and slower. The Lagg-3 and Yak-1 fighter pilots of Major-General Khryukin's air force discovered that unescorted Ju 87 Stukas were easy targets. Reinforcements in the form of machine-gun battalions were on the way also. Chuikov counter-attacked the Mamayev Kurgan, but failed to retake the summit. But it

was also untenable for the Germans, and the hill became a no-man's land.

That evening Soviet reserves were deployed behind Sixty-Second Army as *Stavka* wondered if Chuikov's soldiers would hold. With most of the cargo ferries lost, movement of fresh men up to the front and evacuating the wounded became increasingly difficult.

By now the German attackers and Soviet defenders of Stalingrad had almost reached stalemate, with neither force capable of delivering a knock-out blow. The Soviet writer Konstantin Simonov wrote during the fighting in Stalingrad: 'Houses all over the city were burning and at night their smoky glow filled the horizon. Day and night the earth was shaken by the thunder of the bombing and the artillery barrage. The wreckage of crashed bombers lay scattered in the streets and the air screamed with shells from the ack-ack, but not for a moment did the bombing stop. The besiegers were trying to turn Stalingrad into a hell on earth. But it was impossible to remain inactive – you had to fight, you had to defend the city amid the fire, the smoke and the blood. This was the only way you could live, the only way you had to live.'

On the same day Hoffman wrote 'Our regiment, and the whole division, are today celebrating victory. Together with our tank crews we have taken the southern part of the city and reached the Volga. We paid dearly for our victory. In three weeks we have occupied about five and a half square miles. The commander has congratulated us on our victory. ...'

On 29 September the 14th Panzer and 94th Infantry Divisions advanced down into *balkas* running down to the Volga and into the *Krasny Oktyabr* Factory cemetery. The Soviet forces pulled back from the cemetery leaving the German soldiers the grim prospect of digging-in among the headstones and graves.

On 30 September Hitler spoke at The Winter Relief Rally at the *Sportspalast* in Berlin. The speech was broadcast to a wider German audience:

'When Mr Eden or some other fool declares that they have a belief, we cannot talk with them, as their idea of belief seems to be different from ours ... They believed that Dunkirk was one of the greatest victories in the world's history ... What have we to offer them? If we advance 1000 kilometres, it is nothing. It is a veritable failure ... If we could cross the Don, thrust to the Volga, attack Stalingrad – and it

Left: A Stalingrad family attempts to survive in the late summer of 1942. Grimly this father, mother and daughter would probably not survive the winter and, if they did, would be seen as suspect by the Soviet authorities because of their enforced contact with the Nazi occupiers.

MG-34 MACHINE GUN

The MG34 machine gun, commonly known in the West as the Spandau, was the section automatic weapon with which the German forces entered World War II. Designed by Louis Stange of Rheinmetall, it was the world's first General Purpose Machine Gun (GPMG), a weapon that could be used in the light role firing from its bipod, or in the sustained-fire role on a folding tripod with an optical sight. Its design drew on German experience in World War I, where water-cooled Maxim machine guns were too cumbersome to be used effectively in the trenches.

The tripod of the MG34 gave greater stability and consequently a longer effective range – however, if the crew were attacked from another direction it was difficult to dismount the gun and redeploy it quickly. The MG34 could also be used as a light AA gun with a ring sight on a special mount. Tanks and other AFVs were equipped with the MG34. Infantry crews carried two spare barrels in a metal tubular container, which were changed after they had fired 250 rounds. The air-cooled weapon was 121.9cm (48in) long with a 62.7cm (24.75in) barrel, weighing 11.9kg (26.7lb) in the light role and 31.07kg (68.5lbs) on the sustained-fire mount. With a muzzle velocity of 755m (2480ft) per second it had a maximum range of 2000m (2187 yards) and a cyclic rate of 800–900 rounds per minute. It fired from a 75-round saddle drum magazine or 50-round non-disintegrating belts that could be reloaded for subsequent use and carried in two or more ammunition boxes.

Above: The MG34 was a superbly engineered weapon; however, this made it expensive and it was replaced by the MG42, which could be mass-produced by unskilled workers.

Above: A soldier leans cautiously out of a window to display a Swastika flag. This shows that the building is in German hands to men on the ground and also hopefully the Luftwaffe as well as being a good propaganda gesture.

will be taken, you may be sure of that – then it is nothing. It is nothing if we advance to the Caucasus, occupy the Ukraine and the Donetz basin … We had three objectives. One – to take away the last great Russian wheat territory. Two – to take away the last district of coking coal. Three – to approach the oil district, paralyse it, and at least cut it off. Our offensive then went on to the enemy's great transport artery, the Volga and Stalingrad. You may rest assured that once there, no one will push us out of that spot …'

He was almost correct. Swastika flags fluttered over the shattered remains of the stores and public buildings in the city and machine gunners could fire on the ferries crossing the Volga from the Soviet-held east bank. Despite this the 39th Guards Infantry Division managed to cross the Volga

early in the morning, at half strength, and dug in between the Silicate Factory and Zuyvskaya Street.

On the last day of September Hitler also re-issued Field Marshal Manstein's Order of the Day of 20 November 1941, which reminded all German troops that they were facing 'not merely a fighter according to the rules of the act of war, but also the bearer of a ruthless ideology'. The German soldier must therefore understand 'the necessity for a severe but just revenge on sub-human Jewry'.

CHAPTER FOUR

THE FINAL EFFORT

Though neither the German nor the Soviet forces locked in combat in Stalingrad realized it at the time, October would be the critical month in the fighting for the city and ultimately for the fate of the Sixth Army. There would be a week to 10 days in the month that would be the last opportunity that the Germans would have of grasping victory. During this time only incredibly tough leadership and extraordinary courage would keep the Soviet Sixty-Second Army hanging on to its toehold on the west bank of the Volga.

THE ONCE-FORMIDABLE *LUFTFLOTTE* IV had by October been weakened considerably by the months of intense combat, and the Russian Air Force had almost wrested air superiority from the Germans, as both more and newer equipment arrived. In addition, as the Germans captured more and more of Stalingrad, the Red Air Force could more easily bomb the city. *Stavka* also dispatched General A.A. Novikov to help co-ordinate air operations for the planned counter-attack at Stalingrad. He became such a valued team member that when he stated that the air forces were not yet prepared, Zhukhov delayed the opening of the offensive.

In preparation for a large-scale assault on the city on 1 October the Germans attacked the Orlovka salient that projected westwards from the northern suburb of Rynok. The attack by the 60th Motorized Division from the north and the 100th Infantry Division from the south trapped a battalion of the 115th Rifle Brigade that fought on for five

Left: Near a wrecked farm, men of a German PK (propaganda) company prepare a meal by their 4x2 Typ 320 WK vehicle. They have dug a basic trench in which they can take cover in the event of air or artillery attack.

PTRD 1941 ANTI-TANK RIFLE

Introduced in 1941, the 14.5mm (0.57in) Degtyarev-PTRD anti-tank rifle fired a very powerful steel-cored or tungsten bullet that could penetrate 25mm (1in) of armour at 500m (547 yards). The single-shot weapon with a semi-automatic action could deliver eight to 10 rounds per minute. It was 196.6cm (78.74in) long, weighed 17.44kg (38lb) and had a muzzle velocity of 1010m (3320ft) per second. Though thicker tank armour would be proof against it, it remained in service throughout the war since it was a valuable weapon in street fighting. In Stalingrad a battalion commander, Captain Ilgachkin, teamed up with a Private Repa, a man remembered as 'gaunt and melancholy', to modify the PTRD as an anti-aircraft weapon. They fixed it to the spokes of a cartwheel and mounted it on a tall stake driven into the ground. The officer worked out the velocity of the round in relation to the speed of a diving Stuka. Whether Repa used this information is open to question, but what is not is that he downed three dive-bombers with this contraption. Master sniper Vasily Zaitsev also experimented with the anti-tank rifle and a telescopic sight as a long-range sniping weapon against machine gun bunkers. However, its mass-produced ammunition did not produce consistent performance at long ranges.

days. Two other battalions from the Soviet brigade attempted a relief attack from the east but were caught in a massive German artillery barrage as well as by concentrated air strikes. Some divisions of the Sixty-Second Army were now down to only 2000 men, and the *Luftwaffe* was attacking the city's oil reserves.

THE FACTORIES DISTRICT

In the factories district the Germans launched heavy attacks against the 193rd Rifle Division near the *Krasny Oktyabr* (Red October) steel works that had been providing the armour plate for the T-34s that were being built at the Tractor Factory. The Soviet 284th Rifle and 13th Guards Divisions were under pressure as the Germans attempted to reach the Volga, but the 13th Guards blocked German attempts via the Krutoy and Dolgi Gullies. During the night the German 295th Infantry Division sent a strong assault force of 300 men, according to some accounts disguised as Soviet soldiers, into the Krutoy Gully and down to the banks of the Volga. Here they swung south into the rear of the 13th Guards. They dug in and waited until dawn when they attacked the Soviet positions from the front and rear. As his defences began to break up, Chuikov ordered the 39th Guards to hold and fortify the *Krasny Oktyabr* factory.

Since attacks began on 13 September the Sixth Army had suffered 40,000 casualties while the Sixty-Second had lost 78,000 men. However, the Soviet command had a shorter supply line than the Germans and had 950 guns, 500 mortars and 80 tanks within the city. Supplies were being shipped across the Volga, and a narrow pontoon bridge built around barrels and planking that linked Zaitsevsky Island to the west bank had been constructed by a battalion of Volga boatmen from Yaroslavl. It was wide enough for porters to carry rations and ammunition on their backs, but too narrow for German artillery spotters to call down accurate fire on it. For the porters the nightly dash across the constantly moving bridge must have been a terrifying experience.

INTO THE *KRASNY OKTYABR*

On 2 October the *Krasny Oktyabr* Factory and city centre came under German attack. The 295th Infantry Division launched an attack at 06:00 against the rear and right wing of the 13th Guards Division. The Soviet forces hung on, fighting hard, and eventually eliminated the enemy force that had infiltrated into their position. Heavy attacks were launched against the factory positions where the 112th Rifle Division was hard-pressed, suffering heavy losses. The 193rd Rifle Division fought in the *Krasny Oktyabr* kitchens, bath house and workers' flats, while the 39th Guards held the factory complex. One survivor of the fighting for the plant described it as 'A ghastly place for a battle ... heavy metal panels creaking in the wind', with walls and supporting columns on the verge of collapse. On the southern flank, southwest of Yelshanka, the Soviet Sixty-Fourth Army launched a counter-attack with four rifle divisions in an effort to link up with the Sixty-Second Army but were repulsed after a day of hard fighting.

After locating the area in which they believed that Chuikov had his headquarters German artillery bombarded the industrial area of the city and hit the oil storage tanks. Everyone had believed that they were empty and it was therefore a shock to both Soviet and German forces alike when they exploded, sending flames down the river and huge columns of black smoke into the sky. Chuikov hung on in this HQ for three days. With telephone lines burnt out he kept in contact with his troops by radio. Across the Volga Yeremenko's chief of staff of the Stalingrad Front sent a stream of radio requests to Chuikov's HQ for a location report, in reality to check that the Sixty-Second Army was still a coherent force. There was a worrying silence and then a signaller at the Sixty-Second Army HQ transmitted this terse report: 'We're where the most smoke and flames are.'

Reinforcements continued to arrive for the Sixty-Second Army. The 308th Rifle Division was ferried across the Volga during the night of 2/3 October and moved into positions in the *Barrikady* Factory, near the Tractor Factory between the 112th and 308th Divisions. Yeremenko sent over the 37th Guards Division under Major-General Zholudev. They arrived but without their anti-tank guns. The 84th Armoured Brigade followed but since their T-34s were too big for the barges they could only transport light tanks which were used as pillboxes in the rubble.

On 3 October the hard battle for Orlovka reached its climax as the 115th Rifle Brigade struggled to repulse attacks by the XIV Panzer Corps. The Soviets had suffered cruelly but planned to break out through the Orlovka Gully to the factories. In the factory areas the 308th Rifle Division launched counter-attacks that drove the Germans back into the Silicate Factory.

Chuikov commented that 'The infantry and the tanks which had broken through were destroyed separately: the tanks were unable to do very much without infantry and, without achieving anything, they would turn back after suffering big losses ... Counter-attacks always caused the enemy heavy losses, frequently forcing him to abandon his

Below: In a picture probably posed after the battle, Soviet soldiers man a 12.7mm (0.5in) DshK1938 heavy machine gun at the Krasny Oktyabr Factory as Soviet aircraft fly overhead. The DshK was a formidable weapon that was mounted on tanks and small coastal craft.

THE STALINGRAD ARMSHIELD

Hitler had authorized a metal Crimean Shield, a Narvik Shield and a Cholm Shield to be worn by veterans of these actions on the upper sleeve of their tunics and so he proposed that one should be designed for the soldiers who had fought at Stalingrad. Paulus agreed but others were against the idea, Chief of Staff Schmidt saying that Stalingrad was not captured yet and the decorations had to wait.

Paulus ordered Propaganda Company 637 to produce a shield and they commissioned the war artist Ernst Eigener to prepare the design. Eigener had been in the war from the very beginning, in Poland, France, the invasion of Russia and now Stalingrad. He was to be met everywhere, in tanks and trucks and in the mud with the infantry. He loved life and all living creatures, and therefore he hated war. Friends said of him that he could not laugh; this was not quite true – they meant that they had never seen him laugh. Eigener was interested in much that other men pass by without a glance; ruins, which others might ignore, appealed to his artist's eye. He examined where most were merely bored; gunfire and clouds, sun and mud, the clear nights, the Volga mist. He thought of no man as his enemy, and he hoped one day to return to Russia and to live in a house in the hills near Kalach beside the Don.

In the centre of the shield Ernst Eigener drew the Grain Elevator, amidst the ruins of the city beside the Volga. Turned towards it was the face of a dead soldier. Around the soldier's helmet was a crown of barbed wire and right across the design, in bold letters, the single word 'Stalingrad'. This design was turned down by the OKW with the comment 'Too demoralizing'. A design showing the Elevator with the words 'Stalingrad' and 'Wolga' and surmounted by a German eagle was accepted by the OKW. It was said that this conventional design was the work of General Paulus.

On 20 November 1942, a day filled with sunshine, the soldier and artist Ernst Eigener was killed in action close to where he had hoped one day to build himself a house after the war. He was 37 years old. Three hours before he was killed he wrote in a letter to a friend 'The stars are eternal, but men behave as though they will be gone tomorrow.'

---

attack in a given area and rush up and down the front searching for a weak point in our defences, lose time and lower his rate of advance. ... We often had the aim not only of causing the enemy losses, but, by surprise attack with infantry and tanks, with artillery and air support, to penetrate into the enemy's starting positions, upset his formations, break his attack and gain time.'

The latest German offensive at Stalingrad began to bog down as German forces reached the Volga at several points. Resistance by the Sixty-Second Army remained strong as several bridgeheads in the south and central sectors continued to hold out, but near the factory complexes Sixty-Second Army was pushed back to the bank of the Volga. Casualties on both sides were very heavy.

ALL-OUT ATTACK

Hitler now ordered that Stalingrad be taken whatever the cost to German forces. General Kurt Zeitzler, Chief of the General Staff, was totally opposed to the idea, urging Hitler to permit the Sixth Army to withdraw from Stalingrad to the Don bend, where the broken front could be restored. Hitler refused and on the radio he told the German people 'You may rest assured that nobody will ever drive us out of Stalingrad.' When General Gustav von Wietersheim,

commander of the XIV Panzer Corps, complained about the high casualty rates, Paulus replaced him with General Hans Hube. However, Paulus, who had lost 40,000 soldiers since entering the city, was running out of fighting men and on 4 October he made a desperate plea to Hitler for reinforcements.

On the Soviet side there had been a total mobilization of the whole community to prosecute the war. General Chuikov remarked: 'It is no exaggeration to say that women fought alongside men everywhere in the war ... Anyone who visited the front would see women acting as gunners in anti-artillery units, as pilots of aircraft doing battle with the German air aces, as captains of armoured boats, in the Volga fleet, for example, carrying cargoes from the left bank to the right and back again in unbelievably difficult conditions. ... The majority of gun crews in the Stalingrad anti-aircraft defence corps, in both anti-aircraft batteries and on searchlights, consisted of women ... They would stick to their

Right: The second assault on Stalingrad reduced the Orlovka salient to the north and so made the northern ferry routes vulnerable to artillery fire. In the attack on the salient the Germans were able to use their tanks and air support effectively; in the battle for the factories in northern Stalingrad they would not enjoy these advantages.

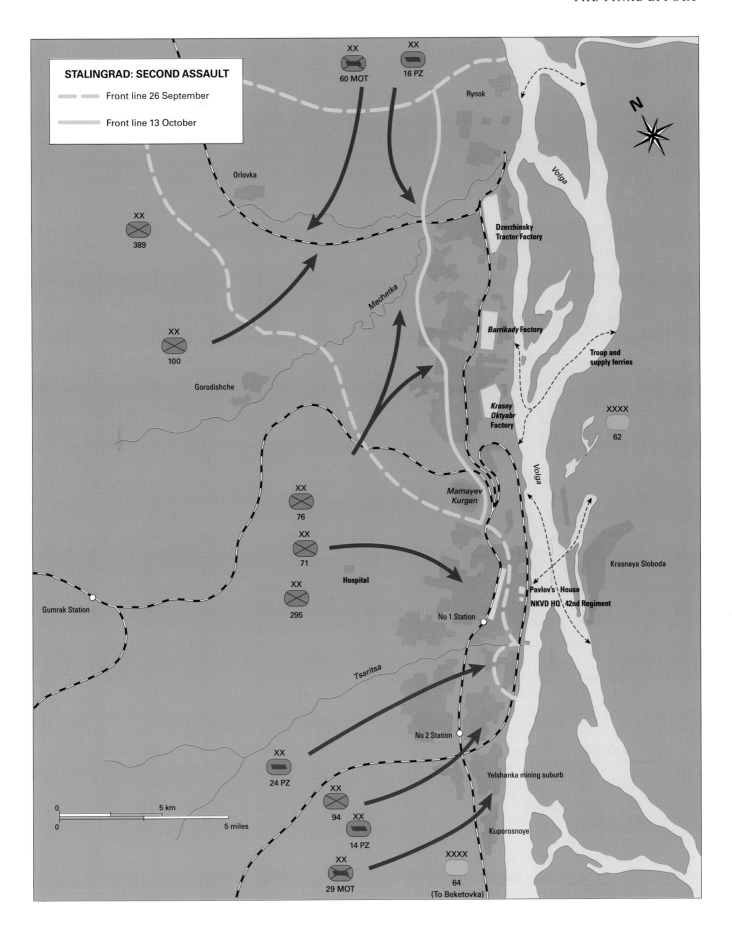

STALINGRAD: SECOND ASSAULT

Front line 26 September

Front line 13 October

Rynok

Orlovka

Dzerzhinsky Tractor Factory

XX
60 MOT

XX
16 PZ

Volga

XX
389

Mechetka

Barrikady Factory

XX
100

Troop and supply ferries

Gorodishche

Krasny Oktyabr Factory

XXXX
62

Volga

XX
76

Mamayev Kurgan

XX
71

Krasnaya Sloboda

Hospital

Gumrak Station

XX
295

Pavlov's House
NKVD HQ 42nd Regiment

No 1 Station

Tsaritsa

No 2 Station

XX
24 PZ

Yelshanka mining suburb

XX
94

0   5 km

0   5 miles

XX
14 PZ

Kuporosnoye

XX
29 MOT

XXXX
64
(To Beketovka)

75

Above: PzKpfw III tanks move past the gutted remains of workers' flats on the outer fringes of Stalingrad. Tanks would be at a serious disadvantage when they attempted to push into the wrecked factories where ranges were shorter, the going poor and the enemy difficult to locate.

guns and go on firing when bombs were exploding all around them, when it seemed impossible not merely to fire accurately, but even to stay with the guns. In the fire and smoke, amid bursting bombs, seemingly unaware of the columns of earth exploding into the air all about them, they stood their ground to the last. The [*Luftwaffe*] raids on the city, therefore, in spite of heavy losses among the anti-aircraft personnel, were always met by concentrated fire, which as a rule took a heavy toll among attacking aircraft. Our women anti-aircraft gunners shot down dozens of enemy planes over the blazing city.'

There were, however, few women who served as front-line soldiers in Stalingrad, though one notable exception was Yekaterina Petlyuk who was a member of a tank crew.

On 4 October Paulus launched his second major offensive on Stalingrad. Assault pioneers and police units were used because of their street fighting expertise. The German LI Corps attacked positions in the *Barrikady*, *Krasny Oktyabr* and Tractor Factories.

For Hoffman the reality of the offensive began with a night march on 3 October:

'We have established ourselves in a shrub-covered gully. We are apparently going to attack the factories, the chimneys of which we can see clearly. Behind them is the Volga. We

have entered a new area. It was night but we saw many crosses with our helmets on top. Have we really lost so many men? Damn this Stalingrad!

'4 October. Our regiment is attacking the Barrikady settlement. A lot of Russian tommy-gunners have appeared. Where are they bringing them from?

'5 October. Our battalion has gone into the attack four times, and got stopped each time. Russian snipers hit anyone who shows himself carelessly from behind shelter.'

In Berlin Hitler announced that he wanted Stalingrad taken by 15 October and that, after the city had been completely captured, Paulus would be promoted to be his new chief of staff.

On the night of 4 October the 84th Tank Brigade crossed the Volga and entered the battle. It had a total of 49 tanks –

Right: Private Kalmikov loads a 76.2mm (3in) Field Gun M1939 in October 1942. The gun layer is Private Ovchinnikov. The gun is sited in a building for cover and camouflage.

Above: Men of a 62nd Army Storm Group armed with PPSh-41 submachine guns and dressed in camouflaged snipers' smocks. The men taking aim are supporting the weapon with their left hand under the magazine to give greater stability.

five KVs, 24 T-34s and 20 T-70s. The shortage of ferry boats meant that the some men had to wait for the next night to make the crossing. The boats now showed numerous signs of the hazards of crossing the Volga. For example, a fire-fighting launch pressed into service in the Volga flotilla was reported to have received 436 bullet and shell holes in one outward and return trip and only a single square metre was undamaged.

In Moscow Stalin was beginning to wonder if Stalingrad could be held and so on 5 October he sent special orders to Yeremenko emphasizing the need to hold the city. *Stavka* sent reinforcements, including light anti-aircraft regiments that had a mix of triple Maxim machine guns and light guns from the Moscow Defence Zone to beef up the anti-aircraft defences on the Volga islands of Sporny, Zaitsevsky, Golodny and Sarpinsky. They were further reinforced by a full

My God, why have you forsaken us?

Anonymous lieutenant in a Panzer Division, Stalingrad, October 1942.

regiment of 12 37mm (1.45in) anti-aircraft guns. In early October the islands would be designated a special defence command under Popov's II Tank Corps. By 12 October two cavalry divisions (the 61st and 81st) from the IV Corps and the VII Rifle Corps had reached Yeremenko's Front. The 169th Rifle Division, supported by light anti-aircraft regiments, also arrived.

One further rifle division, the 45th, was posted from *Stavka* reserve and put under Popov's special command. Popov then received orders to set up three defensive zones on the eastern bank. The first would be from the mouth of the Akhtuba River to the suburb of Krasnaya Sloboda, the second from Golodny and Sarpinsky and the third running north from the mouth of the Akhtuba.

Across the river the fighting continued, and Chuikov's HQ signals log for 15 October gives an indication of the intensity of the fighting during that day:

Above: The Soviet SVT-40 automatic rifle evolved from the Tokarev SVT-38. Captured weapons were used by the Germans under the designation 7.62mm SIGew 259(r). It had a 10-round magazine and could fire 30 rounds a minute.

'05:30. As yesterday the enemy has again begun heavy shelling.

'08:00. The enemy launched an attack with tanks and infantry. There is fighting along the entire front.

'09:30. The attack on the Tractor Works has been beaten off. Ten Nazi tanks are burning in the factory yard.

'10:00. The 109th Guards Regiment of the 37th Division has been crushed by enemy tanks and infantry.

'11:30. The left flank of the 524th Regiment of the 95th Division has been smashed and about 50 German tanks are "steamrolling" the position.

'11:50. The enemy has seized an area of the Tractor Works. Some of our units, which have been cut off, are fighting in encirclement.

'12:00. Major Andreyev, commander of the 117th Regiment, has been killed.

'12:00. A radio message from the hexagonal district from a unit of the 416th Regiment:

"Encirclement. Ammunition and water we have. Shall die but not surrender!"

'12:30. General Zholudev's command post is being attacked by Stuka dive-bombers. General Zholudev has no working communications: his dugout is half buried. We shall now have to maintain contact with the units of his division.

'13:10. Two dugouts of the army command post have caved in. One of the officers got his legs trapped. The others were unable to release him.

STORM GROUPS

Storm Groups were platoon-sized or larger units developed by the Sixty-Second Army tailored to the mission of active defence. They would launch assaults on forward German positions. Storm Groups appeared when the Sixty-Second Army was desperately trying to hold on to Stalingrad in September 1942, and their organization grew out of the use of traditional rifle groups, which did not have the firepower to maximize assault tactics. The Germans never did manage to counter Storm Group tactics, and they were used right up to the liberation of Stalingrad.

Storm Groups were built around two or more Assault Teams, consisting of a leader and between eight and 10 men. Supporting them was a Reinforcement Group that included anti-tank gun or rifle teams, mortar crews, machine gunners, and specialists, such as demolition teams, snipers or flame-thrower crews. The Reinforcement Group would also carry explosives, crowbars and picks to assist in the fortification of the recently captured building. Providing further support was a Reserve Detachment organized into two or more Assault Teams. They would also block off the flanks against enemy counter-attacks and if the operation failed would cover the withdrawal of the Assault and Reinforcement parties.

In action, the Assault Teams would use stealth and speed to approach a German position, holding their fire if possible until they were right on top of their objective. Then they would use grenades, submachine guns and even entrenching tools and shovels to disrupt and suppress and ultimately kill or drive out the German soldiers there. Once they were on the objective, they would signal the Reinforcement Group to move up and secure the flanks. During this time, the Assault Teams would be cleaning up the objective, and fortifying it against counter-attack, or as a staging point for the next Storm Group operation.

Other missions performed by Storm Groups include raids on enemy supply lines, and even tunnelling under German positions to place explosive charges. In defence they would site anti-tank weapons on the ground floor of a building, machine guns on the upper storeys and infantry at all levels including the basement.

Storm Groups were eventually found in every division that fought in Stalingrad and were one of the reasons that the city became known as the 'University of Street Fighting'.

'14:40. All telephone communications have broken down. We have switched over to radio communication and are duplicating our messages by sending liaison officers. Our aircraft cannot take off because the *Luftwaffe* is blocking the airfields.

'15:25. The army headquarters guard has been thrown into action.

'16:00. All contact with the 114th Guards Regiment has been lost. The situation there is unknown.

'16:20. Lieutenant Colonel Ustinov, regimental commander, requests artillery fire on his command post – it has been surrounded by German sub-machine gunners.

'17:00. The radio operators can hardly keep up with the flow of radio messages from units fighting in enemy encirclement.'

COUNTER-ATTACK

On 5 October a worried Stalin wrote to Yeremenko at the Stalingrad Front HQ: 'The enemy is in a position to realize his plans, since he occupies the landing-stages for the Volga to the north, in the centre and to the south of Stalingrad. To eliminate that danger, it is necessary to slice the enemy away from the Volga and re-occupy those streets and houses in Stalingrad which the enemy has wrested from you. It is therefore essential to turn each house and each street in Stalingrad into a fortress … Stalingrad must not be taken by the enemy. That part of Stalingrad which has been captured must be liberated.'

With over 300 guns sited on the east bank of the Volga, the Sixty-Second Army was able to bring down a *kontropodgotovka*, a counter-preparation barrage, on German forces bunched in the factory area. The fire included heavy mortars and five regiments of *Katyusha* rocket launchers. The opening salvoes lasted 10 minutes followed by 20 minutes of observed fire corrected by artillery observation posts on both banks of the Volga and ending with 10 minutes of final massed fire from all available guns. However, the *Luftwaffe* launched 2000 sorties against Soviet positions, concentrating 700 attacks on the Tractor Factory; and on the ground the Germans recaptured the Silicate Factory, isolating the 42nd and 92nd Rifle Brigades and the 6th Guards Tank Brigade.

As the East Prussians of the 24th Panzer Division pushed towards the Tractor Factory, Chuikov was forced to relocate his headquarters again. He moving 500m (547 yards) closer to the complex on the bank of the Volga River as the entrance of his previous HQ had come under accurate and sustained mortar and machine gun fire. The new HQ was in the

bunker of Saryev, the commander of the 10th NKVD Division, who was being sent back to the east bank to re-form his division. Of the NKVD formation only the 282nd Regiment remained to fight on in Stalingrad.

The Germans heavily outnumbered the defenders, but the Soviet command had developed tactics based on small 'Storm Groups' of men with light and heavy machine guns and PPSh submachine guns, who created what in modern terminology are called 'killing zones' of heavily mined houses and squares. The Germans were obliged to advance through canalized areas under intense fire, taking enormous casualties. The fighting from a German perspective was summed up by General Doerr:

'The time for conducting large-scale operations was gone forever; from the wide expanses of steppe land, the war moved to the jagged gullies of the Volga hills with their copses and ravines, into the factory area of Stalingrad, spread out over uneven, pitted, rugged country, covered with iron, concrete and stone buildings. The kilometre as a measure of distance was replaced by the metre. G.H.Q.'s map was the map of the city.

'For every house, workshop, water tower, railway embankment, wall, cellar and even pile of ruins, a bitter battle was fought, without equal even in the First World War with its vast expenditure of munitions. The distance between the enemy's army and ours was as small as it could be.

Above: In what is probably a pre-war exercise, Soviet general officers identified as Chuikov and Yeremenko study a situation map. Stalin's purges before the war had removed many talented officers – some were executed and others survived in gulags to return later to serve their country.

Despite the concentrated aircraft and artillery, it was impossible to break out of the area of close fighting. The Russians surpassed the Germans in their use of the terrain and camouflage, and were more experienced in barricade warfare for individual buildings.'

On 5 October the last of 160,000 Russian soldiers crossed the Volga to defend the city.

> Those who do not assist the Red Army in every way, and do not support its order and discipline, are traitors and must be killed without pity.
>
> *Josef Stalin*

PROGRESS

On 6 October two German divisions hit the 37th Guards Rifle Division at the Tractor Worker Settlement; they gained ground with heavy losses being suffered on both sides. During heavy air attacks a *Luftwaffe* bomber hit the HQ of the German 339th Infantry Regiment, causing heavy casualties. While this may have been, in the modern phrase, 'friendly fire', it may have been the result of some ingenious work by Soviet troops who were using captured German flares to send misleading pyrotechnic signals to *Luftwaffe* aircraft. Chuikov again moved his HQ, this time to the Tractor Factory, which itself was under threat. He withdrew the 10th NKVD Division since it was now down to a mere handful of men.

The OKW issued orders on 6 October that read 'The situation at Stalingrad, the capture of which the *Führer* has again described as the most important objective of the Army Group, demands the concentration of all available forces. All other objectives must take second place.' However, von Weichs stressed to Paulus that it was vital that the Sixty-Second Army was eliminated to allow German forces to be transferred to cover the thinly held flanks north and south of the city.

The fighting at Stalingrad now centred on the battle for the Tractor Factory. The Germans sent in two infantry divisions backed by tanks against the 37th Guards Division. The fighting raged in the workers' housing areas around the factory, with gains measured in rooms. By the end of the day the Germans had taken only one block of apartments in the

Below: In the early Autumn of 1942, a convoy of BM-13 Katyusha multiple rocket launchers mounted on US-supplied camouflaged 6 x 4 Studebaker trucks moves up to the front line, just east of Stalingrad. In typical relaxed Soviet style, even though the vehicles are moving the launchers are loaded.

BM-13 *KATYUSHA*

The BM-13 *Katyusha*, developed in 1933, was a 16-rail 132mm (5.19in) multiple rocket launcher. The use of aircraft rockets in a surface-to-surface role had been examined by a team of engineers under Petropavlovsk at the Leningrad Gas Dynamics Laboratory. Following the death of Petropavlovsk in 1935, research was continued by A. Kostikov and the weapon initially known as Kostikov's Gun, or the BM-13, was mounted on the Zis-5 truck and test-fired in March 1941. It proved very impressive and an order was signed in June for mass production to start. The BM-13 mounting was soon switched to the Zis-6 truck because of the added stability the rear dual wheels allowed. Later variants were mounted on Lend-Lease US-built 6 x 4 Studebaker trucks (BM-13N). They were also mounted on old T-60 hulls. The first successful combat use occurred at Orsha, near Smolensk, on 7 July 1941 where their salvos caused panic among the Germans troops.

Soviet soldiers called it *Katyusha* ('Little Katie') after 'Katerina' a popular song composed by Isakovskiy. The BM-13 could deliver a terrifying punch, and its distinctive howl – a metallic sound generated at launch as the rockets left their rails – earned it the nickname 'Stalin Organ' from German soldiers. The rails for the M-13 launcher were 487.7cm (192in) long and could be elevated to 45° and traversed 10° or 20° according to the chassis. The standard Soviet MP41 mortar sight was used for aiming. The rockets were aimed by aligning the vehicle in the direction of fire and adjusting the rocket rack up or down with the hydraulic ram for range. Initially the rockets were just armed with high explosive warheads, but later armour-piercing, illumination, incendiary and signalling rockets were introduced.

The rockets had an 18.5kg (41lb) warhead and, travelling at 355m (1165ft) per second, had a maximum range of 8.5km (5.28 miles). The 7.08kg (15.6lb) propellant was probably solventless cordite but there are also references to Soviet munitions factories using black powder instead.

Below: The Katyusha *ready to fire – at Stalingrad launch trucks were backed to the Volga river so their rear wheels overhung the bank to give the launch rails greater elevation and the rockets longer range.*

housing estate. At 18:00 a lucky salvo from a *Katyusha* battery caught a German battalion in the open west of the railway bridge across the Mechetka River, annihilated it, and stopped the attack. The rocket launcher trucks under the command of Colonel Yerokhin had been driven to the edge of the steep Volga bank, backing over it with rear wheels hanging in midair to fire at maximum elevation. During the day it cost the Germans four battalions and 16 tanks to take one block of flats.

A lieutenant in the 24th Panzer Division wrote: 'We have fought for 15 days for a single house, with mortars, grenades, machine-guns and bayonets. Already by the third day 54 German corpses are strewn in the cellars, on the landings, and the staircases. The front is a corridor between burnt-out rooms; it is the thin ceiling between two floors. Help comes from neighbouring houses by fire escapes and chimneys. There is a ceaseless struggle from noon to night. From story to story, faces black with sweat, we bombard each other with grenades in the middle of explosions, clouds of dust and smoke, heaps of mortar, floods of blood, fragments of furniture and human beings. Ask any soldier what half an hour of hand-to-hand struggle means in such a fight. And imagine Stalingrad; 80 days and 80 nights of hand-to-hand struggles. The street is no longer measured by metres but by corpses ... Stalingrad is no longer a town. By day it is an enormous cloud of burning, blinding smoke; it is a vast furnace lit by the reflection of the flames. And when night arrives, one of those scorching, howling, bleeding nights, the dogs plunge into the Volga and swim desperately to gain the other bank. The nights of Stalingrad are a terror for them.

Animals flee this hell; the hardest stones cannot bear it for long; only men endure.'

The Russian author Konstantin Smirnov wrote in a report for the American news magazine *Time*:

'It is evening and we are standing on the outskirts of the city. Before us is the battlefield: smoking hillocks and flaming streets. Everywhere there is a bluish-black smoke cut by fairy arrows of mortar fire from our guards. Ashes float in the air. White German flares light up the long circular front. First we hear the Nazi bombers, then the explosions of their bombs. Next comes the roar of our bombers sailing west. They drop yellow flares to illuminate the German position, and a few seconds later they drop cargoes of death. On the East bank of the Volga we see the supply system in operation. Our ferryboat is overloaded with five trucks full of munitions, a company of Red Army men, and a number of nurses. Bombs are whistling all around. Next to me sits a doctor's assistant, a young Ukrainian woman named Victoria Tshepnya. This is her fifth crossing. As the ferryboat approaches the landing stage, Victoria confesses: "You know me, always a little frightened to get out. I've already been wounded twice, once very seriously. But I don't believe I'll die yet because I haven't begun to live." It must be frightful to have been wounded twice, to have fought for 15 months, and now to make a fifth trip to a flaming city. In 15 minutes she will pass through burning buildings, and somewhere under the rain of shrapnel and bombs will pick up a wounded man and bring him back to the ferryboat. Then she will make her sixth trip. We are in the city. Near the river the streets are still black, except when the bombs land. In that moment the outline of

Right: A German infantry lieutenant armed with a captured PPSh-41 scans the twisted steel and rubble of Stalingrad. Terrain like this was an ideal hunting ground for snipers who could remain still for hours, waiting for an incautious move by the enemy.

Below: An officer gives quick orders to his platoon. The men are wearing a basic assault order with ground sheets, water bottles, entrenching tool and ammunition – enough to survive for a few days on the battlefield as long as rations are brought up to them.

STURMGESCHÜTZ – ASSAULT GUN, STUG III

The reliable *Panzerkampfwagen* III (PzKpfw III) provided the chassis for most of the *Sturmgeschütz* assault guns. These turretless vehicles, with a low silhouette, were designed to give close support for infantry with direct fire on point targets. During the war, production increased as the vehicles were less complex than tanks and kept the PzKpfw III production line running. In 1940 some 184 vehicles were produced, rising to 550 in 1941. In 1942 it went up to 828, and in 1943, following the defeat at Stalingrad, Germany geared up for full production and the figure jumped to 3319; in 1944 it was 7628 and StuG IIIs were still being produced in 1945.

The first vehicle, the StuG III Ausf A, had a crew of four and was armed with a short-barrelled 75mm (2.9in) KwK L/24 gun. It was intended to give supporting fire for tanks or infantry. It weighed 10,163kg (19.5 tons) and had 50mm (1.9in) of frontal armour. It was powered by a Maybach HL120 TRM V-12 petrol engine that gave a maximum road speed of 40km/h (24.8mph) and a maximum cross-country range of 100km (62 miles). The *Sturmgeschütz* III Ausf B bis D SdKgfz 142 assault gun had 50mm (1.9in) frontal and 30mm (1.2in) hull armour and a limited traverse short-barrelled 75mm

(2.95in) StuK L/24 or L/33 gun but initially no hull-mounted machine gun. In the F to G marks this was rectified and frontal armour was increased to 70mm (2.75in). The StuG III B to D had a range of 90km (55.9 miles) cross-country and 140km (86.9 miles) on roads; in the F to G this was reduced to 80km (49.7 miles) and 130km (80.7 miles) respectively.

Below: The 75mm (2.95in) StuG III Ausf C assault gun, which appeared at the end of 1942. It had a longer gun and thicker frontal armour than earlier marks as well as seven episcopes on the commander's cupola.

---

the buildings is silhouetted against the sky and reminds one of a fortress. Indeed Stalingrad is a fortress. Underground we enter the staff headquarters. Telegraph girls, their faces pale from sleepless nights and explosion dust, tap out dots and dashes. I try to light a match, but it is quickly smothered. Here underground there is not enough oxygen. Now we are riding through the streets in a dilapidated Gazik [old Soviet-made car] to a command point. We pass a gate through

The Germans themselves now call Stalingrad the Russian Verdun. But Verdun was a fortress. Stalingrad is an open city … This is not a battle for a locality or a river, but for street crossings and houses. Stalingrad has defeated Hitler's armies. Poland was conquered in 28 days. In 28 days in Stalingrad the Germans took several houses. France was defeated in 38 days. In Stalingrad it took the Germans 38 days to advance from one side of the street to the other.

BBC broadcast, October 1942

which roll squeaking wagons loaded with fresh bread. Evidently the building houses a bakery. The city is still alive.'

The commander of the 100 men and women who made up the Sixty-Second Army's sanitary company was Zinaida Georgevna Gavrielova, an 18-year-old medical student. Her medical orderlies, who were in their teens and early 20s, had to crawl often under fire to recover wounded soldiers. They then pulled or carried them to forward aid stations.

One of the orderlies with the 214th Rifle Division in the Twenty-Fourth Army on the northern flank was 20-year-old Gulya Koroleva who came from a well-known Moscow literary family, but had volunteered as a nurse, leaving her infant son with her family. A strikingly beautiful woman, she was killed in action and posthumously awarded the Order of the Red Banner. Before she died she recovered over 100 wounded and 'killed 15 fascists herself'. In the Soviet Army medical orderlies were not non-combatants. Before the war, Natalya Kachnevskaya, a nurse with a Guards Rifle Regiment, had been a drama student in Moscow. In a single day she recovered 20 wounded soldiers and 'threw grenades at the Germans'.

On the night of 6 October an overloaded boat crossing the Volga capsized and 16 out of the 21 men on board were drowned. Soon afterwards the skipper of a craft landed his passengers on a stretch of the right bank that had been mined, but not marked – 34 men were killed in the explosions in the darkness.

Incredibly, on 7 October the survivors of the isolated battalion of the 115th Rifle Brigade at Orlovka, now down from an initial 500 men with two days' rations and 200 rounds per rifle to only 120 men, broke through the gully under their commander Colonel Andryusenko. They linked up with the 112th Rifle Division on the northern flank of the Sixty-Second Army. In the city in the morning a heavy attack by two German infantry divisions hit the Tractor Factory. The Soviet 37th Guards Division holding the workers' flats came under heavy pressure and were finally forced out by XIV Panzer Corps. Though the Germans captured the bath house near the *Krasny Oktyabr* Factory, the 193rd Rifle Division counter-attacked and the bath house changed hands five times that day.

Fierce fighting continued in the factories on 8 October. The Soviet 193rd Rifle Division suffered heavy casualties when German infantry again penetrated into the *Krasny Oktyabr* bath house. XIV Panzer Corps pushed the 37th Guards back into the sports stadium near the Tractor Factory.

SOVIET DISCIPLINE

On 8 October 1942, the Political Department of the Stalingrad Front reported to Moscow that in the city 'the defeatist mood is almost eliminated and the number of treasonous incidents is getting lower'. The reality behind these words was incredibly harsh discipline.

By the close of the fighting in Stalingrad the total of summary and judicial executions stood at 13,500. Some men were executed for failing to kill their comrades who were

Below: A StuG III Ausf E assault gun gives a lift to a squad of infantrymen while a work party of Soviet prisoners shuffle past. The box on the StuG III may be spare ammunition for the short 75mm (2.95in) gun.

attempting to surrender. Men who failed in their attempts to desert were sometimes executed publicly, but death was often a brief private affair at the hands of an NKVD Special Department squad. The soldier was told to remove his boots and uniform so that they could be reused. To undertake this grim duty the NKVD execution squads were often primed with vodka. The relatives of a deserter would also suffer since they could be prosecuted under Order No 270. Malingerers and those suffering from self-inflicted wounds were classified as guilty of desertion by dishonesty.

Despite all this pressure and coercion the Soviet writer Vasily Grossman rejected the idea that soldiers at Stalingrad were brutalized and had ceased to value life. 'Life is not easy for a Russian, but in his heart he does not feel that this is unavoidable. During the war at the front, I observed just two feelings towards events: either an incredible optimism or a complete gloom. No one can bear the thought that the war is going to last a long time, and anyone who says that only months and months of hard work will lead to victory is not believed.' He would elevate the Soviet soldier to a secular saint: 'In war the Russian man puts a white shirt on his soul. He lives sinfully, but he dies like a saint. At the front, the

Above: Men of the Sixty-Second Army in quilted winter uniforms in the autumn of 1942. The rifleman is about to throw a RGD-33 grenade and immediately after the explosion the submachine gunner will follow up with a burst of fire at the survivors.

thoughts and souls of many men are pure and there is even a monk-like modesty.'

Long after the war, Aleksandr Smirnov, a sergeant in the Sixty-Second Army, recalled 'We Russians were ideologically prepared for the battle of Stalingrad. Above all, we had no illusions about the cost and were prepared to pay it.'

A LULL IN THE FIGHTING

There was a lull in fighting on 9 October as the Germans started digging in awaiting reinforcements. Although they had 334,000 men in the area, only 67,000 were front-line combat soldiers. The Sixth Army communiqué for the day stated 'No particular fighting to report in Stalingrad'. On the Soviet side Chuikov took the opportunity to redeploy and reinforce his forces in anticipation of renewed German attacks. He estimated that he was faced with nine German divisions with a main assault force of 90,000 men, 2000 guns and mortars, plus 300 tanks supported by the 1000 aircraft of *Luftflotte* IV. Chuikov had 55,000 men, 950 guns, 500 mortars and 80 tanks. The Eighth Air Army under General Khryukin could put 24 fighters, 63 dive-bombers and 101 bombers into the air to support the Sixty-Second Army. Chuikov moved the 95th Rifle Division with 3000 men away from the Mamayev Kurgan into the factories where it took up position between the 37th Guards and 308th Rifle Divisions in the *Krasny Oktyabr* Factory. The 42nd Rifle Brigade, now reduced to 900 men, was incorporated into the 95th Rifle Division and Chuikov also moved the 2300-strong 112th Rifle Division into the Tractor Factory.

Late at night, according to Soviet accounts, a German soldier, a signaller named Willi Brandt, was captured by a Russian fighting patrol tasked with taking a prisoner who could explain the German troop movements that had begun earlier that day. The four-man patrol was a forward artillery observation post who had been in cover in a wrecked coal wagon on the railway near the Mamayev Kurgan and the *Krasny Oktyabr* Factory. They had observed the movement of men and vehicles and, having located a German field telephone line, cut it, took cover and waited until a signaller appeared to repair the break in the line. He was quickly killed and one of the Russians donned his uniform and took up position near the break in the telephone cable. When Brandt appeared he was quickly knocked down, secured and interrogated.

The soldier told them that Hitler had ordered that Stalingrad be taken by 15 October. Instead of taking the soldier back as prisoner or killing him, the Russians released him. As Brandt walked back towards the German lines he nervously waved goodbye to the patrol – both he and the patrol knew that both sides routinely killed prisoners after they had been interrogated.

The lull continued in Stalingrad for two days. On 10 October Chuikov was alerted to the new planned German

PAVLOV'S HOUSE

Nicknamed the 'Houseowner' by his comrades, Sergeant Jacob Pavlov, Hero of the Soviet Union and pre-war accountant, held a battered four-storey brick apartment block at Solechnaya Street for 58 days. It remains today in Volgograd as a mute testimony to the savagery of the fighting.

During the street fighting in late September Colonel Yelin, commanding the 42nd Regiment, had identified the block as a potential strongpoint. He despatched Sergeant Pavlov with three men – Privates Alexandrov, Glushchenko and Chernogolovy – to secure it. On the night of 29 September a messenger sent by Pavlov reported back to the Divisional HQ and then led 20 men to join the squad. They prepared the building for defence, breaking down the walls between the cellars, and reinforced by four more men began an active defence of the building, sniping at the Germans.

By chance the group of Soviet soldiers were representative of many of the republics of the USSR and included men from Georgia, Kazakhstan, Uzbekistan and the Ukraine. They were reinforced by Lieutenant Afanasyev's machine-gun platoon of seven men with a Maxim machine gun and six men with three anti-tank rifles under the command of Senior Sergeant Sabgaida, and three submachine gunners. They were further reinforced by four men with two 50mm (1.9in) mortars under the command of Lieutenant Chernushenko. During the lulls in the fighting the men hunted through the building for food and water and found an ancient wind-up gramophone and with it one surviving record. It was a tune unknown to them, but as a distraction it was very welcome – so much so that they played it until the steel needle wore through the fragile disc.

The Germans continued to probe and attack the building that was now known in Soviet command posts as '*Dom Pavlov*' – 'Pavlov's House'. It was a well-chosen strongpoint with wide fields of fire that dominated the approaches to the Volga only 250m (273 yards) away.

In October four German tanks entered Lenin Square and blasted Pavlov's House, but the wily sergeant moved his small force to the fourth floor or the cellar where at close range the tank guns could not reach due to the restriction on their elevation. A fighting patrol with a 14.5mm (0.57in) PTRD anti-tank rifle slipped out and knocked out one of the tanks and the survivors withdrew. Before the fighting ended *Dom Pavlov* became a reference point on the Sixty-Second Army HQ maps and Pavlov received the code-name 'Lighthouse'.

Pavlov survived Stalingrad and went on to serve in the forces that captured Berlin in 1945. He became a Hero of the Soviet Union for his stand at Stalingrad. Pavlov discovered his God somewhere in this devastation and bloodshed, as he joined the Russian Orthodox priesthood after the war. He lived out the rest of his life in peace as the Archimandrite Kyrill, a man of God determined to kill no more.

offensive. He ordered some localized counter-attacks on several specific German positions to disrupt their preparations. He was reinforced with the IV Cavalry Corps, VII Rifle Corps as Front reserve and the 93rd, 96th and 97th Rifle Brigades which deployed at Dubrovka.

Soviet close-combat tactics were paying off, Hoffman noted: 'The Russians are so close to us that our planes cannot bomb them. We are preparing for a decisive attack. The *Führer* has ordered the whole of Stalingrad to be taken as rapidly as possible.'

STRUGGLE FOR THE TRACTOR FACTORY

On 10 October, *Feldwebel* Dragutin Podobnik was awarded the Iron Cross 1st Class for his role in the 30 September battle in the *Krasny Oktyabr* Factory. He had captured a Soviet position and allowed the German 54th Regiment to occupy a section of the factory, capturing three artillery pieces, one Maxim machine gun, two mortars and a quantity of small arms. What made the award unusual was that Podobnik was a Croat serving with the 369th Croat Reinforced Infantry Regiment, 100th *Jäger* Division, XI Army Corps. His regiment was made up of Croats and Bosnian Muslims from Yugoslavia. He had earlier received the Iron Cross 2nd Class on 24 September for his role in the *Proljet Kultura Kolkhoz* (collective farm) battle in the Ukraine, an all-night, hand-to-hand engagement. He may even have received it from his national leader, or *Poglavnik* of Croatia, Dr Ante Pavelic, who had flown out to the Sixth Army. He was met by General Paulus and a guard of honour formed by *Luftwaffe* ground troops. Podobnik was later listed as 'missing and presumed dead' and never returned from Stalingrad.

On the same day that Podobnik received his Iron Cross, Helmut Weltz, an officer commanding a battalion of combat engineers, recorded his memories of fighting in the Tractor Factory:

'Finally, you could notice movement. A soldier jumped over the edge of a gully. A German soldier. He was running back. Of course, he would be a runner carrying a message. But no, he was followed by another soldier, yet another and others too. They were all running back with several combat engineers in their wake. So the Germans were withdrawing. In two or three minutes we sighted the first few Russian

Left: On the western outskirts of Stalingrad an elderly babushka *(grandmother) attempts to cook using the remains of her stove. Many of the wooden single storey houses in the area were burned down in the air attacks of the summer of 1942.*

helmets. The Russians assembled and regrouped to pursue the German combat engineers retreating in disorder. Where were the other men of the five battalions? Were these men all that was left of those units? The Russians were now approaching our starting position. We opened a hurricane fire on them as we had done in the morning. The Russian advance halted. The lines were consolidated and everything returned to its original state. As it had been before the

Below: The dangerous and unstable ruins of an apartment block provide cover for a Soviet assault group. During the heavy fighting smoke from explosions and fires and dust from rubble reduced visibility to a few metres.

Opposite: The low silhouette of the 50mm (2in) PaK 38 anti-tank gun made it a hard target for Soviet tanks, but meant that the crew either had to dig a shallow trench, or squat behind the double splinter shield.

assault, as it was yesterday, and a week ago. It was very much like a dream. Had I dreamed the whole battle? Five fresh battalions had gone into the attack, just as at home on a training ground. And what was the result? Most of them had been killed, some were wounded and all the rest were routed, utterly routed. A cursed place! Though we tried hard to capture it, it was like granite.'

On 11 October the Romanian Third Army moved into position to protect the left flank of the German Sixth Army at Stalingrad, taking over positions from VIII Corps which was released to join the fighting in Stalingrad. Units that had been exhausted in Stalingrad were also redeployed to the flanks.

The strain was intense for both sides and on 12 October an NKVD patrol searching houses along the Volga entered the village of Tumak looking for deserters and discovered a 'disgraceful scene'. A captain, a commissar and stores sergeant, a corporal from the Volga flotilla and local secretary of the Communist Party had 'drunk themselves out of consciousness', the patrol reported, and were lying on the floor 'in a sleeping state with women'. Still drunk, the group was dragged in front of Major-General Rogatin, the chief of NKVD troops in Stalingrad.

On 13 October Stalin began to panic about the situation in the city. He raged at Yeremenko. Instead of giving Chuikov all the help he could, Yeremenko was holding back troops on the east bank – troops that Stalin said he had specifically assigned for the defence of Stalingrad. He instructed Yeremenko 'in the name of the *Stavka*' to make a personal visit to Chuikov's HQ to investigate the situation and established the 'true position'.

Mindful of the experiences of the previous winter in Russia, Hitler ordered his armed forces on the Eastern Front to take up defensive postures, and hold their current positions throughout the season.

To the north and south of Stalingrad the Red Army began to build up its forces in preparation for the counter-offensive that would capitalize on the bitter Russian winter. At Stalingrad during the day the temperature fluctuated between -20° and -35°C (-4° and -31°F) but at night it could plunge down to as low as -44°C (-47°F). The wind from the steppe added to the discomfort of the Sixth Army. They were fighting the old Russian ally 'General Winter'.

CHAPTER FIVE
HARD FIGHTING

The critical week for the combatants at Stalingrad began on Monday 14 October at 08:00 in light rain as a new German attack was launched against the factory district in northern Stalingrad. The coal-fired Power Station that had continued to operate, supplying electricity for factories in the north, was hit by heavy artillery and air attacks. It had operated at night so that the smoke from its chimneys would not be seen and attract artillery fire.

BY MIDDAY THE NOISE FROM ARTILLERY FIRE and 2000 *Luftwaffe* sorties was so intense that individual explosions could no longer be distinguished in the all-consuming roar. Visibility in the smoke and dust was reduced to a few metres. From the vantage point of his dugout on the Mamayev Kurgan a Soviet soldier, Pyotr Deriabin, watched the *Luftwaffe* in action. The Stukas peeled off to attack and as their bombs exploded amongst the smoke and flame he watched as chunks of masonry and machine parts from the factories pirouetted into the sky. A German soldier with the 389th Infantry Division saw the same images. 'The whole sky was full of aircraft, every flak gun firing, bombs roaring down, aircraft crashing, an enormous piece of theatre which we followed with very mixed feelings from our trenches.'

Paulus had committed two panzer divisions, the 14th and 24th, and three infantry divisions, the 100th *Jäger*, 60th Motorized and the 389th, on a 4km (2.4 mile) front hitting both the Tractor Factory and the *Barrikady* Factory.

Left: During a lull in the fighting an infantry section moves through the smashed remains of a captured factory. The loose metal sheets and girders made tactical movement difficult as well as producing eerie creaks and rattling sounds.

Above: A platoon watches as Stukas roar overhead to attack Soviet positions. In the foreground the officer has Stielhandgranate *39 stick grenades tucked in his belt – his rank badges and pistol holster make him an obvious target for a sniper.*

THE TRACTOR FACTORY

By noon on the 14th 200 tanks and supporting infantry had reached the walls of the Tractor Factory and were turning into the rear of the 112th Division. By late afternoon General Zholudev's 37th and 112th Divisions were surrounded, while the right flank of the 308th had been pounded to pieces. Zholudev was buried alive in his HQ after it received several hits and he was dug out by the men of the Guard Company. There were casualties at Chuikov's HQ below the river bluff, a position that blocked his radio communications. His signallers resolved the situation by transmitting to stations on the east bank that in turn rebroadcast to the units within the city. Afterwards Chuikov would recall: 'They bombed and stormed our troops without a moment's respite. The German guns and mortars showered us with shells and bombs from morning until night. It was a sunny day, but owing to the smoke and soot, visibility was reduced to 100m [109 yards]. Our dugouts were shaking and crumbling like a house of cards. By 11:30 180 tanks broke through to the

stadium of the Tractor Plant. By 16:00 the troops were encircled but still fighting.'

'It was a terrible, exhausting battle,' wrote an officer of the 14th Panzer Division, 'on and below ground, in ruins, cellars, and factory sewers. Tanks climbed mounds of rubble and scrap, and crept screeching through chaotically destroyed workshops and fired at point-blank range in narrow yards. Many of the tanks shook or exploded from the force of an exploding enemy mine.'

Losses were very heavy on both sides as the Soviet forces were forced to give ground. The XLVIII Panzer Corps reached the Volga in the southern part of Stalingrad, while Soviet troops counter-attacked in the factory areas. An NCO in the 305th Infantry Division recalled that 'Our support from heavy weapons was unusually strong. Several batteries of *Nebelwerfer*, Stukas shuttle-bombing and self-propelled assault guns in quantities never seen before bombarded the Russians, who in their fanaticism put up a tremendous resistance.'

Above: The Stuka's eye view of the Stalingrad factory area. The tactics of the Sixty-Second Army were to keep as close to the Sixth Army as possible so that close air support would be impossible since the bombers risked hitting their own side.

By nightfall, the factory was surrounded on three sides and fighting was going on in the outer workshops. The area between the Red Barricade and Tractor Factories defended by the 37th Guards and 95th Rifle Divisions had changed hands several times during the day. The fighting continued into the night as German forces surrounded the Tractor Factory on three sides, and under intense pressure the Sixty-Second Army was split, allowing the enemy to reach the Volga on a 2000m (2187 yard) front.

On the right wing of the Sixty-Second Army the isolated 112th Rifle Division, 2nd Motorized Brigade, 115th, 124th and 149th Rifle Brigades fought on, though the 37th Guards had been virtually annihilated. That night, 3500 seriously wounded Soviet soldiers were evacuated across the Volga

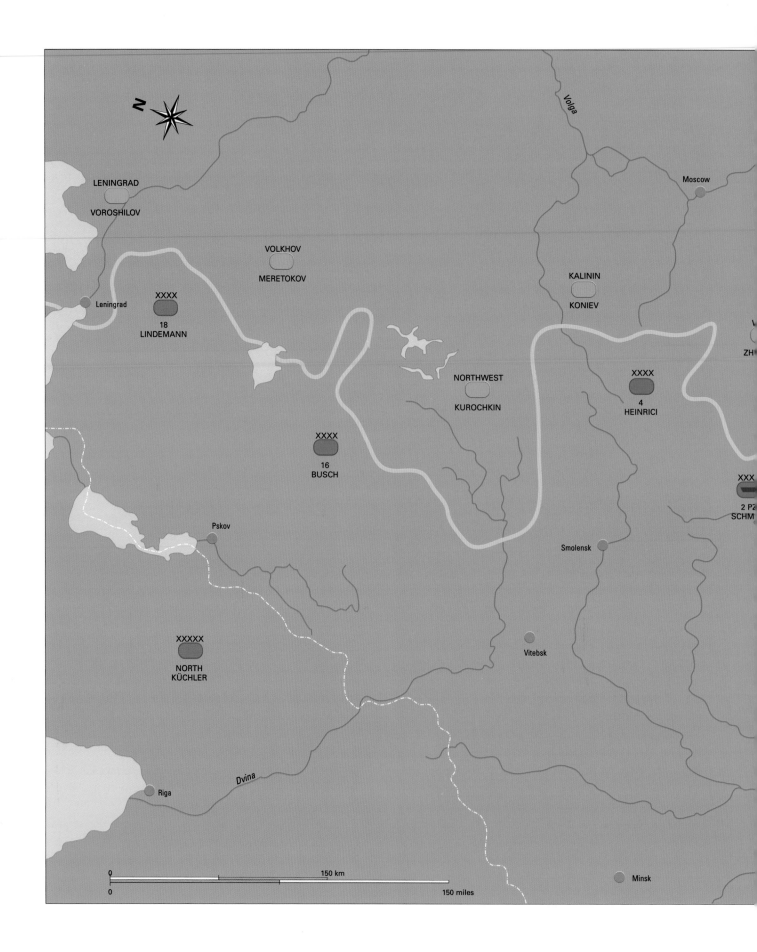

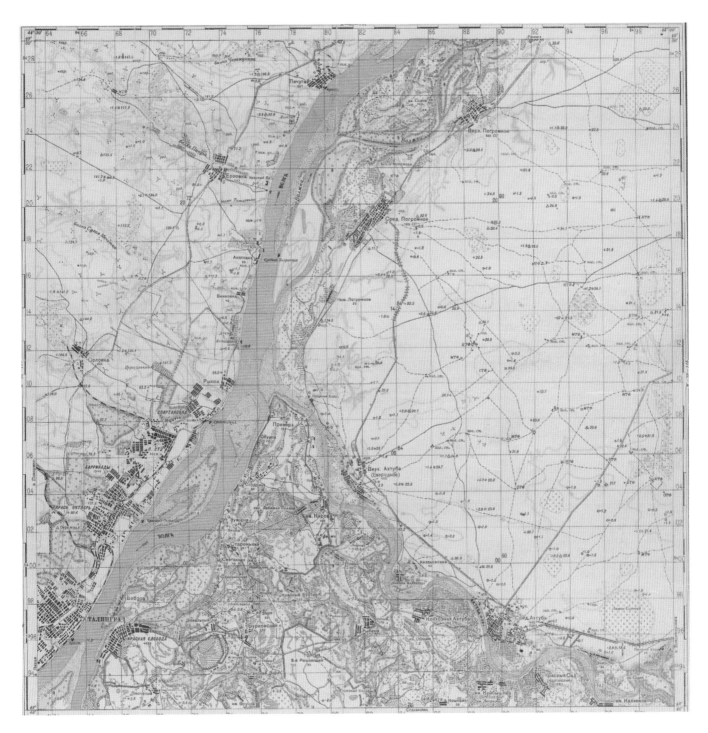

Above: The Volga gave Soviet forces a natural barrier that the Germans could not bypass and beyond which reinforcements and supplies could be brought forward with relative safety to Stalingrad, situated on the east bank of the river. The critical moment for the Sixty-Second Army would be when the river began to freeze and supplies could not be brought across – when it was completely frozen it would become an ice bridge. The German Sixth Army was at the end of a long and vulnerable logistic chain that even without partisan attacks could break down.

Right: While Stalingrad absorbed men and resources in the fighting throughout the autumn of 1942, elsewhere on the Eastern Front things began to slow down. While the Germans welcomed this since they saw it as a chance to finish off the city before the onset of winter, the Soviet high command, Stavka, were also pleased. They knew that if they could play for time and keep the Germans focused on Stalingrad they would be able to build up reserves for a winter counter-attack on a bigger scale than the one that had saved Moscow in 1941–42.

GERMAN INFANTRY WEAPONS

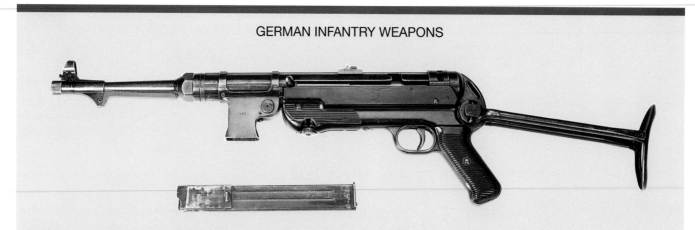

The German *Maschinenpistole* MP38 and MP40 submachine guns, originally manufactured at the Erma-Werke at Erfurt, had several revolutionary features. No wood was used in their construction, only steel and plastic, and they had folding metal stocks, which made them ideal for paratroopers and armoured vehicle crews. The weapons were universally known as *Schmeissers* by the Allies, but despite this accolade the German small-arms engineer Hugo Schmeisser had no part in their design. The 9mm (0.35in) calibre MP38 and MP40 both fired from a 32-round box magazine with a distinctive cyclic rate of 500 rounds a minute. They were 83.3cm (32.6in) long with the butt extended and 63cm (24.8in) with it folded. Manufacturing changes to increase production reduced machining and replaced it with welding and steel pressings. This reduced the weight of the MP40 to 4.027kg (8.87lb), compared to 4.086kg (9lb) for the MP38.

The German Kar 98k rifle was developed from the Mauser commercial rifle called the Standard model that was first produced in 1924. The Kar 98k, first produced in 1935, weighed 3.9kg (8.6lb), was 110.75cm (43.6in) long, and in its 10-year production life it was manufactured in thousands in Germany, by FN in Belgium and Brno in Czechoslovakia. Another rifle based on the Standard model and almost identical to the Kar 98k was the Chinese Model Chiang Kai-Shek, or 'Generalissimo', which was also first produced in 1935 and saw extensive service in the Far East. A trained soldier armed with a Kar 98k could fire 15 rounds per minute,

Above: The MP38/40 was a typical example of German weapons design. It used new materials like plastic, was tough and reliable and was the first SMG to have a folding stock. However like the MG34 it was expensive to produce.

but like the *Gewehr* 98 the new rifle had only a five-round magazine, which could be a liability in a firefight. Like all the 7.92mm (0.31in) calibre rifles the maximum effective range of the Kar 98k was 800 metres (1500 yards).

The Kar 98k was widely used as a sniper's weapon. It was fitted with the little ZF-41 and later the x4 ZF-42 and ZF-42W telescopic sights. The Germans made several types of silencer for the Kar 98k and these were used with special low-velocity ammunition. German snipers had three colours of tracer ammunition as well as ball, incendiary and armour-piercing. The tracer was used for target designation for machine gun crews, while ball and armour-piercing were used against men and equipment.

Several types of grenade launcher could be fitted, including the 30mm (1.18in) *Schießbecher* that could fire explosive, illuminating and hollow-charge anti-tank grenades between 45 and 90m (49 and 98 yards). The rifle grenades came boxed with either a blank cartridge or a cartridge with a wooden bullet taped to their side. The cartridge was used to propel the grenade. Experience on the Eastern Front led to the development of a winter trigger that could be operated by a man wearing gloves or mittens.

and the 138th Rifle Division crossed from the east bank and was directed to the *Barrikady* Factory.

At the Tractor Factory one of the toughest militia defenders was Olga Kovalova, a foul-mouthed woman who had worked at the plant for 20 years and had become the first female steel foundry worker. Her battalion commander tried

to send her to the rear, insisting that the front line was no place for a woman. She stayed and continued to yell at militiamen whom she considered lazy or ineffective. She died fighting in the factory.

An aide-de-camp in the Sixth Army, Colonel Adam, recalled the tenacity of the defence in his memoirs: 'The

Soviet troops fought for every inch of land. We found it hard to believe a report of General of the tank corps von Wietersheim who said that Red Army units had launched a counter-attack. The population took up arms. Lying on the battlefields were workers in overalls still clasping a rifle or pistol in their stiff hands. The dead in workers' clothes leaned over the controls of smashed tanks. Never ever have we seen anything of the kind.'

The detachments of armed workers who had hitherto fought independently had been put formally under Red Army command on 5 October and assigned to defending the *Krasny Oktyabr*, *Barrikady* and Tractor Factories. These men and women were invaluable with their detailed local knowledge and skill at improvising and repairing weapons.

On the first day of the major attack young Hoffman was

optimistic, noting: '14 October. It has been fantastic since morning: our aeroplanes and artillery have been hammering the Russian position for hours on end; everything in sight is being blotted from the face of the earth. …'

From his HQ at Vinnitsa Hitler issued *Operationsbefehl Nr 1* that ordered the suspension of all offensive action on the Eastern Front. Army Groups were to make a resolute defence of present positions and to ensure success in the 'winter campaign' they were to 'consider their present lines springboards for a German offensive in 1943 and hold them

Below: Two German senior NCOs take shelter in a bomb crater; while one observes, the other calls forward troops to support them. Both men are armed with MP38s, ideal weapons for close-range fighting in built-up areas.

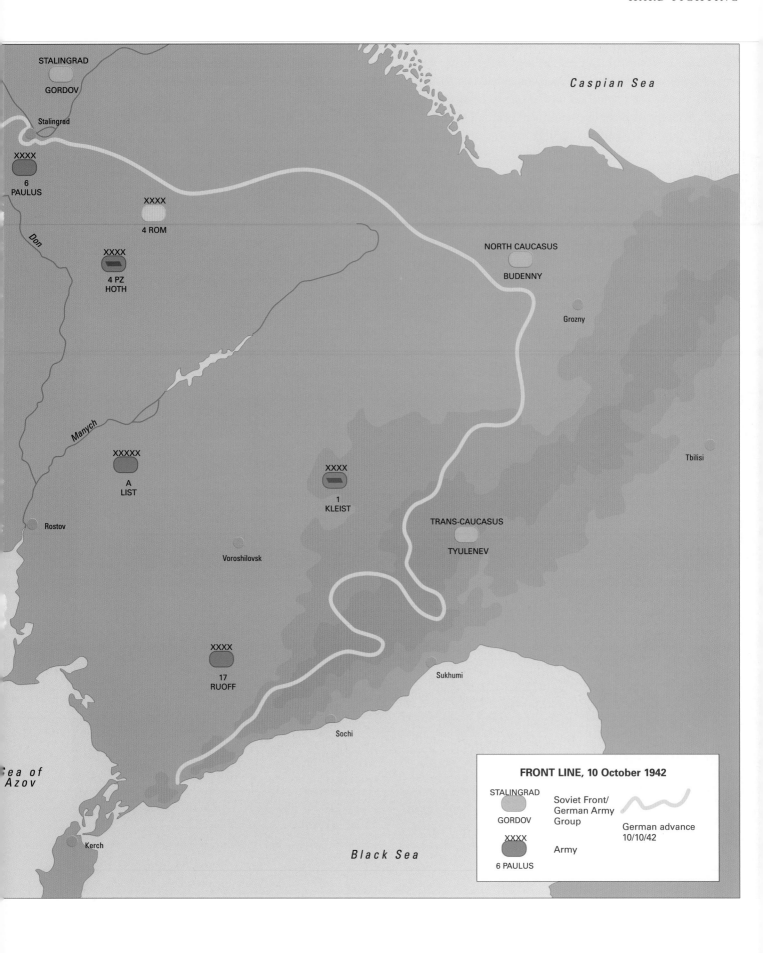

STALINGRAD

GORDOV

Stalingrad

XXXX
6
PAULUS

Don

XXXX
4 ROM

XXXX
4 PZ
HOTH

NORTH CAUCASUS

BUDENNY

Grozny

Caspian Sea

Manych

XXXXX
A
LIST

XXXX
1
KLEIST

Tbilisi

Rostov

Voroshilovsk

TRANS-CAUCASUS

TYULENEV

XXXX
17
RUOFF

Sukhumi

Sochi

Sea of
Azov

Kerch

Black Sea

FRONT LINE, 10 October 1942

STALINGRAD

GORDOV

Soviet Front/
German Army
Group

German advance
10/10/42

XXXX
6 PAULUS

Army

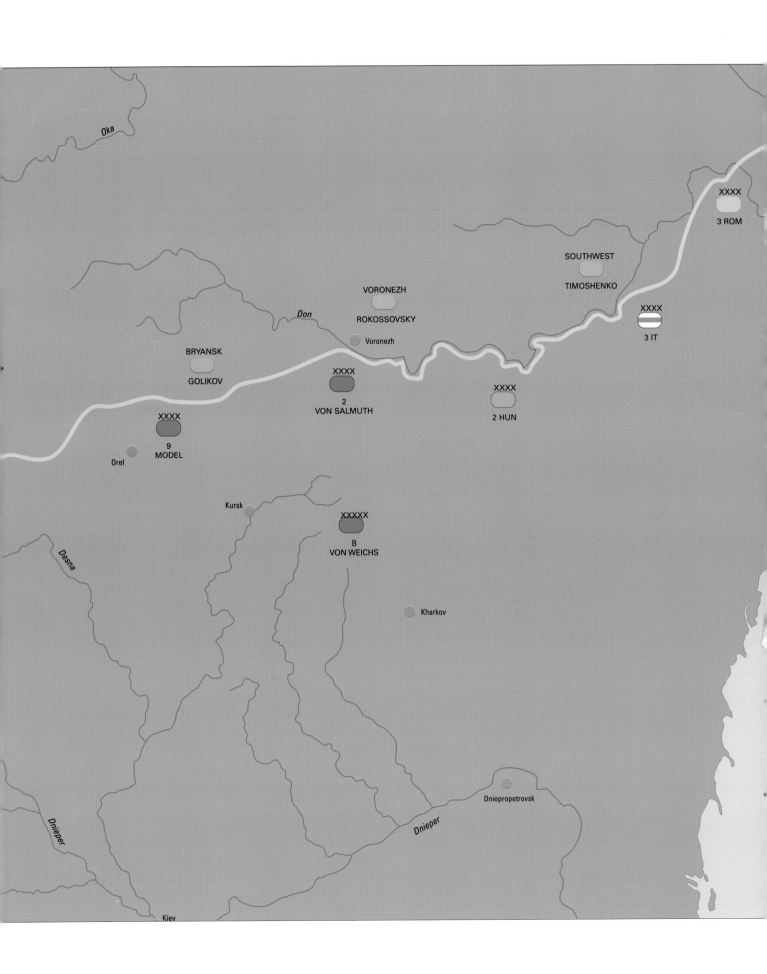

SNIPERISM

To the German soldiers, the ruthlessly efficient Soviet snipers at Stalingrad were the objects of fear and hatred. In contrast in Moscow their operations, described as 'sniperism', were celebrated by the Soviet propaganda machine. Many were experienced hunters and were equipped with a Mosin Nagant Model 1891/30 rifle with a x4 PE telescopic sight. The M1891/30 weighed 4kg (8.8lb) empty, had a muzzle velocity of 811m (2661ft) per second, and though a modernization of an old design it was robust and reliable. The sights were offset, mounted on the left of the receiver to allow the empty cases to be ejected when the bolt was worked. Until 1930 the iron sights on the rifle were graduated in the archaic linear measurement of *arshins* (0.71m/27in) but the Soviet government redesigned the back sight in metres and so the modified weapon became the 1891/30. The other rifle issued to snipers was the Tokarev SVT-40 automatic rifle fitted with a x3.5 PV telescopic sight. It weighed 3.95kg (8.7lb) and had a 20-round box magazine. Early models were unreliable, but the 1940 version was modified and eventually two million were manufactured. Soviet snipers usually worked in pairs at a low tactical level, assigned directly to companies and platoons.

The most famous sniper of them all, although not the highest scorer, was Vasily Zaitsev in Batyuk's division, who, during the October Revolution celebrations, raised his tally of kills to 149 Germans. The highest scorer, identified only as 'Zikan', had killed 224 Germans by 20 November. For the Sixty-Second Army, the taciturn Zaitsev, a shepherd from the foothills of the Urals, represented much more than any sporting hero. News of further additions to his score passed from mouth to mouth along the front. Zaitsev, whose name means 'hare' in Russian, was subsequently put in charge of training young snipers, and his pupils became known as *zaichata*, or 'leverets'. This was the start of the 'sniper movement' in the Sixty-Second Army. Conferences were arranged to spread the doctrine of 'sniperism', and exchange ideas on technique. Soviet snipers' preferred targets were the Germans carrying insulated food containers to the front-line soldiers, or water-carriers. If those

are killed, Zaitsev told his students, the Germans must drink polluted water, and suffer dysentery.

The Don and Southwest Fronts took up the 'sniper movement', and produced their star shots, such as Sergeant Passar of Twenty-First Army who was especially proud of his head shots and was credited with 103 kills. Non-Russian snipers were also singled out for praise and included Kucherenko, a Ukrainian, who killed 19 Germans, and an Uzbek from 169th Rifle Division who killed five in three days. In Sixty-Fourth Army, Sniper Kovbasa (the Ukrainian word for sausage) worked from a network of at least three trenches, one for sleeping and two fire trenches, all connected. In addition, he dug fake positions out to the side in front of neighbouring platoons. In these he installed white flags attached to levers, which he waved from a distance with cords. Kovbasa proudly claimed that as soon as a German saw one of his little white flags waving, he could not help raising himself in his trench to take a better look, and shout '*Rus, komm, komm!*' Kovbasa then got him from an angle.

The most prized targets were German artillery spotters. 'For two days [Corporal Studentov] tracked an observation officer and killed him with the first shot.' Studentov vowed to raise his score to 170 Germans from 124 by the anniversary of the Russian Revolution. All the star snipers had their own techniques and favourite hiding places. 'Noble sniper' Ilin, who was credited with '185 Fritzes', sometimes used an old barrel, or a pipe, as a hide. Ilin, a commissar from a Guards Rifle Regiment, operated on the *Krasny Oktyabr* sector. 'Fascists should know the strength of weapons in the hands of Soviet supermen,' he proclaimed, promising to train 10 other snipers.

Though popularized after the war, the sniper duel between Zaitsev and Major Koenig, the head of the German sniper school at Zossen, that was the basis for the $85 million film 'Enemy at the Gates' released in 2001, was probably a Soviet propaganda invention. Zaitsev, played by Jude Law, existed, but the sinister Koenig, played by Ed Harris, was almost certainly fictional.

at all costs'. The exception was the fighting for Stalingrad and the Terek River in the Caucasus that was to continue. Zeitzler expanded *Operationsbefehl Nr 1* on 23 October with *Erganzung zum Operationsbefehl Nr 1* that stressed that the Soviets 'were in no position to mount a major counter-offensive with any far-reaching objective'.

THE ASSAULT BEGINS

By the evening the Sixty-Second Army had evacuated 3500 wounded across the Volga. As they waited on the west bank the soldiers could see the water churning with hits by artillery and machine gun fire. When some of the boats reached Stalingrad all of the crews were either dead or

Above: Nuriy Shakirov, a sniper with the 207th Rifle Regiment, takes aim through a x4 PE telescopic sight mounted on his 7.62mm (0.3in) Mosin Nagant M1891/30 rifle. He has used the hole in the brick wall for concealment.

wounded. The next day the 305th Infantry attacked the Tractor Factory, and split the Sixty-Second Army. The tanks of 24th Panzer reached the bank of the Volga at the north end of the factory. Shelling cut Chuikov's telephone lines, isolating the Sixty-Second Army's commander. German troops attacked Soviet positions from the rear, surrounding 112th Division, battling through wooden housing, which became an inferno in the fighting. The 2nd Battalion of the 103rd Panzergrenadiers found an open street leading to the river, and the tanks of 24th Panzer roared down to the Volga. The battalion's CO, *Hauptmann* Domaschk, received the Knight's Cross for this. The LI Corps reported the destruction of 20 enemy tanks, the capture of 1028 PoWs, four locomotives, 60 freight cars, three disabled railway guns (including an armoured train), plus scores of machine guns, mortars, and light artillery pieces. The Soviet 37th Guards and 95th Rifle Divisions had lost 75 per cent of their men and most of their heavy weapons. The 84th Armoured Brigade was down to a company of tanks.

The defensive lines at the Tractor Factory broke again and fighting was reported 320m (350 yards) from Sixty-Second

Army HQ. The army's HQ Guard Company was thrown forward in a desperate attempt to stem the German advance, and succeeded.

The fighting continued in the northern towns of Rynok and Spartanovka, where the German 16th Panzer Division fought its way towards the 'Mushrooms', two huge bunker complexes with machine guns and light artillery, surrounded by zigzagging slit trenches. The Germans seized the smaller fort, and moved up assault guns for the 'Big Mushroom'. German troops battled from room to room. Assault engineers planted breaching charges so close they were wounded by debris from the explosions. As night fell, cooks and mechanics from 16th Panzer mounted guard for the exhausted combat soldiers. The German 94th Division, weakened by casualties and dysentery, fought to clear the Orlovka Creek. The Germans ran into heavy fire and

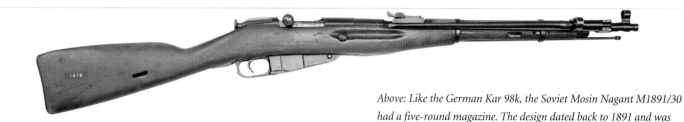

Above: Like the German Kar 98k, the Soviet Mosin Nagant M1891/30 had a five-round magazine. The design dated back to 1891 and was updated in 1938 and 1944 as a short carbine.

minefields and the 274th Infantry Regiment lost nearly every company and battalion officer. In the factories, German troops battled through work halls and narrow streets. Armoured vehicles were trapped and disabled by Soviet anti-tank guns that fired at point-blank range from the rubble. Both the German Sixth Army and the Soviet Sixty-Second were rapidly becoming exhausted. Chuikov requested permission to move some of his HQ staff to the east bank

since they were overcrowded in Stalingrad, but Yeremenko refused since it would be bad for morale.

By the evening of 15 October Sixth Army HQ noted 'The major part of the tractor works is in our hands. There are only some pockets of resistance left behind our front.' One of these was a light artillery regiment whose Commissar Babachenko signalled that the battery was cut off: 'Guns destroyed. Battery surrounded. We fight on and will not

Below: Public art outside the blazing Stalingrad-1 railway station – amid the destruction the rather incongruous figures of Soviet Young Pioneers dancing around a crocodile caught the eye of a German PK photographer in 1942.

Opposite: The third assault on Stalingrad took the Sixth Army to the banks of the Volga and confined the Soviet Sixty-Second to pockets close to the right bank. By now, however, the German forces were exhausted, under strength and demoralized by the continued Soviet resistance.

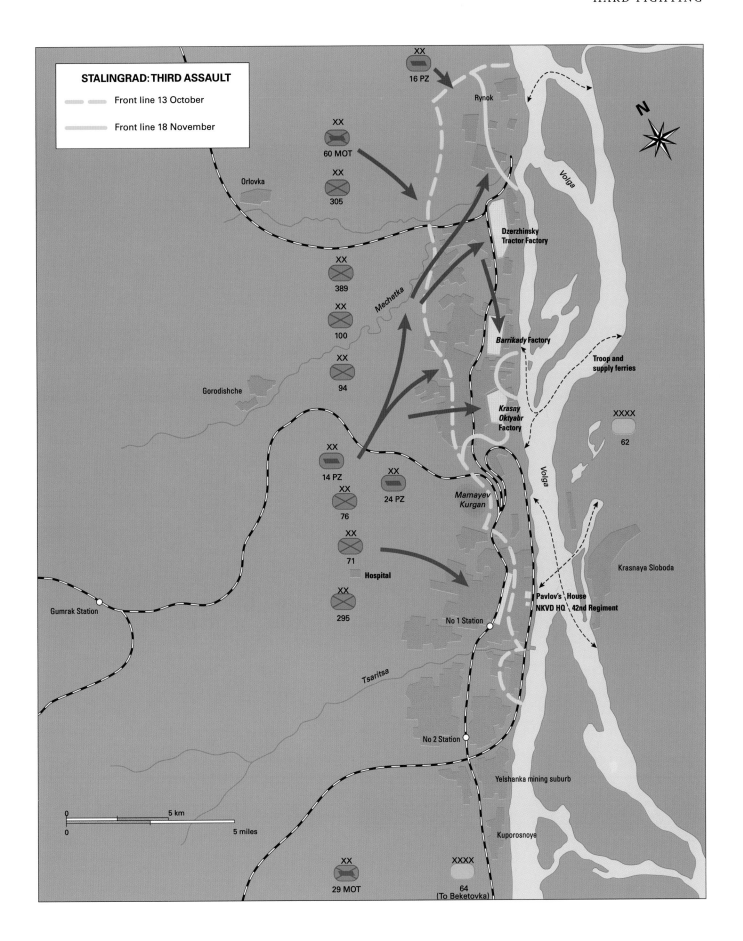

STALINGRAD: THIRD ASSAULT

Front line 13 October

Front line 18 November

16 PZ

Rynok

60 MOT

Orlovka

305

Volga

Dzerzhinsky
Tractor Factory

389

Mechetka

100

Barrikady Factory

94

Gorodishche

Troop and
supply ferries

*Krasny
Oktyabr
Factory*

XXXX

62

14 PZ

XX

24 PZ

76

*Mamayev
Kurgan*

71

Krasnaya Sloboda

Hospital

295

Pavlov's House
NKVD HQ   42nd Regiment

Gumrak Station

No 1 Station

Tsaritsa

No 2 Station

Yelshanka mining suburb

0   5 km

0   5 miles

Kuporosnoye

29 MOT

XXXX

64
(To Beketovka)

Above: These men of the Sixty-Second Army have taken up positions away from the windows in the shadows of this wrecked building. Soviet defenders favoured brick or stone structures that would not burn amidst German air and artillery attack.

Opposite: Armed with an MP40, a German NCO checks the terrain before his MG34 section makes the dash to a new position. Some of the men have attached cloth covers to their helmets to reduce any reflection from the battered steel.

surrender. Best regards to everyone.' Incredibly with only their small arms the gunners broke out and joined the main body of the Sixty-Second Army. Babachenko was made a Hero of the Soviet Union.

However, heroism was not universal. After a pocket of Soviet forces from the 112th Rifle Division and 115th Special Brigade had been cut off north of the Tractor Factory on 15 October, the Sixty-Second Army HQ received a barrage of requests from the two HQs for permission to withdraw across the Volga. They claimed that their regiments had been

wiped out. During a lull in the fighting Chuikov despatched Colonel Kamynin to check the situation. He found that the 112th Rifle Division had 598 men left and the 115th Special Brigade a sizeable 890. Kamynin reported that the senior Commissar 'instead of organizing an active defence ... did not emerge from his bunker and tried in a panic-stricken way to persuade his commander to withdraw across the Volga'.

In the light of Stalin's orders for the defence of the city a request to withdraw was tantamount to treason and so for 'their betrayal of Stalingrad's defence' and 'exceptional cowardice' the senior officers and commissars were later tried by court martial by the Military Council of the Sixty-Second Army. Their fate is not recorded – but it was almost certainly death.

THE CRISIS POINT

On 16 October fighting in the factories reached a peak as the *Luftwaffe* launched a massive raid. Heavy fighting followed as German infantry attacked south from the Tractor Factory

---

ORDERS FROM THE HQ SIXTY-SECOND ARMY FOR 23:50 16 OCTOBER READ:

1. The enemy has taken the Stalingrad Tractor Plant, is developing an attack from the STP [Stalingrad Tractor Plant] to the south along the railway line in an attempt to seize *Barrikady* [Factory].

2. Sixty-Second Army continues to hold its positions, beating off fierce enemy attacks.

3. 138th Red Banner RD [Rifle Division] from 04:00 17.10.42 to occupy and stubbornly defend the line: south of the

Derevensk, Sculpturnyi. Under no circumstances to allow enemy to approach *Leninskii prospect* and *Barrikady* factory.

650th Rifle/Major Pechenyuk: 138th Division to take up positions in the *Barrikady*, establish ring of fire-points and not to permit enemy penetration into the factory.

Signed: Lieutenant-General V. Chuikov
Divisional Commissar K. Gurov
Major-General N. Krylov

---

towards the *Krasny Oktyabr* Factory. They hit the 84th Tank Brigade hard, but the brigade held the Germans on Tramvaynaya Street. In the Tractor Factory the 37th Guards was down to 200 men, but fought on. The Soviet Stalingrad Front reinforced the northern flank with the newly arriving 138th Rifle Division. As the troops came off the boats, they were immediately sent the short distance to the front. Chuikov was informed that ammunition allocations would be halved for his command in the city. Normally this would be bad news, but by now Chuikov recognized this as a sure sign that supplies were being stockpiled for a major offensive in the area and knew that this would relieve the pressure on his forces.

At 03:00 on 16 October Yeremenko with his deputy M.M. Popov arrived at the forward HQ of the Volga River Flotilla and moved off in an armoured sloop from the mouth of the Akhtuba, making for the landing stage at the *Krasny Oktyabr*. On the river *Luftwaffe* flares illuminated the water and on the far bank swathed in smoke and flames were the ruined outlines of the city. Making his way through stumbling and

The buildings in a city are like breakwaters. They broke up the advancing enemy formations and made their forces go along the streets. We therefore held on firmly to strong buildings, and established small garrisons in them, capable of all-around fire if they were encircled. Particularly stout buildings enabled us to create strong defensive positions, from which our men could mow down the advancing Germans with machine-guns and tommy-guns.

Lieutenant-General V.I. Chuikov

crawling wounded who were heading to the landing stage to be evacuated and the newly arrived reinforcements and ammunition porters, Yeremenko found Chuikov's HQ. It was a mass of craters strewn with the wreckage of dugouts and bunkers, timber and logs projecting from the ground covered with a layer of ash. Chuikov discouraged visitors to the battlefield, but had made his way to meet Yeremenko at the landing stage along with Kuzma Gurov, a member of the Stalingrad Military Council.

They finally made contact with Chuikov and with the commanders of the 138th and 95th Divisions whose HQs were nearby. Lyudnikov, who had just taken over command of the 138th, was told by Yeremenko that there would be no retreat. Yeremenko had suffered a leg wound in 1941 and leaned on his walking stick as he surveyed the devastation – Chuikov's HQ had been smashed by artillery fire.

The human cost was obvious when General Zholudev broke down as he described how his Guards Division had been torn apart company by company until only isolated detachments survived fighting in the Tractor Factory. The 114th Guards Regiment had only 84 men left and the 117th just 30. All the divisional artillery, every 45mm (1.7in) gun, mortar and anti-tank rifle had been destroyed. The artillery chief of staff Captain Pavlov had been killed together with most of his divisional staff.

The Sixty-Second Army HQ was relocated in the early hours of 17 October to a position south of the Banni Gully between the *Krasny Oktyabr* Factory and the Mamayev Kurgan. However, this position came under fire and HQ was forced to move to a location 1000m (1094 yards) further on, close to the Mamayev Kurgan. German assault troops broke into the southern edge of the Spartanovka settlement, but Chuikov refused the request by the Soviet brigade commanders to be allowed to withdraw to Sporny Island in the middle of the Volga, replying that any move from the west bank would be treated as desertion. Preliminary attacks by the Germans on the *Krasny Oktyabr* Factory were beaten back but around the *Barrikady* Factory assault parties were moving along the railway line after breaking through between the 138th and 308th Divisions. General Paulus asked his Sixth Army subordinate division commanders for his actual ration strength versus combat strength. The returns indicated that of 334,000 men only 66,549 were combat troops.

The German pressure that had been maintained during the night increased at dawn. Dive-bombers hit positions between the Tractor Factory and *Barrikady* Factory, and tanks and infantry followed up hitting the 84th Armoured Brigade under the command of Colonel Vainrub. The T-34s of the brigade had been dug in covering the road and were almost invisible in the rubble. At a range of 100m (109 yards) the Soviet tank crews opened fire on the enemy vehicles

Above: At the Sixty-Second Army HQ, Krylov, Chuikov and Gurov listen to a report from Rodimtsev and check the information against their situation maps. Because of constant German pressure the HQ was moved on several occasions during the fighting.

Below: Both sides used the steep sides of the balkas *around Stalingrad for accommodation, storage and even hospitals. The bunkers reinforced with timber taken from demolished buildings were hard to hit from the air or with artillery fire. Chuikov's HQ was built in one such bunker.*

moving down Tramvaynaya Street. A dozen German tanks were hit and as the infantry went to ground Soviet guns on the eastern bank and *Katyusha* on the west bombarded the stalled attack. The Germans brought up reinforcements and renewed the attack, but once again it foundered against the guns of the T-34s and supporting artillery fire.

During the day Soviet observers spotted the preparations for a fresh attack on *Krasny Oktyabr*. These moves tallied with intelligence gathered from documents captured from Pioneer troops. In Moscow the Soviet Information Bureau announced: 'Faced with overwhelming pressure from the Germans, our army has been forced to carry out another retreat movement northwest of Stalingrad – the fourth such retreat within 48 hours. Nevertheless reports from the front indicate that the Fascists are paying extremely dearly for their relatively small territorial gains. Reliable sources say that the retreat movements are being conducted in a completely orderly manner and are slight in relation to terrain. Furthermore, it is emphasized that at no point have German troops been able to achieve their objective of penetrating to the Volga.'

In Stalingrad Chuikov sent Lyudnikov holding the *Barrikady* a categorical order to hold the line against the German advance: 'You are responsible for closing the breach with the 308th Rifle Division, securing its right flank, establishing close contact: under no circumstances will you permit enemy penetration of *Barrikady* factory area and at the junction of 308th RD. You are responsible for the junction.'

HANGING ON

On 18 October, German attacks in the factory district at Stalingrad reached a crisis point for the Soviet forces. Under severe attacks, Chuikov, for the first time in the six-week-old battle, ordered a withdrawal of 200m (219 yards). He had little choice in the matter – the 112th Rifle Division was down to 598 men and 115th Special Brigade had only 890. His move stabilized the front, but only just. By the evening, heavy fighting had flared up at the western end of *Barrikady* where German infantry broke through the 'Tramvaynaya Street Line' and fought metre by metre along the track.

Factory militia went into action as front-line troops and by the end of the day only five men were left standing from the *Barrikady* militia. On the right flank, where Gorokhov

Left: This officer has used the camouflaged material from a Soviet Army cape as a helmet cover and secured it in place with a loop of rubber made from the inner tube of a tyre. His PPSh-41 is not merely a trophy, it is a useful weapon in the street fighting.

The Minister [Goebbels] has barred the German Press and Radio from discussing winter clothing for German *Wehrmacht* troops. His intention is to avoid the mishaps that occurred last year when the press and newsreels talked about our fine winter clothing, when in reality almost nothing of the kind has been made ready.

Reich Press Chief, daily keynote address, 14 October 1942

However the Germans too were indulging in wishful thinking. Goebbels ordered all Knight's Cross holders from Stalingrad brought back to Berlin for interviews. Among these holders of one of Nazi Germany's highest decorations was General Jaenecke commanding the IV Corps. A soldier in the 389th Infantry Division wrote home bitterly 'Our General Jeneke [Jaenecke] he's called, received the Knight's Cross the day before yesterday. Now he's achieved his objective.' Goebbels ordered that huge signs should be displayed in German cities showing the distance to

fought virtually surrounded, Chuikov learned from Colonel Kamynin, his special liaison officer on the right wing, that the situation here had been restored. Gorokhov's soldiers were holding the northern outskirts of Rynok and had beaten off the attack on Spartanovka, crucially hanging on to the landing stage close by the mouth of the Mechetka River. The advanced German patrols that had reached Spartanovka were destroyed. Gorokhov now held an area of only about 8 square kilometres (3.08 square miles) on the right flank.

Elsewhere the Soviets held off the German assaults and counter-attacked in the *Krasny Oktyabr* area. Since the battle for Stalingrad started, 17,000 German wounded had been evacuated by train and/or aircraft. However, even the *Luftwaffe* pilots were beginning to wonder about the effectiveness of their attacks and the German tactics. 'I cannot understand how men can survive such a hell. Yet the Russians sit tight in the ruins, and holes and cellars, and a chaos of steel skeletons which used to be factories,' wrote Herbert Pabst on 18 October. To the south the advance by Seventeenth Army of Army Group A, towards the Black Sea port of Tuapse, was halted due to difficult terrain and stubborn Soviet resistance.

On 19 October German troops kept pushing on towards the factories in Stalingrad, while Chuikov scraped the bottom of his replacement barrel. He turned his supply and service companies on the east bank into infantry formations, and shipped the blacksmiths, cobblers and mechanics across the river to fight. In the city, weary Soviet troops picked up rumours that Stalin himself had arrived in the city to direct the defence. These may well have been generated by political officers to sustain morale, but one veteran of the Civil War who had fought at Tsaritsyn asserted he had seen Stalin in the city.

Right: Medics support front-line troops amidst the ruins of Stalingrad. Soviet medical support was often rudimentary and the responsibility of young nurses and medical students who were expected to work close to the front line and recover wounded men, often under fire.

Stalingrad, to demonstrate to the now war-weary German population just how far the *Wehrmacht* had advanced. However, on 22 October he insisted that no references should be made to the tough fighting in the factories that bore the name 'Red' since this might encourage 'Communist-infected circles'.

Northwest of Stalingrad, the Don Front launched a counter-attack, and the Sixty-Fourth Army did the same in the south. These gained little ground, but took the pressure off Sixty-Second Army. Fighting died down in Stalingrad,

giving Chuikov time to move exhausted regiments across the Volga to train replacements. Interrogation of German prisoners indicated that the morale in the Sixth Army had fallen to a new low.

PAVLOV'S HOUSE

On Tuesday 20 October at the four-storey 'Pavlov's House' 300m (328 yards) from the Volga, the tiny garrison engaged a probing force of four German tanks supporting a group of infantry. They put one tank out of action and scattered the

SECRET REPORT OF THE *SICHERHEITSDIENST* ON INTERNAL AFFAIRS, NO 328 OF 22 OCTOBER 1942 [EXTRACT]

1. News of the onset of bad weather on the Eastern Front has caused many Germans to draw comparisons between the military and political situation at the start of this winter and the situation at the same time last year.

The extremely strong, repeated Russian offensives in the central and northern sectors have confirmed the universal conviction that Russia still has vast reserves of manpower and equipment to draw on. The fighting on the Eastern Front has, Germans believe, largely bogged down into trench warfare and Stalingrad especially has become a second Verdun. Evidently the situation on the North African front has come to a similar deadlock.

Below: Flame jets from a Soviet flame-thrower. As a weapon it had a psychological impact that was often greater than its tactical effect. Bursts of flame were often of a short duration and constrained by how much could be held in the fuel tank.

infantry who ran for cover. Sergeant Jacob Pavlov of the 42nd Guards Regiment led the defence engaging German tanks with machine guns and anti-tank rifles from the top storeys, which were higher than the German tanks could elevate their main guns. Several civilians in the basement joined in the fight, including Mariya Ulyanova. Pavlov's men would eventually kill more German soldiers than the Germans lost in the capture of Paris in 1940.

Soviet soldiers favoured defending burnt-out stone or brick buildings, because there was nothing that the German forces could set fire to during attacks. There were strongpoints of many different sizes – some defended by a small squad of men, some by a whole battalion. Strongpoints were constructed to give all-round defence and to keep fighting even if cut off for several days. The soldiers dug communication trenches and used sewers to link the strongpoints to surrounding buildings. Soldiers from the Sixth Army who attempted to pass between these strongpoints would be caught in a crossfire, or else would be blocked by obstacles or minefields. Chuikov wrote: 'A group of strongpoints, with a common firing network, under a single administration and also supplied for all-round defence, constituted a centre of resistance.'

Above: A German mortar detachment prepares to move off in the factory area. They are manpacking the 8cm (3.1in) mortar, which has been broken down into three loads, while one man has a 5cm (2in) light mortar on his shoulder.

LETTERS HOME

Even at the height of the fighting Soviet soldiers still managed to find time to write letters home. Soviet letters were often one page, and three themes dominated, the family at home, reassurance, and preoccupation with the battle. Lieutenant Charnosov of the 384th Artillery Regiment sent his love to his wife Shura and 'kisses to our two little birds, Slavik and Lydusia. I am in good health. I have been wounded twice but these are just scratches and so I still manage to direct my battery all right. The time of hard fighting has come to the city of Stalin. During these days of hard fighting I am avenging my beloved birthplace of Smolensk, but at night I go down to the basement where two fair-haired children sit on my lap. They remind me of Slavik and Lyda.' The letter was the last he ever wrote. It was found on his body, along with a note from Shura, saying 'I am very happy that you are fighting so well, and that you have been awarded a medal. Fight to the last drop of your blood, and don't let them capture you, because prison camp is worse than death.'

Soviet soldiers also wrote about the importance of the battle. One Soviet lieutenant told his wife 'People might reproach me, if they read this letter about the reason why I am fighting for you. But I can't distinguish where you end, and where the Motherland begins. You and it are the same for me.'

However, not all the letters were so brave or confident. Many writers complained about poor rations, and front-line soldiers, aware that their life-expectancy was very short, had few fears about describing conditions as they found them. A soldier in the 245th Regiment wrote 'In the rear they must be

A PARALLEL STRUGGLE

Before dawn on 23 October, thousands of kilometres to the south in North Africa, the battle of El Alamein opened as, preceded by a 1000-gun barrage, General Montgomery unleashed the British Eighth Army against the German lines. After 20 minutes of bombardment, the British XXX Corps sent four of its infantry divisions forward into the German minefields on a 10km (6-mile) front. The 8th Australian and 51st Highland Divisions attacked toward 'Kidney Ridge' while slightly to the south, the New Zealand Division supported by 1st South African Division struck towards the Miteirya Ridge.

The following day, the 1st and 10th Armoured Divisions were committed to the XXX Corps breaches that had been punched through the German minefield. Feint attacks to the south by XIII Corps kept the 21st Panzer Division pinned down but by dawn, 15th Panzer Division launched counter-attacks against the XXX Corps breaches. Fighting was intense throughout the day. By nightfall, lead elements of the 1st Armoured Division began to emerge from the minefield, but 10th Armoured to the south was still mired in the mines. Congestion was severe and German artillery was taking a heavy toll.

By 26 October, both sides continued to attack but the only advances made were by the 9th Australian Division toward the coast. Allied air superiority began to show its effects as German tanks were ravaged. Fuel shortages were becoming critical for the Axis armoured formations and they only got worse when two tankers making the hazardous run from Italy to North Africa, the *Proserpina*

and *Tergesta*, were sunk – almost certainly on the basis of ULTRA intercepts.

During the night, mounting casualties and delays in clearing the minefields in the southern corridor led to a crisis in the British command. However, Montgomery ordered the attack to continue, and by morning the lead brigade of 10th Armoured Division emerged into the clear. Montgomery made one change in plan and sent the 9th Australian Division north to cut off the Italian and German formations still manning the lines between the northern breakthrough and the coast. Rommel, suffering from jaundice and on sick leave in Germany, returned to take command of the hard-pressed *Afrika Korps*.

On the 29th, Montgomery switched his attack toward the centre of the El Alamein line as the Germans reinforced the north end along the coastal road. German counter-attacks in the area were halted by tenacious Australian defences. A day later, the Australian 9th Division broke the German lines and occupied the coastal highway, cutting off several Axis formations.

By 2 November, with an immense logistical advantage, Montgomery launched a second armoured attack, which was repelled by German anti-tank gunnery. Rommel responded impetuously with his own massed armoured counter-attack, and the German armoured formations were virtually annihilated that day by expert British gunnery and air attacks. So ended Rommel's African dream, and the beginning of the end of the *Afrika Korps* in North Africa.

shouting that everything should be for the front, but at the front we have nothing. The food is bad and there is little of it. The things they say are not true.' Other Soviet soldiers told their families of dire food shortages, of scrounging for food, and of suffering from dysentery. The Sixty-Second Army censors reported that from 1 October to 15 October 'military secrets' were divulged in 12,747 letters. One lieutenant who wrote 'German aircraft are very good ... Our anti-aircraft people shoot down only a very few of them', was arrested for treason.

The tone of the letters that German soldiers wrote home was often hurt and disabused, even disbelieving. *Leutnant* Otten wrote to his wife 'I often ask myself what all this suffering is for. Has mankind gone crazy? This terrible time

will mark many of us for ever.' The young *Gefreiter* Gelman wrote to his father 'You kept telling me: "Be faithful to your standard and you'll win." You will not forget these words because the time has come for every sensible man in Germany to curse the madness of this war. It's impossible to describe what is happening here. Everyone in Stalingrad who possesses a head and hands, women as well as men, carries on fighting.' Another soldier reflected the gloomy fatalism that was beginning to infect the Sixth Army: 'Don't worry,

Opposite: By mid-November, the Sixth Army believed it would soon hold the whole of Stalingrad. The Soviet Sixty-Second had been forced out of the Barrikady *Factory and was now hanging on in isolated pockets along the bank of the Volga.*

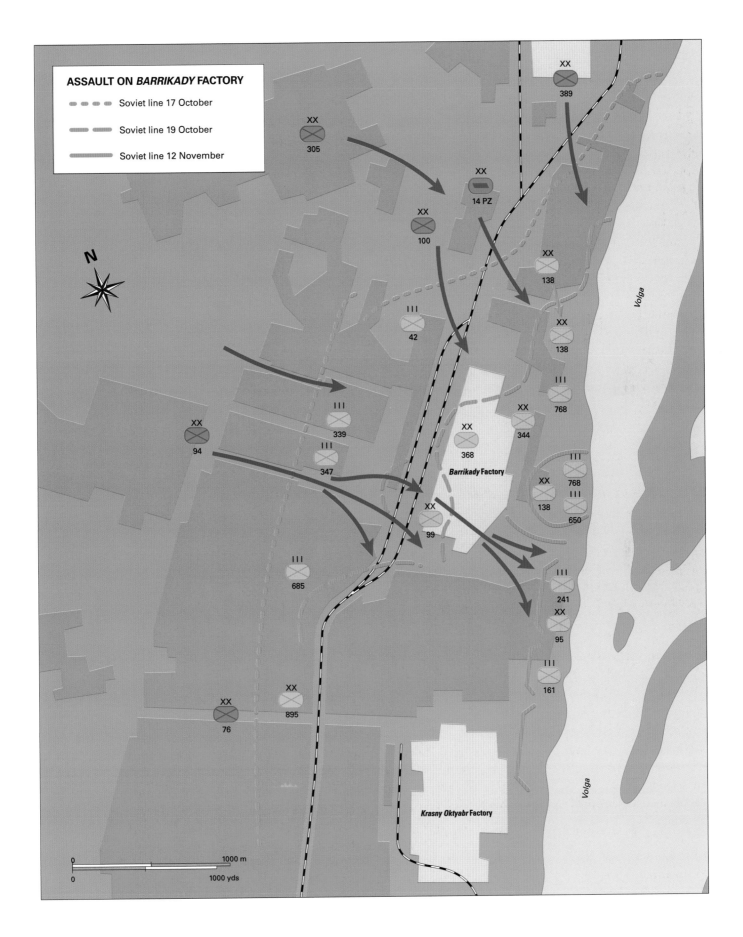

ASSAULT ON *BARRIKADY* FACTORY

- Soviet line 17 October
- Soviet line 19 October
- Soviet line 12 November

XX 389

XX 305

XX 100

14 PZ

XX 138

III 42

XX 138

III 768

III 339

XX 344

XX 368

Barrikady Factory

III 347

XX 94

III 768

XX 138

III 650

XX 99

III 685

III 241

XX 95

III 161

XX 895

XX 76

Krasny Oktyabr Factory

Volga

Volga

0 — 1000 m

0 — 1000 yds

Opposite: Laden with equipment including mess tins, tent sections, ration bags as well as weapons and ammunition, a German platoon moves up through a factory. The heat from earlier fires has twisted the metal sheets of either a fuel tank or the roof of the building.

Above: The body of a German machine gunner lies on the Mamayev Kurgan *as a soldier from an NKVD unit moves up the shell-ravaged hillside. After the war the former Tartar grave would become a huge war memorial.*

don't be upset, because the sooner I am under the ground, the less I will suffer. We often think that Russia should capitulate, but these uneducated people are too stupid to realize it.' In Berlin the Reich Press Chief, recalling the grim Russian winter of 1941–42, announced: 'Winter has already set in at several points on the Eastern Front. For the time being we are maintaining silence about the theme "winter" so long as the OKW report does not issue an official announcement on the subject.'

OPTIMISM

The Germans concentrated their attacks on the *Barrikady* Factory and housing estate on 21 October, capturing over half of it in a two-day struggle. They also made gains in the *Krasny Oktyabr* area.

However, Soviet aircraft were now dominating the night sky over Stalingrad, much to German surprise. At Hitler's headquarters, optimism over Stalingrad was high. Field Marshal Wilhelm Keitel noted 'The *Führer* is convinced the

JUNKERS JU 87 D-1

The two-seater single-engined Ju 87 dive-bomber, universally known as the Stuka from the German acronym for *Sturzkampfflugzeug* – diving warplane, developed a reputation as an awesome instrument of war during the Polish campaign. The scream of the diving aircraft was terrifying to men attacked on the ground. Some aircraft were fitted with sirens called *Jericho-Trompeten*, the Trumpets of Jericho, fitted to the spatted undercarriage to enhance the psychological shock. The aircraft was powered by one 1400hp Junkers Jumo 211J-1 that gave a maximum speed at 3840m (12,600ft) of 410km/h (255mph) and maximum range of 1535km (954 miles). It weighed 3900kg (8598lb) empty, with a maximum loaded weight of 6600kg (14,550lb). The wing span was 13.8m (45ft 3in), length 11.50m (37ft 8in) and height 3.90m (12ft 9in). The armament consisted of two fixed forward-firing 7.92mm (0.31in) MG17s in the wings, twin flexible MG81Zs in the rear cockpit, and a maximum bomb load of 1800kg (3968lb). It was superb in a close-support role where AA defence was negligible and where hostile fighters were not present. However, Soviet AA batteries developed tactics to counter the Stukas that approached at an altitude of between 1000 and 2000m (3280 and 6562ft) and then half-rolled to drop at an angle of about 70°. They pulled out of the dive at just under 900m (2953ft). The AA gunners learned to put up a barrage to hit them either at the point of the dive or when the dive brakes had slowed them down as they were pulling out.

Russians are collapsing. He says that 20 millions will have to starve.'

Optimism likewise increased at Sixth Army HQ when on 22 October the Germans reinforced their attacks on the *Krasny Oktyabr* Factory with the 79th Infantry Division supported by armour; after heavy fighting, they broke the Soviet lines, driving the defenders from the complex. The Germans were not stopped before they secured a foothold in the northwest corner of the *Krasny Oktyabr* Factory.

The Germans now held the Tractor Factory and most of the *Barrikady* Factory. However, it was at a terrible price. Hoffman noted in his diary: 'We have lost so many men; every time you move you have to jump over bodies. You can scarcely breathe in the daytime: there is nowhere and no one to remove the bodies, so they are left there to rot. Who would have thought three months ago that instead of the joy of victory we would have to endure such sacrifice and torture, the end of which is nowhere in sight? ... The soldiers are calling Stalingrad the mass grave of the *Wehrmacht*. There are very few men left in the companies. We have been told we are soon going to be withdrawn to be brought back up to strength.'

Fighting continued in the *Barrikady* and *Krasny Oktyabr* factories, with Soviet forces holding the furnaces and the Germans at the far end of the foundry and *Barrikady* Factory. The Soviet 37th Guards, 193rd and 308th Rifle Divisions, which had numbered 20,000 men a week ago, now fielded only a few hundred. For *Leutnant* Joachim Stempel of the 108th Panzer Grenadier Regiment, part of the 14th Panzer Division, the day would be remembered for the attack that captured the administration building of the Central Bakery:

'And then it is time. In front of us is the administration building of the "Bread factory". And here they come – our Stukas! We're attacking! Meter by meter we crawl forward, following the bombs that the Stukas are dropping in front of us. The howling of sirens, explosions, breaking, splitting, fountains of mud by the exploding bombs! Gun salvoes from the machines that are pulling up, that partially impact near us – around us – with their nauseating explosions force us to take cover for the moment. And then it howls overhead – hopefully not short – our own artillery! But also over from the other side! Whole series of salvoes by the Soviet artillery make the earth shake, with a exploding sound they impact

Left: A Soviet anti-aircraft sentry watches for approaching Luftwaffe aircraft. He is dressed for the winter in shapka-ushanka *synthetic fur hat,* telogreika *quilted uniform and* valenki *felt boots. He has a gas mask slung over his shoulder.*

Above: The Junkers Ju 87 dive-bomber was a superb close-support aircraft but vulnerable to either determined AA fire or, because of its low speed, to enemy fighters. AA gunners would open fire when it was at its slowest – before and after the dive.

in the factory walls that still are standing over there and spread a noise – like that of an underground train entering a station. Unbelievable, one cannot understand anything anymore. We continue to jump from shell crater to shell crater, from earth pile to the next remains of a wall! Now quickly to the block of [a] house, to the next cover. And once again it comes down on us – the fire of Soviet salvo guns! Onwards! – we have to seize the last hundred metres to the Volga! But the Russians are hanging tough and bitterly contest every hole in the earth and every pile of rubble – and

STICK GRENADE

The German *Stielgranate 24*, the Stick Grenade, was 35.6cm (14in) long, 7cm (2.75in) in diameter, and weighed 0.596kg (1.31lb) of which 0.17kg (0.37lb) was explosive filling. Once the metal cap at the base of the handle had been unscrewed, the porcelain ball on the end of the friction igniter cord fell clear. When it was given a sharp tug, there was a 4.5-second delay before the grenade exploded, producing a blast radius of 13 square metres (43 square feet). The practical distance that the *Stielgranate 24* could be thrown varied according to the tactical situation but it was about 35m (115ft), which was further than the range of a British No 36 Grenade. The relatively thin casing of the *Stielgranate 24* meant that in modern terminology the grenade was both 'offensive' and 'defensive' so the thrower did not need to take cover to avoid injury from fragments.

snipers, who with their fire, that hits us in the flank, inflict bloody losses, are lurking everywhere. They are hiding all around, but they cannot be spotted at all …'

SCORCHED LANDSCAPE

As the German 100th Division was in its forming-up position along a railway embankment on 25 October in preparation to attack in the *Barrikady* area, it was hit in error by a preparatory Stuka attack and the assault failed. The Germans captured the centre of Spartanovka and nearly reached the Volga but were pushed back by the timely arrival of ships of the Volga Flotilla delivering direct fire support.

A section of the Soviet 124th Special Brigade, made up of militia and Tractor Factory workers, tried to cross over to the Germans lines. A single sentry was against the idea, but agreed to join them. At the last minute, he ran back to Soviet lines. He was court-martialled 'for not taking decisive measures to inform his commanders of the forthcoming crime and preventing the traitors from deserting'.

The ruthlessness that characterized the fighting even extended to children. The Sixth Army soldiers used orphaned Russians for daily tasks like filling water bottles, but when Soviet snipers realized that these children were working for the Germans, albeit to stay alive, they shot them. Children foraged for grain from the ruins of the elevator and attempted to steal German rations. The carcasses of recently killed horses were quickly cut up by women and children – before the dogs and rats reached them.

As the weather began to turn, the Germans started digging in for the coming winter. Safe behind the lines, officers of a

HIWI

By 1942 German divisions on the Eastern Front were being reinforced by 'Hilfswillige', voluntary assistants or 'Hiwi', Soviet PoWs or civilians who had volunteered to serve with the Germans. In Sixth Army alone, there were 70,000 Hiwi. The 71st and 76th Infantry Divisions had over 8000 Hiwi each, roughly the same number of men by mid-November as their total German strength. There are no exact figures, but by the end of the war approximately 1,500,000 Soviet citizens had served in the Wehrmacht. From the first day of the war in the East large numbers of Soviet captives and deserters offered to assist the Germans in subsidiary services as drivers, cooks, hospital attendants and stable-men in the rear. This freed more Germans to serve in front-line units. In the battle sub-units, Soviet volunteers served as ammunition carriers, pioneers and messengers. Hiwi carried small arms for self-defence.

Originally Hiwi continued to wear Soviet uniform and badges of rank, but gradually they were given the German uniform. Sometimes only the armband with the words 'Im Dienst der Deutschen Wehrmacht' was the proof of the fact that a Hiwi belonged to Wehrmacht. These Russians received harsh discipline – they were shot if they fell out on the march – and were also marked down by Soviet authorities for harsh treatment if recaptured. Soviet authorities referred to Hiwi as 'former Russians'. Though some Hiwi assisted the German forces out of anti-Communist conviction, many men did so to escape from slow death in PoW camps and simply to stay alive. Colonel Groscurth of the XI Corps observed in a letter to General Beck 'It is disturbing that we are forced to strengthen our fighting troops with Russian prisoners of war, who already are being turned into gunners. It's an odd state of affairs that the "Beasts" we have been fighting against are now living with us in the closest harmony.' On 12 December 1942 the von Stumpfeld Division was formed from Hiwi inside the Stalingrad pocket. The division was largely armed with captured Soviet weapons, with some added anti-tank support provided by the 9th Flak Division. The division was initially commanded by German officers down to company level, but these positions came to be taken over by former Soviet officers. For example Kamenberg, the original commander of the Kamenberg Battalion, was later replaced by the former Red Army Major Tuchimov. The division was destroyed at Stalingrad, fighting in defence of the Tractor Factory, in February 1943.

regiment in the Bavarian 376th Infantry Division invited the division CO, General Edler von Daniels, to a Munich *Oktoberfest* shooting contest. Elsewhere, Soviet PoWs and *Hiwi* started digging trenches and bunkers as winter quarters. 'It's not an enticing picture out here,' wrote a German soldier in the 113th Infantry Division. 'For far and wide there are no villages, no woodland, neither tree nor shrub, and not a drop of water.' Divisions sent trucks and working parties to find wooden beams in damaged houses for their bunkers. The 275th Division dug man-made caves into the sides of *balkas* to form stables, stores and an entire field hospital.

From the lowliest *Landser* to Hitler himself, all Germans were now aware of the oncoming winter. Hitler issued orders for tanks to be dug in and protected in concrete bunkers, but the equipment to make them never arrived. The Sixth Army staff made plans for the coming winter, even ordering a Finnish training film 'How to build a Sauna in the Field'. German quartermasters started issuing winter kit to their troops. Some men received *Umkehrbare Winteranzug des deutschen Herres*, the excellent reversible white and field-grey quilted trousers and hooded jackets.

Most troops, however, had nowhere to wash, and spent their free time killing the lice that had collected in the seams of their summer weight uniforms that they nicknamed 'little partisans'. 'For a time being there was no point in even thinking of washing,' wrote a German soldier. 'Today I killed my first batch of eight lice.' *Hiwi* told the Germans to bury each article of clothing with just one corner left above the ground. The lice would collect there and could be burned off. The Sixth Army sent its 150,000 draft horses, oxen and camels back to the rear, to save on fodder. Motor transport and repair units were also sent back behind the Don. This move, which at the time seemed logical, would, however, immobilize the horse-drawn ambulance units.

German morale that was already low sank further, being dependent on mail from home, and the staff at Sixth Army HQ tried to relieve this with leave rosters, which prioritized soldiers who had been at the front since June 1941.

FIGHT FOR THE *BARRIKADY* FACTORY

The 14th Panzer Division's 36th Panzer Regiment attacked the bread factory that was part of the *Barrikady* Factory complex. The Germans ran into heavy fire. Sergeant Esser found himself the senior ranking man when his company commander and platoon leader were both killed. He leapt to his feet, screamed 'Forward!' and the platoon followed him through a 55m (60-yard) courtyard, under fire. They reached the opposing wall, positioned a breaching charge and blasted a hole through. Esser led his men into the building, and in close-range fire their MP40 submachine guns cut down the defending Soviets. Esser pressed on with his 12 survivors to take the building with 80 prisoners, an anti-tank gun and 16 heavy machine guns.

Across the street, the 103rd Rifle Regiment also struggled through ruined buildings and bomb craters, led by Lieutenant Stempel, detached from regimental headquarters to replace all the dead officers. Stempel led the 103rd through the ruins, taking enormous casualties. Some two dozen men

reached the Volga River, to face counter-attacks by determined Soviets. He called for reinforcements, and 70 German troops arrived. But the Soviets continued to counter-attack, determined to keep the Germans from the river's edge.

HEAVY FIGHTING

Heavy fighting was once again reported in Stalingrad on 26 October as the German 79th Infantry Division drove against the newly arrived 39th Guards Rifle Division. The Sixty-

Below: The gutted and twisted remains of the Stalingrad fuel tanks that caught fire on 2 October and burned for days, producing a huge column of smoke. Blazing fuel threatened Chuikov's HQ as well as streaming into the Volga.

Second Army HQ came under fire and its Guard Company was once more despatched to shore up the lines. German forces were now between the *Barrikady* plant and the *Krasny Oktyabr* Factory, less than 400m (437 yards) from the Volga. This meant the last remaining Soviet ferry landings on the western shore were under the direct fire of the Germans. Soldiers in the 100th Division cheered, convinced now that the battle for Stalingrad was over.

In a factory shop in the *Barrikady* plant a squad of 10 signallers from Combat Group Engelke, part of the German 100th Division, were setting up their station when they realized that there were Soviet troops in the room above them. The Germans threw charges upstairs but the Soviets caught them and threw them back, injuring several of the Germans. Night was falling and the Germans were very tired so they decided to leave the Soviets alone. They slept the sleep of the exhausted and the Soviets were silent. The following morning the German signallers requested assistance: 'This is Sea Rose. We are in the third white house … we need reinforcements urgently.' However, it took 12 hours before reinforcements arrived. The day had thankfully been quiet, punctuated only by the crack of rifle fire from German snipers in a building across the road. With each report the signallers could hear a scream from the room above them. Finally, backed by reinforcements, they went upstairs and smashed in the locked door. Inside lay seven dead Soviet soldiers, each with a bullet hole in his head. The signallers went downstairs and went to sleep.

On the same day that the signallers were caught up in this intimate battle Deputy Chief Quartermaster Karl Binder with the 305th Division, who had organized a grain collecting detail at the wrecked silos, made his way to the *Barrikady* Factory. Here in a forward observation post he watched a German combat group fight their way into part of the factory. On his return he met an old friend and Sixth Army staff officer Lieutenant-Colonel Codre who asked him for his opinion of the situation in the city. 'The same as yours,' said the quartermaster. Both men knew that for weeks the battle in Stalingrad had become futile.

On 27 October German forces drove hard for the last ferry crossing not under direct German fire. Two battalions of Sokolov's 45th Rifle Division were rushed across the Volga to the landing site and as the soldiers disembarked they were

Right: A squad of German infantrymen pauses by the remains of the Tractor Factory. Their equipment indicates that they are about to be committed to an attack. Many of the factories in Stalingrad, like this one, were modern designs with glazed roofs.

39TH GUARDS RIFLE DIVISION

The 39th Guards Rifle Division was part of the Sixty-Second Soviet Army, which was formed from the inactive Seventh Reserve Army in July 1942. The Sixty-Second Army was assigned to forces resisting the German thrust towards Stalingrad. Command of the Sixty-Second Army was placed in the hands of Major-General V. I. Kopakchi, who was then replaced by General I. A. Lopatin at the end of July. According to official Soviet histories from the Battle of Stalingrad, the 39th was officially credited with entering the 'Stalingrad Theatre' on 12 August 1942 and they would stay there until 2 February 1943. The division arrived on the eastern bank of the Volga, having fought through the German forces attempting to surround the city. It had been responsible for maintaining the 'Volga Corridor', preventing the Germans from completely closing all access. By the time the 39th was committed to combat on 30 September, it could muster less than half of its original strength. At this time, Lieutenant-General Chuikov assumed command of the Sixty-Second Army. The mission of the 39th was to defend the *Krasny Oktyabr* Factory. From 30 September to 2 February, the division fought in almost continuous combat, often in hand-to-hand fighting, against superior German forces. On 14 October

1942, the Germans staged a major counter-attack, sending three complete infantry divisions and two panzer divisions, and 3000 aircraft sorties against a Soviet front 4.8km (3 miles) long by 1.6km (1 mile) wide. Enemy artillery and mortar bombardment began at sunrise and continued until twilight, the dust and rubble cutting visibility to less than 90m (100 yards). The 39th Division held out for weeks, then months, fighting amongst the rooms of the *Krasny Oktyabr* Factory, never leaving an area which was approximately 1000m (1094 yards) deep and 3000m (3280 yards) long. Major battles were fought in each building and room of the factory, with success being measured by which office or which storage area the 39th captured or held on to. When the Germans surrendered at the beginning of February 1943 the few remnants of the division and the rest of the Sixty-Second Army were transferred into the reserve, to be rebuilt prior to April 1943, when they became part of the new Eighth Guards Army.

Below: Members of the 39th Guards Rifle division take up a defensive stance in the ruins of the Krasny Oktyabr *Factory, October 1942. They are armed with two classic Soviet infantry weapons: a Mosin Nagant rifle (foreground) and a DP light machine gun.*

Above: A StuG III assault gun rumbles past infantry of a support weapons company sheltering in bomb craters. In the distance – behind the ruined workshops in the foreground – appears to be the entrance to the Tractor Factory.

rushed forward to the lines only a few hundred metres ahead. By the end of the day the division had suffered 50 per cent casualties. German troops of the 79th Division pushed through towards the *Krasny Oktyabr* Factory, and hurled hand grenades into the HQ of Guryev's 39th Division.

LAST STAND

Chuikov despatched his last reserve, the Sixty-Second Army's HQ Guard Company, to retrieve the situation. They had saved the situation for the moment but had to dig in at the *Krasny Oktyabr* Factory. German machine gunners reached a point between the *Barrikady* and *Krasny Oktyabr* Factories about 366m (400 yards) from the Volga, and were able to fire on Sixty-Second Army's last remaining ferry landing. The Germans now held nine-tenths of the city. There was now no

place in Stalingrad on which they could not call down fire. However, one ingeniously sited Soviet *Katyusha* position in the *Krasny Oktyabr* Factory continued to defy them. It was actually being used in a direct-fire role and German forward troops of the 100th Rifle Division discovered that it was mounted on a crane. It was reloaded in a cellar and then raised and fired. A forward observation officer of the German 83rd Artillery Regiment located the position and made the relevant calculations for the guns to fire a counter-battery mission.

However, the flight of the shells when the German battery fired gave the Russians enough time to lower their launcher into safety. Chuikov's men now only held parts of the Mamayev Kurgan, a few factory buildings, and a narrow strip of the Volga bank, several kilometres long but only a few hundred metres deep. German victory seemed inevitable.

THE END IN SIGHT

On 28 October the balance between the opposing forces in Stalingrad had become increasingly delicate. Though more

Above: A Soviet soldier from western Russia shares a cigarette with an Asian comrade amidst the rubble of Stalingrad. Rolled in newspaper and made from makhorka, *the rough strong tobacco, the cigarettes helped kill hunger pangs.*

reinforcements were on their way to the Russians, the Germans were moving slowly in the direction of the Volga. However, Hoffman wrote:

'27 October. Our troops have captured the whole of the *Barrikady* factory, but we cannot break through to the Volga. The Russians are not men, but some kind of cast-iron creatures; they never get tired and are not afraid of fire. We are absolutely exhausted; our regiment now has barely the strength of a company. The Russian artillery at the other side of the Volga won't let you lift your head. …

'28 October. Every soldier sees himself as a condemned man. The only hope is to be wounded and taken back to the rear. …'

More and more German troops were falling out and dying from dysentery, typhus and paratyphus. Jaundice cases were sent home, so many German troops hoped to contract it. Half of those who died due to sickness were the youngest soldiers, aged between 17 and 22. Doctors in Berlin were puzzled that well-trained soldiers eating balanced rations, and engaged in physical activity, could be dropping so

quickly. They attributed the high sickness and death rate to cumulative stress and short rations.

On the German right and left flanks, Romanian troops resisted probing attacks and patrols by Soviet forces. On one of these Senior Lieutenant Aleksandr Nevsky led a company of submachine gunners through the Romanian lines, and raided the headquarters of 1st Romanian Infantry Division, causing chaos. Nevsky was wounded twice in the action. The Stalingrad Front political department decided that Nevsky must be related to the great Russian military hero, and followed the new Party line of invoking Russian history. Nevsky, the 'fearless commander, the full inheritor of his ancestor's glory', was awarded the Order of the Red Banner.

THE HIGH-WATER MARK

By 29 October the Germans were holding nine-tenths of the city and the other tenth was under heavy fire. The Soviets were still on Mamayev Kurgan and they were holding a few buildings and a narrow strip of the bank of the Volga. Far to the south, the Germans captured Nalchik in the Caucasus, only 80km (50 miles) from the valuable strategic target of the Grozny oilfields.

On 30 October the Sixth Army communiqué reported 'The Sixth Army will continue its attack on Stalingrad, first dealing with resistance groups in the south of the city'. German forces finally cleared the *Krasny Oktyabr* Factory complex.

On the last day of October *Fremde Heere Ost* – Foreign Armies East, the German army department responsible for evaluating all military intelligence from the Soviet Union, reported what appeared to be a Soviet build-up around Serafimovich, in the Romanian Third Army sector. General Reinhard Gehlen, heading *Fremde Heere Ost*, did not believe the build-up meant a Soviet counter-offensive. Aerial reconnaissance by the *Luftwaffe* also confirmed that the Sixty-Fifth Soviet Army was crossing the Don and establishing itself in a deep bridgehead on the southern bank of the river. With their forces locked in combat in Stalingrad or thinly scattered, the Germans could do nothing about it.

> We have fought for 15 days for a single house with mortars, grenades, machine-guns and bayonets. Already by the third day, 54 German corpses are strewn in the cellars, on the landings, and the staircases. The front is a corridor between burnt-out rooms; it is the thin ceiling between two floors. Help comes from neighbouring houses by fire escapes and chimneys. There is a ceaseless struggle from noon to night. From one floor to the next, faces black with sweat, we bombed each other with grenades in the middle of explosions, clouds of dust and smoke.
>
> *Anonymous junior officer, 14th Panzer Division*

Four days earlier Lieutenant Karl Ostarhild, a young intelligence officer with the 376th Division HQ, had briefed Generals Paulus and Schmidt: 'We have seen a large number of men and material concentrated in the region of Kletskaya. Our orders to conduct a reconnaissance of this concentration was [*sic*] fulfilled ... This is an attack army, heavily armed and of considerable size. We have information about the units ... their weapons, where they have come from, up to the names of their commanders. We also know their attack plans which extend to the Black Sea.' Paulus

TANYA CHERNOVA

Nineteen-year-old Tanya Chernova had once dreamed of becoming a ballerina. But after serving as a partisan in her native Belorussia, she made her way to Stalingrad, grimly determined to kill as many Germans as possible. The bitter warfare and the savage German reprisals had led her to totally dehumanize her enemy. She no longer thought of the Germans as enemy soldiers, but referred to them as 'sticks', fit only for breaking.

Tanya and her companions, intent upon joining a Red Army unit, evaded the Germans by working their way through the sewer system of Stalingrad. Utterly lost in the maze of tunnels, they emerged from a foul passage behind German lines. Hiding their weapons, they brazenly joined the meal queue at a *Wehrmacht* field kitchen, hoping to get a bowl of soup. Fresh from the sewers, their stench quickly attracted attention. One German soldier exclaimed 'What is that horrible smell?' Tanya and her friends were saved by a *Hiwi* who claimed that they were working for him. Despite his help, Tanya made no

attempt to hide her loathing for him or for any other *Hiwi* who worked for the Germans. She wolfed down the bread and soup he gave them, and quietly determined to kill this man at the first opportunity. To her, he was worse than the 'sticks' she was intent on breaking.

Later, she was part of a five-man fighting patrol tasked with dynamiting a forward German command post in the *Krasny Oktyabr* Factory area. Following at the rear of the patrol, she was grabbed by a German soldier who had spotted her moving through the rubble. In the ensuing struggle she kicked him in the groin, cracked his face on her knee and began to strangle him before one of the patrol turned back and smashed in her assailant's skull. Tanya eventually became a student at the special school for snipers under Vasily Zaitsev. She continued her vendetta against the Germans remorselessly, until she herself was wounded. She awoke in a field hospital, recovering from surgery for an abdominal wound that left her unable to bear children.

REINHARD GEHLEN – THE SURVIVOR (1902-1979)

Major-General Reinhard Gehlen, who headed the *Fremde Heere Ost* (Foreign Armies East) section of the *Abwehr*, directed towards the Soviet Union, began planning his surrender to the United States at least as early as the autumn of 1944. In early March 1945 a group of Gehlen's senior officers microfilmed their material on the USSR, packed the film in steel drums and buried it in the Austrian Alps. On 22 May 1945 Gehlen and his top aides surrendered to an American Counter-Intelligence Corps (CIC) team. After the war, the United States recognized that it did not have an intelligence capability directed against the USSR, a wartime ally. Gehlen negotiated an agreement with the United States that allowed his operation to continue in existence despite post-war de-nazification programmes. The group was known as the Gehlen Organization. Reconstituted as a functioning espionage network under US control, it became the CIA's eyes and ears in Eastern Europe and the USSR. Hundreds of German Army and SS officers were released from internment to join Gehlen's headquarters in the Spessart Mountains in central Germany. When the staff grew to 3000, the Bureau Gehlen moved to a 25-acre compound near Pullach, south of Munich, operating under the innocent name of the South German Industrial Development Organization. In the early 1950s it was estimated that the organization employed up to 4000 intelligence specialists in Germany, mainly former army and SS officers, and that more than 4000 V-men (undercover agents) were active throughout the Soviet-bloc countries. In April 1956 control of the Gehlen Organization shifted to the newly sovereign West German Federal Republic as the BND (*Bundesnachrichtendienst* – Federal Intelligence Service). Gehlen remained chief of the West German intelligence service until he retired in 1968.

looked at the corroborating information for the report and then asked 'Is this information known to my intelligence staff?' Schmidt replied that it was but in less detail.

Within the city of Stalingrad the fighting had died down. Both sides were suffering from supply shortages and the troops were exhausted. While the Sixty-Second Army had to move all their men and equipment by ferryboat across the Volga River, often under German fire, the Sixth Army had to draw its rations, fuel, and ammunition from a thin logistic chain of repaired railways and rough roads stretching hundreds of kilometres across the steppes. The ferocity of the fighting and vast numbers of men and guns at the front

meant that Sixth Army was using up food and ammunition almost as soon as it was delivered. There was little in reserve but this did not prevent Paulus, in a moment of tragic hubris, issuing an order of the day:

'The summer and autumn offensive is successfully terminated after taking Stalingrad. The Sixth Army has played a significant role and held the Russians in check. The action of the leadership and the troops during the offensive will enter into history as an especially glorious page. Winter is upon us. The Russians will take advantage of it. It is unlikely that the Russians will fight with the same strength as last winter.'

Opposite: The remarkable resilience of the population of Stalingrad is demonstrated by this picture of a primary school in the spring of 1943. Many of the children who survived the fighting were, however, severely traumatized.

Below: In the winter of 1942 Soviet troops manhandle artillery and stores onto a ferry on the right bank of the Volga. The onset of poor weather reduced the effectiveness of the Luftwaffe *and made the crossing less hazardous for Soviet forces.*

CHAPTER SIX

DESPERATION

The onset of the Russian autumn and its quick transition into winter held hopes and fears for both sides. For the Soviet forces there was the prospect of a winter counter-offensive that might finally see the German pressure removed from the exhausted defenders, while for the Germans the thought that, with the Volga clogged with ice floes, they might finally capture the city and then dig in to see the winter out.

AT THE BEGINNING OF NOVEMBER 1942, Colonel Helmuth Groscurth, the chief of staff of the XI Corps, wrote home: 'The Führer has ordered us to defend our positions to the last man, something we would do of our own accord, since the loss of a position would hardly improve our situation. We know what it would be like to be stranded without shelter in the open steppe.' Groscurth, the son of a pastor and an anti-Nazi, was in trouble with his superiors for filing complaints and taking action against SS *Einsatzgruppen* who had been massacring Jews.

Troops returning from leave knew they were re-entering horror when they passed a sign on the main road into Stalingrad that read 'Entry to the city forbidden. Onlookers put their own lives and those of comrades in danger.'

The Sixth Army HQ had established two administrative *Kommandantur* for the battered city. One was responsible for the centre and north of Stalingrad and the other for the area south of the Tsaritsa. Each had a company of *Feldgendarmerie* – military police, known to the *Landsers* as 'Chained Dogs' because of the metal gorget that hung

Left: Russian women emerge from dugouts in a corner of Fallen Fighters Square, known to the Germans as Red Square. The gutted buildings offer little cover from the elements, and falling masonry makes them dangerous for these survivors.

around their chests on a metal chain when they were on duty. They were responsible in the city for guarding against sabotage and registering and evacuating civilians. Anyone who failed to register would be shot.

They worked closely with a more sinister organization, the *Geheime Feldpolizie* – the Secret Field Police, under *Kommissar* Wilhelm Möritz. Their tasks included selection of suitable civilians for forced labour in Germany and handing over Communist activists and Jews to the *Sicherheitsdienst* (SD) – the Security Service of the SS. According to Soviet sources the Germans executed over 3000 civilians during the fighting and transported 60,000 civilians from Stalingrad to the Reich to work as slave labourers.

THE *EINSATZGRUPPEN*

Behind the armies came the sinister *Einsatzgruppen des Sicherheitsdienstes* (SD) *und der Sicherheitspolizei* (*Sipo*) – Operational Squads of the Security Service and the Security Police, a task force of mobile murder units operating in German-occupied territories during World War II. *Einsatzgruppe* C consisted of *Sonderkommandos* SK4a and SK4b, and *Einsatzkommandos* EK5 and EK6.4. The first commander of *Einsatzgruppe* C, SS-*Standartenführer* Dr Emil

Otto Rasch, had 700 men under his command; the *Einsatzgruppe* was attached to Army Group South and covered the southern and central Ukraine.

Sonderkommando 4a followed behind the Sixth Army in the summer of 1942 and had reached Nizhne-Chirskaya by 25 August. Here, under the command of SS-*Obersturmbannführer* Eugen Steimle, its members executed two truckloads of children, 'the majority between six and twelve', as well as Communist officials and NKVD informers who had been denounced by Cossacks who had suffered under the Communists. The *Sonderkommando* remained in the Stalingrad area until almost the end of September. It already had a ghastly record, having carried out massacres in Dubno and Kremenets. On 29 and 30 September 1941 *Sonderkommando* 4a, commanded by Paul Blobel, perpetrated the mass slaughter of Kiev's Jews at Babi Yar. This unit was also responsible for the murder of Kharkov's Jews, in early January 1942.

Below: Smoke and dirt geyser upwards from the Krasny Oktyabr *Factory as it comes under artillery fire. The heavy air and artillery bombardment delighted German infantry and convinced them that the enemy had been eliminated.*

Right: Fatigue lines the face of a German soldier as he cleans his Kar 98k rifle. Extreme cold made mineral oils viscous and it came as a revelation to the Germans that the Soviet forces often used sunflower oil for lubrication in the winter.

The method that the *Einsatzgruppen* used was to shoot their victims in ravines, abandoned quarries, mines, anti-tank ditches, or trenches that had been dug for this purpose. The killing by shooting, especially of women and children, had a devastating effect on the murderers' mental state, which even heavy drinking of hard liquor (of which they were given a generous supply) could not suppress.

This was among the primary factors that led the RSHA in Berlin, in August 1941, to look for an alternative method of execution. It was found in the form of gas vans – heavy trucks with hermetically sealed vans into which the trucks' exhaust fumes were piped. Within a short time these trucks were supplied to all the *Einsatzgruppen*. The *Einsatzgruppen* units operated in daylight and in the presence of the local population; only when the Germans began their retreat was an effort made to erase the traces of their crimes.

VON RICHTHOFEN

Meanwhile the fighting in the wrecked city continued. German troops were exhausted and short of ammunition. The 79th Infantry Division made another attack on the *Krasny Oktyabr* Factory, but the Soviet defenders brought down heavy artillery barrages, stopping the attack. 'The effect of massed enemy artillery has decisively weakened the division's attacking strength,' Sixth Army noted.

At Spartanovka, the 94th Infantry also suffered heavy casualties. German troops installed wire netting over windows and embrasures in their bunkers, so that hand grenades would bounce off. The Soviet soldiers needed small-calibre artillery to break the netting, but these guns could not be shipped across the Volga, so they improvised hooks on their grenades to catch in the netting. By now

German troops held 90 per cent of Stalingrad, while Chuikov's 20,000 defenders held only two patches of ground – a portion of the northern suburbs and parts of the *Krasny Oktyabr* Factory. Chuikov was suffering from stress-induced eczema, which was so painful he had to bandage his hands to cover the open sores. His opponent Paulus was also suffering from stress and had developed a nervous twitch.

NEBELWERFER

In German, 'Nebelwerfer' means 'smoke launcher', a name chosen to confuse the enemy but has probably caused more confusion after the war. When development started in the early 1930s, the programme to give Germany rocket-based artillery was top secret, and to conceal its true purpose it got the designation 'Nebelwerfer', although the system did have a marginal smoke-laying capability. The first attempt, the Do-Gerät 38, was unsuccessful, being inaccurate and dangerous to its crew.

The next one, the NbW 451, by contrast, was very effective and became synonymous with 'Nebelwerfer'. The 15cm (5.9in) NbW 451 six-barrelled rocket launcher weighed 540kg (1188lb) in action, with elevation from –5.5° to +45° and traversed through 24°. It had a range of 6700m (4.16 miles) and a 2.5kg (5.51lb) warhead that produced a massive blast effect. The NbW 451 was mounted on a modified version of the split-trail 37mm (1.4in) Pak 35/36 carriage. The tubes had to be fired individually, a complete firing cycle taking 10 seconds, to prevent the weapon from overturning. Though inaccurate, it could be reloaded in 90 seconds and was highly manoeuvrable.

The rockets were of an unusual design, with the solid fuel motor mounted at the front and venting through a ring of 26 angled venturis positioned about two-thirds from the nose of the projectile. By the end of World War II the Germans had 150 Werferregimenter, in part because the rounds were much more cost-effective than 10.5cm (4.1in) leFH 18 shells – rockets came in at RM 3350 and shells at RM 16,400.

To the west of Stalingrad, von Richthofen, commander of VIII *Fliegerkorps*, was equally stressed. His bombers had provided the Sixth Army with ample air support, but the aviator was frustrated by the ground forces' slow progress. With rain coming and temperatures dropping, Richthofen was eager to finish off the Soviets. He flew out to the Sixth Army Tactical HQ to tell Paulus that *Luftwaffe* support was pointless, because he complained 'the artillery don't fire and the infantry don't exploit our air attacks. We drop our bombs on enemy positions less than a hand grenade's throw from the infantry, but they do nothing.'

Paulus, now suffering diarrhoea brought on from exhaustion and poor sanitation, blamed the problems on numerical weakness – his battalions were considerably under strength – the lack of training in close-quarters urban combat, and ammunition shortages. Richthofen wrote 'They trotted out all the same old and stupid excuses'. However, he offered additional air transport planes to bring up ammunition, and called the *Luftwaffe* high command in Berlin to demand the immediate despatch of four *Luftwaffe* pioneer assault battalions. He told Paulus 'The real reasons for the slackening pace lie in the weariness of both command and troops and in that rigid army formalism, which tolerates only 1000 men in the front line out of a division ration strength of 12,000.' He added 'Generals are content merely to issue orders, without going into any detail or making sure that preparations are properly made.' While they talked, Richthofen's Stukas hit Russian positions. However, 'Following the raids by all Stuka wings,' Richthofen wrote, 'the army struck with a force of only 37 men, and they promptly stopped again after initial losses!'

At Hitler's HQ on 2 November the *Führer* saw fresh *Luftwaffe* reconnaissance photographs showing new bridges built by the Soviets across the Don in the Romanian Third Army's sector. He ordered heavy air attacks against the bridge sites and concentration areas in the forests on the Don's northern bank. Discussing the deployment of *Luftwaffe* field divisions to Stalingrad, he said they should 'only be used in defensive fighting until such time as they have gained cohesion and combat experience'. He recalled his experiences at the First Battle of Ypres and the '*Kindermord*', where a generation of eager but inexperienced young German soldiers were slaughtered in attacks on British positions in 1914: 'Volunteer units were prematurely committed in offensive actions and, because of their

In sending you this letter from the trenches, we swear to you, dear Joseph Vissarionovich, that to the last drop of blood, to the last breath, to the last heart-beat, we shall defend Stalingrad ... We swear that we shall not disgrace the glory of Russian arms and shall fight to the end. Under your leadership our fathers won the Battle of Tsaritsyn. Under your leadership we shall win the great Battle of Stalingrad.

'Oath of the Defenders of Stalingrad', Pravda, 6 November 1942 (25th anniversary of the Bolshevik Revolution)

inadequate training, suffered dreadful losses.' With this in mind, he cancelled the transfer of *Luftwaffe* field divisions to Romanian Third Army.

On 4 November Hitler ordered the 6th Panzer Division and two infantry divisions, including the 306th, to be transferred from France to Army Group B in the East, to serve as tactical reserves behind the Romanian Third Army and the Italian Eighth Army. The orders were transmitted immediately – but it would take the three divisions a month to reach their destination. Meanwhile, the assault engineer battalions Richthofen requested for Stalingrad arrived in the city. Heavy snowfalls and colder temperatures made take-offs and landings difficult for Richthofen's weary aircrew, but they continued to attack railway lines and installations east of the Volga.

TWO ANNIVERSARIES

German intelligence provided its latest assessments on the Russian Front to the OKW. The Soviet counter-offensive would hit Army Group Centre, but an attack might also be launched against Army Group B and the Romanian Third Army, with the objective of cutting the railroad to Stalingrad and compelling a withdrawal from the city.

Hitler ordered Paulus to take the two remaining pockets in Stalingrad east of the gun factory and the *Krasny Oktyabr* Factory and signalled 'Only after the bank of the Volga is entirely in our hands in those places is the assault on the [Lazur] chemical plant to be begun'. Hitler ordered Paulus to attack with smaller shock troop units. The area between the factories would be attacked by newly formed battle groups of the 71st, 79th, 100th, 295th, 305th, 398th Infantry Divisions and 14th and 24th Panzer Divisions. They would be assisted by five extra battalions of the 50th, a Panzer Pioneer Battalion and the 162nd, 294th, 336th and 389th Pioneer Battalions from the 161st Division and 294th Division. The battalions, based in Millerovo and Rossosh near Voronezh on the Don, about 480km (300 miles) west of Stalingrad, were

ПЬЁМ ВОДУ РОДНОГО ДНЕПРА, БУДЕМ ПИТЬ ИЗ ПРУТА, НЕМАНА И БУГА! ОЧИСТИМ СОВЕТСКУЮ ЗЕМЛЮ ОТ ФАШИСТСКОЙ НЕЧИСТИ!

Above: Patriotism became the driving motive for many Russians faced by the German invasion. The Communist Party would later claim that the victory at Stalingrad was inspired by party loyalty; however, most Russians wanted to liberate their country.

flown to the city on 6 November. In overall command of the pioneer battalions was Colonel Herbert Selle, the senior combat engineer officer at Sixth Army HQ. At Stalingrad, Groscurth wrote to his brother 'Along the whole of the

Above: Soviet infantry wait on the east bank of the Volga, dressed in great coats and armed with Mosin Nagant rifles. The original Soviet caption reads 'Waiting to cross the Volga'. In reality many soldiers were far less eager and this is probably a posed propaganda photograph.

eastern front, we are expecting today a general offensive in honour of the anniversary of the October Revolution.'

There was no attack but Soviet soldiers were urged to 'exceed their socialist promises to destroy Fritzes which they made in socialist competition'. In Fifty-Seventh Army, the *Komsomol* members took the exhortation to heart so that out of 1697 Young Communists only 678 were reported to have not yet killed a German. But other celebrations of the October Revolution were more traditional. A 45th Rifle Division battalion commander and his executive officer 'got drunk' while leading reinforcements to Stalingrad and were 'missing for 13 hours'. The unfortunate men of the battalion wandered around aimlessly on the Volga's east bank for a day.

But most Stalingrad Front divisions did not receive the promised special vodka ration, or even their food ration. But many resourceful Soviet soldiers made home brews from a variety of questionable liquids. Late in the evening, 28 soldiers from the 248th Rifle Division died in an approach march in the Kalmyk Steppe. Nobody called for medical assistance and nobody admitted the cause of death. The officers assumed the soldiers had died from cold and exhaustion, and submitted that as their report. The NKVD ordered autopsies on 24 bodies and found that death had been caused by consuming 'anti-chemical liquids'. The soldiers had drunk large amounts of a solution that contained small amounts of alcohol that was meant to be taken in small quantities as an antidote to the effects of a chemical attack.

The NKVD interrogated the unit's survivors, and found out that the men believed it to be 'some sort of wine'. On the surface, it appeared to be a case of theft of army material and drunken soldiers. However, the NKVD did not accept this obvious solution and reported it as 'an act of sabotage to poison soldiers', and started pursuing the traitor or traitors in this non-existent plot. Meanwhile Stalin made a rare broadcast speech, giving his Order of the Day for the October Revolution's anniversary. His speech intrigued and cheered the Russians with its cryptic reference to the

Below: A Soviet 120-HM 38 120mm (4.7in) mortar crew of the Thirty-Second Army near Stalingrad prepare to fire on German positions using a rudimentary system of hand signals.

upcoming Soviet counter-offensive: 'There will be a holiday in our street, too.'

In Germany, the Nazis were also celebrating an anniversary. In Munich on the evening of 8 November the surviving '*Alte Kampfer*' – 'Old Fighters' – of the 1923 Beer Hall Putsch packed the *Lowenbraukeller*, wearing their SA Brownshirts. The *Lowenbraukeller* had been chosen because the actual *Burgerbraukeller* was still in ruins following the bomb attack during the 1939 Beer Hall rally, which failed to kill the *Führer*. Swastika flags hung from the arches of the *Lowenbraukeller*'s main hall; the stage was covered with flowers, above which were massive gold eagles. When the band broke into the Badenweiler March the crowds rose to their feet as the *Führer* entered.

In the course of a long broadcast speech that reviewed the state of the war Hitler said of Stalingrad: 'I wanted to reach the Volga, to be precise, at a particular spot, at a particular city. By chance it bore the name of Stalin himself. But don't think that I marched there just for that reason, it was because it occupies a very important position … I wanted to capture it and, you should know, we are quite content, we have as good as got it! There are only a couple of small bits left. Some say: "Why aren't they fighting faster?" That's because I don't

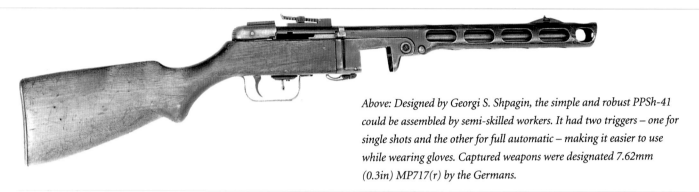

Above: Designed by Georgi S. Shpagin, the simple and robust PPSh-41 could be assembled by semi-skilled workers. It had two triggers – one for single shots and the other for full automatic – making it easier to use while wearing gloves. Captured weapons were designated 7.62mm (0.3in) MP717(r) by the Germans.

want a second Verdun, and prefer instead to do the job with small assault groups. Time is of no importance to me. No more ships are coming up the Volga. And that is the decisive point!'

In Stalingrad some German troops who were dug deep in cellars, foxholes, and ruins heard the speech with growing disbelief on their *Volkensangers* (cheap German radios tuned exclusively to *Deutsche Rundfunk*). One joked 'If only he had made it to the rank of full corporal!'

THE 'COMMISSAR'S HOUSE'

The five battalions of assault engineers arrived in Stalingrad. Equipped with flame-throwers, MP40 submachine guns and explosives, these men were considered the German Army's experts on street fighting. On the train carrying the 336th Battalion to Stalingrad Wilhelm Giebeler, a cook, listened to his comrades grumbling about their new mission – like every soldier in history. The 336th Engineer Battalion was met by their commanding officer, Major Josef Linden, and assigned to a location across the street from the *Barrikady* Factory. In a pre-attack reconnaissance Linden inspected his battlefield, and found it ghastly. 'Loosely hanging corrugated steel sheets, that creaked eerily in the wind, T-beams, huge craters … cellars turned into strongpoints … over all a

never-ceasing crescendo of noise from all types of guns and bombs.' Inside the factory, Major Eugen Rettenmaier, just back from leave, returned to take over his battalion, and found that out of a paper strength of 400, only 37 men now answered roll call. The rest were killed, wounded, or presumed dead.

Rettenmaier summoned Linden and the 336th to reinforce his own group, and spent part of the day planning how to drive from the factory to the Volga. The two main Soviet strongpoints were nicknamed the 'Chemist's Shop' and the 'Commissar's House' – the latter a clumsy brick fortress that dominated the terrain. Linden's orders were to clear the Russian strongpoints inside the factories and the neighbouring major buildings. The attack would be on a 5km (3.1-mile) wide front between Volkhovstroyevskaya Street and the Banni ravine. The assault would commence at 09:00 on 9 November and continue until the 12th, the objectives being the 'Commissar's House' and the 'Chemist's Shop' and the *Krasny Oktyabr*, *Barrikady* and Tractor Factories.

Opposite: Taking aim through the simple hinged L-shaped sights of his PPSh-41, a Soviet soldier uses the cover and camouflage of a wrecked building in the autumn of 1942. The PPSh-41 had a rate of fire that was almost double that of the MP38/40.

PISTOLET-PULEMET SHPAGINA O1941G

Soviet troops were principally armed with the robust and very effective *Pistolet-Pulemet Shpagina o1941g*, or PPSh-41 submachine gun. Designed by G.S. Shpagin, this weapon used barrels taken from bolt-action Mosin Nagant M1891/30 rifles that were chromed to reduce corrosion and wear, and was produced using simple techniques of stamping and brazing. Firing 7.62mm (0.29in) pistol ammunition, it weighed 3.56kg (7.8lbs) and had a 71-round drum or 35-round box magazine. It

fired at 900 rounds per minute, a rate of fire that in Korea would earn it the nickname of 'Burp Gun'. By 1945 some five million had been produced. During the siege of Leningrad, where there were munitions factories but wood was almost unobtainable, A.I. Sudarev designed the *Pistolet-Pulemet Sudareva 01943g* or PPS-43 submachine gun, an all-metal weapon with a folding stock and a 35-round box magazine. This modern design continued in production after the war.

Above: By November 1942 the Luftwaffe *were using all manner of aircraft to fulfil their commitments due to a chronic shortage of serviceable planes. Here, amidst freezing conditions, ground crew prepare an obsolete Henschel Hs 123 for a bombing mission.*

The assault engineers asked Rettenmaier relevant questions about the Soviet defences. However, when he tried to brief them on Soviet tactics, explaining how they used the cellars, they explained that they had encountered these tactics in the fighting for the city of Voronezh. The pioneers and infantry drew extra ammunition and rations, and then started assembling for the assault.

FREEZING OVER

On 9 November in Stalingrad, the temperature dropped to -18° C (0° F). The real Russian winter had arrived at last. The Soviet writer Vasily Grossman watched the Volga River starting to freeze: 'The ice floes collide, crumble and grind against each other, and the swishing sound, like that of shifting sands, can be heard quite a distance from the bank.'

While the eerie sound of crunching ice unnerved the troops, the spectacle of the Volga freezing up was deeply worrying for Chuikov. A partially frozen Volga would be a nightmare for his supply ferryboats, which were coming under increasingly heavy German fire. One Volga River steamer packed with guns and ammunition took a hit and started sinking. Another boat came alongside, and all hands start transferring men and munitions, amid heavy fire. 'The blunt, broad bows of the barges slowly crush the white beneath them, and behind them the black stretches of water are soon covered with a film of ice,' Grossman wrote.

Chuikov's problems were compounded by the Deputy Head of Supply Services, General Vinogradov, who was in charge of supplies on the east bank. He had his own ideas of what was a priority in Stalingrad and began sending over felt boots and winter caps. Chuikov had to persuade Khrushchev to intervene and post the diligent but misguided general away. Chuikov's staff proceeded to beg, borrow or steal whatever ammunition they could acquire. Former Volga sailors and fishermen within the ranks of the Sixty-Second Army were pulled out and tasked with building boats and rafts to supplement the conventional shipping that was crossing the Volga in the last available days. Chuikov knew that food would be vital and his supply staff accumulated a reserve of 12,200kg (12 tons) of chocolate.

While senior officers might build up stocks of high-energy food, most Soviet soldiers kept going on their daily ration of 100g (3.5oz) of vodka. It was awaited eagerly and drunk in a contented silence. Senior Lieutenant Ivan Bezditko, known to the men of his 120-HM 38 120mm (4.7in) mortar battery as 'Ivan the Terrible', had a real craving for spirits. In order to ensure that he had a regular supply he failed to report the death of men in the unit so that their vodka ration continued to be sent up to the battery. He collected the vodka and stowed it in his bunker. On the Volga shore Major Malygin, the quartermaster who handled the supplies, realized that according to the ration returns the mortar battery had enjoyed almost miraculously low casualties. When he contacted the lieutenant and discovered that in fact the unit had suffered heavy losses he told him that the crime would be reported to the Stalingrad Front headquarters. The real sting came at the end of the telephone conversation:

'With effect from today your vodka ration is cancelled'. Bezditko bellowed back 'If I don't get it, you'll get it.'

The quartermaster hung up the field telephone and contacted the HQ to report the fraud and to halt the vodka ration. The lieutenant was true to his word and passed the co-ordinates for a fire mission to his mortar line. Three rounds hit the quartermaster's stores and the major watched as the vodka poured from shattered bottles. 'Ivan the Terrible' was now in serious trouble as Malygin telephoned the headquarters. He was startled when a tired staff officer replied 'Next time give [him] his vodka. He has just been awarded the Order of the Red Star, so just give it to him.'

It was a story that did the rounds of the *frontoviks* who not only shared a similar craving for vodka, but enjoyed the idea of one of their number scoring a victory against the quartermasters. Along with vodka the other craving that

Below: A Soviet assault group in the Tractor Factory. The steel girders and lathes provided bullet-proof cover for German and Soviet forces alike but could also produce ricochets and shrapnel from exploding shells and grenades.

Left: The battle for the Grain Elevator in southern Stalingrad had given the Sixth Army an indication of the ferocity of the defence they could expect as they fought their way into the city. Now it was a haunt for scavenging children and a grain supply for the Germans.

plagued soldiers was the longing for *makhorka*, the rough strong tobacco. Soldiers asserted that the best hand-rolled cigarettes were made from newspaper since the ink added to the flavour. One soldier told Konstantin Simonov 'It's permissible to smoke in action, what's not permissible is to miss your target. Miss it just once and you'll never light up again.' These tough soldiers of the Sixty-Second Army were about to face their final test.

PIONEER ASSAULT

Shortly after midnight on 9 November, German combat groups, based on the five 600-man battalions of assault pioneers, assembled in the battered machine shops of the *Barrikady* Factory ready to attack. The pioneers had seen city fighting before, at Voronezh and Rostov, and were well equipped with demolition and pole charges, flame-throwers, and MP40s. The pioneers, loaded down with charges, shovels, grenades, and belted machine gun ammunition, moved slowly off to their starting line, cocky and cheerful, smoking last-minute cigarettes. A group moved into one of the factory's rooms. There was a massive explosion, followed by screams. Sergeant Ernst Wohlfahrt, a veteran of weeks in the *Barrikady*, charged into the room to find 18 pioneers dead and the shocked survivors subdued and fearful. At 03:30 German artillery opened fire, and the pioneers moved off to attack. The Russians fired back, but the pioneers pushed across the open pitted moonscape towards the 'Commissar's House'. The 'Chemist's Shop' fell quickly, but the 'Commissar's House' was a real fortress with its lower windows and doors blocked by debris. The Russian defenders had cut small embrasures in the walls. The Germans attacked and the Soviet defenders cut them down with automatic fire, pinning down the pioneers.

Further south, the 576th Regiment stormed its way to the Volga, backed by pioneers. German troops hurled grenades at the Soviet bunkers. At the close of the day when the pioneers took a roll call only one man was unwounded. Colonel Selle wrote home to his family 'There will be many tears in Germany … Happy is he who is not responsible for these unwarranted sacrifices.' Despite the increasingly intense cold, the Germans continued small-scale attacks, while the Russians counter-attacked with small assault parties armed with PPSh-41 submachine guns.

SINKING MORALE

German morale was sinking and some *Landsers* tried to desert. One German soldier who crossed the narrow no-man's land to surrender was shot halfway across by a newly arrived Russian. The body lay between the lines for the rest of the day. That evening, a Russian patrol crawled out to retrieve it but found that the Germans had got there first, taking the soldier's rifle and paybook. In a drive to encourage more desertion the Soviet command issued Order No 55, instructing Soviet troops to use loudspeakers and pamphlet barrages to encourage Germans to desert by promising them good treatment.

Despite the continuing failures at Stalingrad, the OKW believed that the Russians were near the end of their reserves. The Germans had some reason for this over-confidence, they occupied land that held 40 per cent of the Soviet Union's population, and the Soviets had suffered gigantic losses in men and equipment. However, the Soviet generals had good news for Stalin: a captured document from the 384th Infantry Division gave *Stavka* its first insight into the state of Sixth Army's morale. It was a signal from the 384th's CO, General Baron von Gablenz, to all of his commanders. 'I am well aware of the state of the division,' it read. 'I know that it

has no strength left. It is not [a] surprise, and I shall make every effort to improve the division's state, but the fighting is cruel and it becomes crueller every day. It is impossible to change the situation. The lethargy of the majority of soldiers must be corrected by more active leadership. Commanders must be more severe. In my order of 3 September 1942, No. 187-42, I stipulated that those who desert their post would be court-martialled ... I will act with all the severity that the law requires. Those who fall asleep at their posts in the front line must be punished with death. There should be no doubt about this. In the same category is disobedience ... expressed in the following ways: lack of care of weapons, body, clothing, horses, and mechanised equipment.' Gablenz told

Opposite: A Sixty-Second Army soldier with an insulated food container strapped to his back makes his way through the rubble of Stalingrad to deliver rations to forward troops. He is armed with a PPD-34, the first SMG to enter service with the Soviet Army.

Below: Salvos of M-30 Katyusha ('Little Katie') rockets streak away from their pre-positioned frame launchers. The M-30 was developed in 1942 from the M-13 rocket, and had a larger, bulbous warhead. The Germans soon learned to fear the sound of a Katyusha attack.

Above: A Polikarpov U-2VS in service with a Polish squadron of the Red Air Force. This slow biplane operated largely at night as it was vulnerable to AA fire and fighters. In the ground attack mode the pilot would glide over the target after cutting the engine and release the bombs.

his officers to warn their men 'they should count on staying in Russia for the whole of the winter.' This was bad news for the Germans, but the Soviets were delighted.

On 10 November, the German 50th Pioneer Battalion made renewed attacks on the 'Commissar's House', and this time broke into the building by using satchel charges. As the Germans charged in, the Russians withdrew to the cellars. The Germans tore up the floor, poured petrol into the cellars, lowered satchel charges into them and detonated them. Outside, German troops set off smoke grenades to blind anyone who might run out of the basement. The building exploded, killing everyone inside.

The Germans had taken the 'Commissar's House'. It was a victory but at a terrible cost: only one battalion could be formed from the survivors of the five pioneer battalions that had gone into the attack.

OPERATION *HUBERTUS*

On 11 November, the Sixth Army launched its final throw in Stalingrad, in an operation code-named 'Hubertus'. Paulus had organized 10 battle groups from the 71st, 79th, 100th, 295th, 305th, and 389th Infantry Divisions, backed by four fresh pioneer battalions. Troops of the 161st and 294th Divisions had been brought in by air and joined the assault. Many of the German troops in the city were hungry, filthy, exhausted, lice ridden and suffering from dysentery, but despite this they went into the attack. Von Richthofen's VIII *Fliegerkorps* roared into battle again, with its Ju 87 Stukas hitting the Russian positions in the Tractor and *Krasny Oktyabr* Factories.

The German attack went in on a 4.8km (3-mile) front between the Banni Gully and Volkhovstroyevskaya Street, amid the blasted factories. The Russians counter-attacked in force, and vicious close-quarter fighting raged for five hours amid the wreckage of the Tractor Factory with point-blank firefights in the vast workshops. German flame-thrower crews won this battle.

Among the Soviet defenders were sailors drafted from the Pacific Fleet in Vladivostok, hardy Siberians who were untroubled by the increasingly cold weather. When Paulus committed his reserves to the battle, they overran the 95th Division and reached the Volga River around the *Krasny Oktyabr* Factory. The Germans finally held a 500m (548 yard) stretch of the river.

The vicious fighting cut off Colonel Lyudnikov's 138th Division from the rest of the Sixty-Second Army and split it into three parts. The 138th dug in behind the *Barrikady* Factory on the Volga, its men down to 30 rounds for each rifle or PPSh and a daily ration of less than 50g (1.76oz) of

The untouchable nightly air dominance of the Russians has increased beyond understanding. The troops cannot rest, their strength is used to the hilt. Our personnel and material losses are too much in the long run. The Army asks *Heeresgruppe* to order additional attacks against enemy airfields day and night to assist the troops fighting in the front lines …

Sixth Army HQ to Army Group B at Golubinka, 19 October 1942

POLIKARPOV U-2VS (PO-2)

With a crew of two or three, the Po-2 first flew in January 1928, and over 13,000 had been built by June 1941. Though it was used primarily for training and liaison, it pioneered night raids. It was powered by one 100hp M-11 that gave a maximum speed at sea level of 150km/h (93mph) and a maximum range of 530km (239 miles). It weighed 635kg (1400lb) empty and 890kg (1962lb) loaded. The upper wing span was 11.4m (37ft 5in) and the lower 10.65m (34ft 11in). It was 8.15m (26ft 9in) long. Production continued into the mid-1950s in Eastern Europe.

Its armament consisted of one 7.62mm (0.3in) ShKAS machine gun in the rear cockpit and it had a maximum under-wing load of 250kg (550lb) of bombs or rockets. The pilots employed a simple night attack tactic of flying to within range of their target and then cutting their engines and gliding in to drop their bombs. For the German soldiers in the front line the silence that presaged the explosion of the modest bomb load was always disconcerting. A number of captured aircraft were flown by ex-Soviet Air Force volunteer personnel for the *Luftwaffe* in night attacks on the Eastern Front. The first Soviet all-female formation to be activated was the 588th Air Regiment that went into action in the summer of 1942. The women often flew the fragile Po-2 biplane. It was terribly vulnerable and so attacks were conducted at night from altitudes of between 1200 and 600m (4000 to 2000ft). By October 1943 its performance had earned it the title 46th Taman Guards Bomber Regiment. The 46th was the only all-women regiment in the Red Army with a total strength of over 200. It was commanded by Major Yevdokiya Bershanskaya throughout the war. The 46th was composed of three squadrons with a training squadron. Thirty air crew were killed during the war and the regiment flew over 24,000 combat missions in 1100 nights. It was the most decorated of the women's formations with 23 members receiving the Gold Star of the Hero of the Soviet Union, the nation's highest award – five posthumously. The Regiment adopted the slogan 'You are a woman, and you should be proud of that'.

To the Germans the Po-2's 100hp radial engine sounded like a malign sewing machine and when they discovered that some of these front-line intruders were piloted by women the pilots of the 46th Guards Regiment earned a new title from the Germans – they were 'The Night Witches'.

dried bread. Chuikov, aware that German signallers were monitoring his transmissions, kept sending Lyudnikov messages that help would soon be coming. In part this was to keep the 138th Division fighting but also to bluff the Germans that the Sixty-Second Army still had more men to commit – in fact they did not and the 138th was forced to give ground building by building. By the close of the day the German 100th Division had destroyed 19 bunkers. The 71st and 295th cleared out some workers' housing near the 'Tennis Racket'.

But the Soviets refused to break, despite taking immense casualties. The 118th Guards Regiment had 250 men at roll call on the morning of the 11th, and lost 244 men in five hours. The 112th Guards Regiment was down to 100 men in each of its battalions. The 193rd Rifle Division was gone. The Germans had suffered equally. In their first day of action, the five new pioneer battalions had lost 440 men. The 389th Infantry Division reported 190 casualties and 189 missing.

That evening, Soviet Po-2 biplanes dropped sacks of ammunition and food to the 138th Division. The food was welcome, but the ammunition was damaged on impact, which caused misfires. The Soviet troops had been instructed to light fires to assist the pilots, but the Germans realized what was happening and lit decoy fires. Meanwhile as Soviet reinforcements came across the Volga in boats, German 20mm (0.78in) Flak guns and MG34 machine guns cut them down. Shellfire capsized boats and hurled heavily laden Russian troops into the Volga River, where they drowned in the bitterly cold water. The ice chunks in the Volga River were illuminated by the flame and thunder of explosions, casting a weird light on the floating corpses.

Among the men of the 138th Division close to the Volga was a squad of four men commanded by a soldier named Rolik. Their fight with the German pioneers became a duel. When the Germans lowered demolition charges over the edge of the river bank the Rolik men cut the cables and let the charges fall into the river. They then returned fire against their tormentors. For the rest of the 138th Division the little group became almost talismanic. When they were silent 'everyone trembled', when the firing resumed there were shouts of 'Rolik's firing! Rolik's firing!'

The Soviet High Command continued its preparations for Operation Uranus, transmitting radio messages to the 'Lucy' Ring in Switzerland: 'Where are the rear defence locations of the Germans on the southwest of Stalingrad and along the Don? Are defence positions being built on sectors Stalingrad-Kletskaya and Stalingrad-Kalach? Their characteristics?' Stalin continued to worry.

On 11 November the Germans in Stalingrad had made their final effort at eliminating the Sixty-Second Army in savage fighting in the city. That evening von Richthofen wrote in his diary that the Sixth Army's attacks were 'dreadful and only reluctantly carried out … Opposite the Romanians on the Don, the Russians are resolutely carrying on with their preparations for an attack. Available elements of VIII *Fliegerkorps*, other *Luftwaffe* units and the Romanian air forces continually hit them. Their reserves have now been concentrated. When will the Russians attack? They have apparently been experiencing ammunition shortages. Artillery preparations, however, are starting to be equipped. I only hope that the Russians don't tear too many large holes in the line.'

On 14 November Chuikov reported to the Front HQ: 'No ships arrived at all. Deliveries of supplies have fallen through for three days running. Reinforcements have not been ferried across, and our units are feeling an acute shortage of ammunition and rations … The drifting ice has completely cut our communications with the left bank.'

Hoffman confided to his diary:

'3 November. In the last few days our battalion has several times tried to attack the Russian positions … to no avail. On this sector also the Russians won't let you lift your head. There have been a number of cases of self-inflicted wounds and malingering among the men. Every day I write two or three reports about them.

Below: By early November, snow had started to dust the ruins of Stalingrad. A Soviet soldier works his way through the rubble while in the foreground is a coil of barbed wire dumped before it could be deployed as an obstacle.

'10 November. A letter from Elsa today. Everyone expects us home for Christmas. In Germany everyone believes we already hold Stalingrad. How wrong they are. If they could only see what Stalingrad has done to our army.

'18 November. Our attack with tanks yesterday had no success. After our attack the field was littered with dead.'

Richthofen rang General Zeitzler at *Führer* headquarters at Rastenburg on 16 November and raged: 'Both the command and the troops are so listless … we shall get nowhere … Let us either fight or abandon the attack altogether. If we can't clear up the situation now, when the Volga is blocked and the Russians are in real difficulty, we shall never be able to. The days are getting shorter and the weather worse.' Zeitzler agreed.

On 17 November Hitler signalled Paulus: 'I know about the difficulties of the battle for Stalingrad … With the ice drifting on the Volga, however, the difficulties are even greater for the Russians. Making use of this [time] span we will avoid a bloodbath later on. I expect therefore that the Supreme Command, with all its repeatedly proven energy, and the troops, with their courage often demonstrated, will do their utmost to break through to the Volga at the metallurgical works and at the gun factory and occupy these parts of town.'

Above: A Focke-Wulf Fw 190 ground attack fighter runs up its engines on a snow-covered airstrip. Though this was the second winter in Russia for the Luftwaffe *it was still less well equipped for these conditions than its enemy.*

By 18 November, the men of the Soviet Sixty-Second Army held only toeholds on the west bank of the Volga River, but this Soviet-controlled territory included the satellite town of Rynok in the north, parts of the huge *Krasny Oktyabr* Factory, as well as much of the area between the railway station and the Volga. The area measured 20km (12.4 miles) at its longest. Soviet forces fought from the cellars and the sewers. Prolonged street fighting and the utter destruction of Stalingrad reduced men to a primitive level of existence. The Germans, who had been the exponents of the fast, mechanized war dubbed *Blitzkrieg* – Lightning War, were now engaged in *Rattenkrieg* – Rat War.

Many of the newly arrived Soviet soldiers in Stalingrad received a leaflet prepared by Chuikov's staff that described the tactics that would neutralize the effectiveness of superior German firepower. They were urged to 'Get Close to the Enemy', 'Crawl', 'Use craters for Cover', 'Dig trenches by Night, Camouflage them by Day'. Some survived to put these

---

A WAR BALLAD

The Soviet war correspondent Alexei Surkov composed a song during the siege in late November. In official circles the last line of the song was condemned as 'too negative' but to *frontoviks* it summed up their feelings.

In our bunker the log fire burns
Weeping resin, it sputters and sighs
The accordion's haunting refrain
Sings of you, your smile and your eyes,
We are light years apart
And divided by snow covered steppes
Though the road to your side is so hard
To death's door it's four easy steps

Six soldiers from a Guards tank unit wrote to Surkov supporting his decision not to bow to official pressure and change the song, saying 'For them you say that death is four thousand English miles away but for us, leave the song as it is. We have counted the steps it takes to die.'

---

simple rules into practice and became veteran *frontoviks*, but many of these barely trained soldiers died standing on the western shore shivering from cold and terror as German bombs and shells ripped into their positions.

DANGER ON THE FLANKS

The best of the German forces were now completely entangled in Stalingrad, and on their northern flank on the Don River bend the front lines were held by less well equipped and trained troops of the Romanian Third Army, under General Dumitrescu, and the Italian Eighth Army. The Romanian Fourth Army under General Constanescu held the front to the south of Stalingrad.

The decision that would prove fatal was at the time probably seen as the best move in the circumstances. The Romanian troops had fought hard at Odessa and Sevastopol in 1941 and 1942 and with the Italians could hold the flanks, while better equipped, motivated and trained Germans captured Stalingrad.

While the possibility of a counter-attack along the long northern flank on the Don had been discussed on several occasions, Hitler's increasingly irrational orders meant no defensive work could be carried out. One particular stretch, the line known because of its shape as the Beketovka 'bell',

did not actually run on the Don but was on the west bank. This left the Red Army several bridgeheads directly in front of the Romanian Third Army, which was stretched out along 150km (93.2 miles) of the front after taking over from German and Italian units. In summer the defences were effective since they included the large water obstacles of two lakes, the Tsatsa and Barmantsak, but in winter the lakes would freeze. The Romanian commander had asked in vain for tanks to support an attack to clear out the pocket on several occasions. With the onset of winter, due to poor administration, the Sixth Army did not receive the new cold weather uniforms that had been developed following the winter of 1941–42. Italian and Romanian troops huddled in greatcoats in the snow. The uniforms were held in depots and had not been sent forward because it was thought that they had a lower priority compared to ammunition and rations necessary to prosecute the offensive.

Forty thousand fur coats, caps and boots were held in depots in Millerovo. In stores in Morosovskaia, Tormosin, Chir, Peskovatka, Tatsinskaya, Oblivskaia and Cherkovo were 2,000,000 shirts, 40,000 hats, 102,000 pairs of felt boots, 83,000 pairs of long pants, 61,000 pairs of quilted trousers, 53,000 quilted jackets, 121,000 greatcoats as well as scarves, mittens, gloves and socks. Some exotic civilian winter clothing did reach Stalingrad, and when men of the 100th Infantry Division kitted themselves out they looked as if they were off to a fancy-dress party and not the front line. The army reporter Heinz Schröter noted grimly 'The scenes which took place at this depot were amongst the few events at which the Stalingrad soldiers were able to laugh.'

As far back as September 1942 Stalin and *Stavka* had realized that the Sixth Army was out on a limb. However, the first priority would be an attempt to relieve the besieged northern city of Leningrad. These attacks were launched in August and ended by September. The plan for Stalingrad would be a double envelopment by attacks on the vulnerable flanks to north and south. In Stalingrad Chuikov was urged to hang on.

His men were going into action inspired or terrified by three slogans:

'Every man a fortress!'
'There's no ground left behind the Volga!'
'Fight or die!'

Opposite: A Soviet assault group armed with PPSh-41 SMGs and a DPM light machine gun move through a ruined building in central Stalingrad. From early November, the Sixty-Second Army became more aggressive in its operations in the city.

CHAPTER SEVEN
AFTERMATH

On 19 November 1942 Marshal Zhukhov launched Operation Uranus, the Soviet counter-attack and encirclement that finally sealed the fate of the Sixth Army in Stalingrad. 'At precisely 07:30 on the morning of 19 November 1942,' recalled Marshal of Artillery V. Kazakov, 'the misty quiet of the dawn was shattered by the thunder of artillery fire. Even we officers, who'd fought a few battles in our time, had never seen anything like this before. The air was filled with the screech of thousands upon thousands of shells and the echo of their explosions.'

THE SOVIET ARTILLERY ARM WAS NOT ONLY POWERFUL, but it was used *en masse*. Huge barrages would crash down on enemy assembly areas and advancing forces and precede the Soviet counter-attacks. It was fire from these guns that had caused so much havoc among German forces in Stalingrad. The principal heavy calibre weapons were the 122mm (4.8in) M1939 and the 152mm (5.9in) M1937 howitzers. The M1939 howitzer had a crew of eight and fired 21.8kg (48lb) HE shells to a maximum range of 11,800m (7.3 miles). An experienced, full-strength crew could fire five to six rounds per minute. The M1937 howitzer weighed 7128kg (7 tons) in action and fired a 43.6kg (96lb) shell to a maximum range of 17,265m (10.7 miles). A trained crew could keep up a rate of fire of four rounds per minute. The guns were backed by massed *Katyusha* batteries. As this crescendo of violence was being unleashed, an exhausted Hitler was enjoying a brief

Left: Columns of prisoners, survivors from the Sixth Army, shuffle through a Russian town on a bright winter's day. Weakened and often diseased, many would die soon after the surrender and the last of the 5000 survivors would return to Germany in the mid-1950s.

Above: Romanian soldiers with their distinctive Dutch helmets and tall sheepskin caps man a 7.92mm (0.31in) Czech-made VZ-37 medium machine gun. The gun was designed to fire single shots or at 500 or 700 rounds a minute.

holiday at the Berghof, his mountain retreat in Berchtesgaden, southern Bavaria. His relaxation came to an abrupt end that afternoon when he took a telephone call from his headquarters in East Prussia.

A clearly agitated Zeitzler, Chief of the Army General Staff, shouted down the line that hundreds of Soviet tanks had shattered the Romanian front exactly where Hitler had earlier predicted and that the Romanian formations were in full flight.

Repeated updates throughout the afternoon convinced Hitler that the situation was serious, although he still felt that

Our troops in the approaches of Stalingrad have gone on the offensive against German forces. The offensive was undertaken at two sectors in the northwest and south of Stalingrad ... our troops have advanced 35 to 40 miles in three days of intense fighting in which they overcame enemy resistance.

Stavka Special Announcement, Monday 23 November 1942

Generallmajor Ferdinand Heim's LXVIII Panzer Corps could, if properly deployed, contain the enemy breakthrough. He promptly ordered *Generaloberst* Maximilian von Weichs, commander of Army Group B, to abandon all further offensive operations within Stalingrad and transfer forces from the city to cover the broken flank.

Zhukhov had positioned the Southwest Front under General Nikolai Vatutin – consisting of the Sixty-Third Army, First Guards Army and Twenty-First Army, totalling one million men, 13,500 guns and 894 tanks – opposite the Romanian and Italian armies. After a short but intense bombardment the Soviet tanks and infantry tore through the Axis forces. The Twenty-First Army initially had a hard fight with the Romanian Army on the northern Don, but punched through them and swung south behind the German Sixth Army.

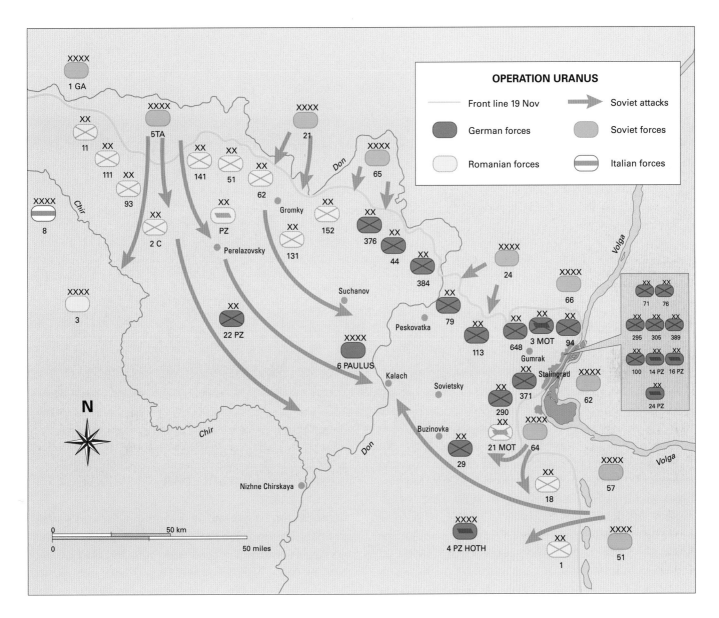

Above: The link-up between Fifth Tank Army and IV Mechanized Corps from Fifty-First Army at Kalach did not seal the fate of the Sixth Army – it might have attempted a break-out but with every day that passed the encirclement became stronger.

OPERATION URANUS

In early November *Luftwaffe* reconnaissance flights had reported a massive build-up of Red Army units just north of the Romanian Third Army, preparing for an offensive. Increasingly desperate messages despatched to the OKW from the Sixth Army HQ were ignored, or returned with admonishments about getting on with the task at hand. Paulus eventually gave up asking and moved the 22nd Panzer Division into position south of the Romanians. However, they arrived in terrible condition with only 50 serviceable tanks, but were nevertheless deployed with the only Romanian tank division to form the newly named XLVIII Armoured Corps.

On 20 November the Stalingrad Front attacked out of the fog and by the end of the day had penetrated up to 50km

(31 miles). The Soviet Fifty-First, Fifty-Seventh and Sixty-Fourth Armies attacked the Romanian Fourth Army and part of the German Fourth Panzer Army. Elements of the 29th Panzergrenadier Division counter-attacked and stalled the offensive for a time until Soviet numbers began to tell. Aware now that they were under serious threat, the Sixth Army headquarters moved from Golubinsky to Nizhne-Chirskaya on the Chir River, and a day later Paulus ordered the HQ to move further eastward to the airfield at Gumrak, closer to Stalingrad. He had ordered the XIV Panzer Corps

from the northern suburbs of Stalingrad to the Don bridgeheads but a shortage of fuel delayed the redeployment.

By the end of the day the situation had changed dramatically. To the north the Romanian Third Army had been comprehensively defeated and was in disorderly retreat towards Kotelnikovo, having suffered casualties amounting to 35,000 men, half its operational strength. In five days the XXVI Tank Corps of the Twenty-First Army had linked up with men of the IV Tank Corps of the Stalingrad Front south of Stalingrad at Kalach on the Don and closed the trap on the Sixth Army.

Though the next priority was to destroy the Fourth Panzer Army and Sixth Army inside the Stalingrad pocket,

Above: Dragging a Maxim machine gun on its Sokolov mounting, soldiers of the Twenty-First Army of the Southwest Front follow behind a T-70 light tank during fighting near the Kalach Bridge. When they captured the bridge they severed the Sixth Army communications.

the Soviet forces were still on the move and relatively under strength. The reduction of the pocket would take time. That evening Paulus held a conference with his chief of staff, Major-General Arthur Schmidt, Hoth of the Fourth Panzer Army and *Luftwaffe* Major-General Wolfgang Pickert, commanding the 9th Flak Division. He did not speak but let Schmidt lead the conference. The chief of staff explained that the Sixth Army did not have enough fuel to break out.

GENERAL NIKOLAI F. VATUTIN (1901–1944)

Born in 1901, Vatutin was Head of General Staff Operations when Germany invaded the USSR. He served with distinction at the Battle of Moscow in 1941. He was appointed commander of the Southwest Front in 1942. His front encircled the Sixth Army at Stalingrad. Following the surrender of the German Army, his forces pushed deep into the occupied interior of the Ukraine. In July 1943 he commanded the Voronezh Front at Kursk. His subsequent offensive liberated Kharkov on 22 August and much of the Ukraine. On 6 November his command, renamed the 1st Ukrainian Front, recaptured Kiev and kept the pressure on the Germans throughout the winter. On 29 February 1944 Vatutin was ambushed by anti-Soviet Ukrainian nationalist partisans near Rovno and fatally wounded. (Zhukhov called these partisans 'Bandera bandits' after Stepan Bandera, the Ukrainian nationalist leader who sided with the Germans.)

For ordinary soldiers like Hoffman the prospects seemed grim:

'21 November. The Russians have gone over to the offensive along the whole front. Fierce fighting is going on. So, there it is – the Volga, victory and soon home to our families! We shall obviously be seeing them next in the other world.

'29 November. We are encircled. It was announced this morning that the *Führer* has said: "The army can trust me to do everything necessary to ensure supplies and rapidly break the encirclement."

'3 December. We are on hunger rations and waiting for the rescue that the *Führer* promised. I send letters home, but there is no reply.

'7 December. Rations have been cut to such an extent that the soldiers are suffering terribly from hunger, they are issuing one loaf of bread for five men.

Below: The crew of a T-34/76D with soldiers of the Twenty-First Army of the Southwest Front huddle on the turret of the tank during Operation Uranus. The Southwest Front under General Nikolai Vatutin initially had a hard fight with the Third Romanian Army.

'11 December. Three questions are obsessing every soldier and officer. When will the Russians stop firing and let us sleep in peace, if only for one night? How and with what are we going to fill our empty stomachs, which, apart from 3½–7 ozs. of bread, receive virtually nothing at all? And when will Hitler take any decisive steps to free our armies from encirclement?

'14 December. Everybody is racked with hunger. Frozen potatoes are the best meal, but to get them out of the ice-covered ground under fire from Russian bullets is not so easy.'

By 25 November the Soviet forces surrounding Stalingrad had erected an inner and outer defensive ring. One to contain the Sixth Army and one to prevent German forces breaking in from outside.

THE GERMAN AIRLIFT

On 26 November Hitler had issued orders that the Sixth Army should make no attempt to break out from Stalingrad. *Reichsmarschall* Hermann Goering, head of the *Luftwaffe*, assured the *Führer* that his aircraft could supply the trapped army – a promise beyond the capability of the *Luftwaffe*. The

SHTURMOVIK

Among the Soviet aircraft that were now harassing German forces within the pocket and further to the west on the main front line was the formidable Il-2 *Shturmovik* ground-attack aircraft that had originally been designed as a fighter. Powered by a 1770hp Mikulin AM-38F engine, it had a top speed of 404km/h (251mph) at 1500m (4920ft) and a normal range of 765km (475 miles). The crew of the two-seater version were well protected by armour and the aircraft was armed with two fixed forward-firing 23mm (0.9in) VYa cannon in the wings, two 7.62mm (0.3in) ShKAS machine guns in the fuselage and a flexible 12.7mm (0.5in) UBT machine gun in the rear cockpit. It could carry up to 600kg (1323lb) of external ordnance.

Sixth Army staff estimated that the pocket would need to receive 762,000kg (750 tons) of supplies per day to survive. However, not only did the *Luftwaffe* not have sufficient aircraft, but six of the airstrips around Stalingrad could only operate by day – and now the long Russian winter nights had set in. Of the airfields inside the Stalingrad pocket, only Pitomnik was properly equipped to handle large-scale operations. It even had lights, flare paths and signal equipment for night operations. To supply the Sixth Army with 304,800kg (300 tons) per day, the absolute minimum amount demanded by the army, would necessitate an average of 150 fully-laden Ju 52s landing in the pocket each day.

Below: The two-seater Shturmovik with its combination of armour protection and powerful armament was a formidable Soviet Air Force ground attack aircraft – arguably one of the best aircraft employed for this role in World War II.

(For 508,000kg – 500 tons – per day, an average of 250 Ju 52s would need to land in the pocket. Including the time taken with loading, unloading, losses, etc., it would mean they needed 500 Ju 52s to realize 508,000kg each day.)

The *Luftwaffe* chief of staff, Hans Jeschonnek, who had deep reservations about the viability of an airlift, postulated two conditions for its success:

1. That the weather conditions made flying possible.
2. That the vital supply airfields at Tatsinskaya and Morosvskaia be held at all costs against Red Army attack.

The lumbering Ju 52 transports did manage to fly out some casualties and bring in supplies, but intense anti-aircraft fire and long flights made it an increasingly hazardous journey. The best delivery that was achieved by the *Luftwaffe* was on 19 December when they flew in 254,000kg (250 tons), but the average during the siege when airfields were open was 91,440kg (90 tons) per day.

Goering aggressively dominated his own staff, driving two of his senior officers to suicide (Ernst Udet in November 1941 and Jeschonnek in August 1943). Yet he proved incapable of standing up to Hitler. He rarely even expressed views contrary to Hitler's (at least in the latter's presence), especially after his obvious failure to defeat Britain from the air in 1940 and to defend Germany's cities from ever increasing Allied air attacks. These failures had steadily reduced his standing in Hitler's eyes throughout 1941 and 1942. Instead, he lapsed into subservience, hoping his slavish loyalty would repair their relationship. It is probable, then, that Goering's unconditional assurances that the *Luftwaffe* could maintain Sixth Army stemmed from his inability to resist Hitler or challenge his views, and from his intense desire to restore his tattered prestige. 'I gained the impression that he was afraid of Hitler,' Field Marshal Milch once wrote.

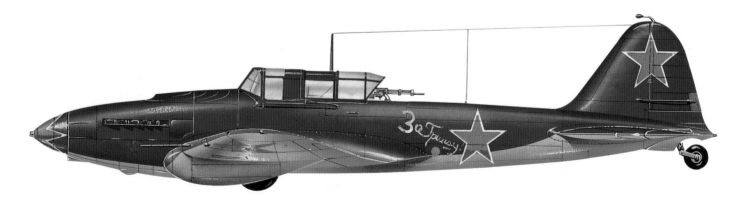

Above: Fuel drums are loaded aboard the rugged and reliable Ju 52 tri-motor transport. Both before and after the war the Ju 52 served as a commercial airliner, but in World War II it became a maid of all work for the Luftwaffe.

As early as 22 November General Martin Fiebig, commander of *Luftflotte* VIII, had told Paulus and Schmidt that an airlift would be impossible. However, the strong-willed Schmidt was unconvinced and Paulus accepted his views. Schmidt would dominate Paulus until the end of the battle.

'WINTER STORM'

On 27 November 1942 Field Marshal von Manstein was appointed to command the newly formed Army Group Don. The force was composed of one *Luftwaffe*, four Panzer and six infantry divisions along with the remnants of a number of Romanian formations. Von Manstein was ordered to break into the encirclement to relieve the Sixth Army. On the same day the staff at the Sixth Army HQ urged Paulus to break out. General von Seydlitz-Kurzbach urged him 'to take the course of the lion', a historical reference to General Karl von Litzmann, who in November 1914 had made a daring break-out against orders when encircled by the Russians. Seydlitz-Kurzbach had ordered his troops to destroy surplus

JUNKERS JU 52/3M G7E

The rugged '*Tante Ju*' – 'Auntie Junkers', with its distinctive corrugated fuselage, was the transport workhorse for the *Luftwaffe* throughout the war. A total of 4850 were built and ironically the largest operator of the type after the Germans was the USSR which had over 80 captured or repaired aircraft. The USAAF had one Ju 52 that they gave the designation C-79 and the RAF had two. It was aboard Ju 52s that German paratroops were carried to Crete for the airborne invasion in 1941. With a crew of three and 18 troops or 12 stretchers, the Ju 52 was powered by three 830hp BMW 132T-2 engines that gave a maximum speed at 1400m (4590ft) of 286km/h (178mph) and a normal range of 1500km (930 miles). It weighed 6500kg (14,328lb) empty and 11,030kg (24,320lb) loaded. The dimensions were 29.2m (95ft 10in) wing span, 18.9m (62ft) length and 4.52m (14ft 10in) height. Armament consisted of one 7.92mm (0.31in) MG15 in an open dorsal position. The Ju 52 was pressed into service as a bomber at Stalingrad during the initial assault and became a vital, if inadequate, life line to the trapped Sixth Army.

Left: A park of abandoned German Panzerjäger 38(t) Pak 36(r) Marder III self-propelled anti-tank guns captured at Stalingrad. The Marder III was a vehicle that combined captured Soviet 76.2mm (3in) FK 296 guns with the chassis of the Czech 38(t) tank.

But Schmidt said 'We must obey'.

'I shall obey,' replied Paulus and sealed the fate of the Sixth Army.

Manstein, on whom Paulus was pinning his hopes, did not attack along the line of the Don at its junction with the Chir, the most direct route to Stalingrad, but in an operation code-named *Wintergewitter* – 'Winter Storm', he chose as his axis the Kotelnikovo-Stalingrad railway to the south. He did not wait for all the units to concentrate but in order to ensure surprise intended to attack on 3 December. However, on 30 November there were renewed Soviet attacks to clear the German forces from the lower Chir. Manstein was forced to detach formations intended for Winter Storm to halt the Soviet attacks. He had an almost impossible series of tasks: the first was to restore the front line which was then in tatters, the second to prevent Soviet forces reaching Rostov and so cutting off Army Group A in the Caucasus, and finally to relieve the Sixth Army in Stalingrad.

At the end of November the Soviet Army's expanded tank strength stood at 4940 AFVs and the Red Air Force had 3100 planes. Opposing them the German *Ostheer* – Army of the East, had 3133 AFVs, of which only a third were operational, and 2450 aircraft, many of which were grounded. At Stalingrad the Don and Stalingrad Fronts launched heavy attacks on 3 December to break into the pocket. Their objective was to link up at the airfield at Gumrak. After five days of heavy fighting they had made virtually no headway and the attacks were called off. A new operation code-named 'Ring' was proposed by *Stavka*. It would be a two-phase operation.

Above: A T-70 light tank of the Twenty-First Army follows a T-34 tank through winter fog during the attack following Operation Uranus. The commander has the hatch open but has turned his back to limit the effect of wind chill.

equipment and he himself had set an example by destroying all his possessions except the uniform he was wearing. All the corps commanders expressed their approval for a break-out in spite of Hitler's orders. It would be better to escape with five divisions than die with 20.

Phase one would be to liquidate the south and west parts of the pocket and the second phase would be a general assault against the remainder. Operation Ring was planned to begin on 16 December.

The Germans launched Winter Storm on 12 December; troops of Group Hoth commanded by General Hermann Hoth, including soldiers of the elite *Waffen-SS*, initially made good progress. However, they encountered fierce resistance from the Fifth Shock Army and this bought time that allowed troops to be deployed from the Stalingrad pocket to take up blocking positions. Winter Storm continued to make good progress on 14 December and the *Luftwaffe* airlift delivered a then record 182,880kg (180 tons) of supplies to Stalingrad.

'LITTLE SATURN' AND 'THUNDERCLAP'

On 16 December the Soviet Voronezh and Southwest Fronts launched 'Little Saturn', an attack on the Italian Eighth Army on the Chir. The Italians were quickly overwhelmed and the key resupply airfield at Tatsinskaya was captured. The 11th Panzer Division halted the Soviet attacks but at considerable cost to themselves. The Volga froze on 17 December and the Soviets were now able to deliver fresh supplies via an 'ice bridge' to the Sixty-Second Army on the west bank.

Two days later to the south, Hoth's troops pushed to within 30km (18.6 miles) of the Stalingrad pocket and reportedly could see on the distant horizon the smoke and explosions around the pocket. However, Manstein never transmitted the code-word 'Thunderclap' to Paulus to break out to the south. The two generals exchanged signals that hedged around the move. The commander of the Sixth Army was only prepared to release some tanks without infantry support so the break-out might not have succeeded. Paulus's reluctance may also have been because of the condition of the infantry in the Sixth Army, who were suffering from the effects of months of fighting. The signals traffic that sealed the fate of the Sixth Army has all the banality of a business conference call.

Manstein: 'How much fuel and supplies would you require before launching "Thunderclap" and on the assumption that once the action began further supplies to meet day-to-day requirements would reach you?'

Paulus: '1000 cubic metres [nearly 250,000 gallons of fuel] and 500 tons of food. If we get that, all my armour and motor vehicles will have enough [the fuel requirements were almost 10 times the quantity that had been delivered by air] …'

Manstein: 'Well, that's a lot. Good luck Paulus.'

Paulus: 'Thank you, sir. And good luck to you too.'

Group Hoth continued to attempt to break through until 23 December, the force reaching the Myshkova River. The troops in Stalingrad, it was said, could hear the gunfire but Winter Storm had blown itself out and a day later the Soviet counter-offensive broadened. The Soviet Fifty-First Army

THE *WAFFEN-SS*

The *Waffen-SS* – Armed SS, were the military arm and largest branch of the SS. The force would eventually number 39 divisions and through its ranks would pass nearly one million men of 15 nationalities. It was formed in 1940 from already existing SS military units, its first three divisions being the *Leibstandarte-SS Adolf Hitler*, *Das Reich* and *Totenkopf*. By the close of the war the SS had become a huge organization that ran the concentration and extermination camps, race and ethnicity, and Reich and overseas intelligence and security. At Nuremberg all members of the SS, with the exception of the *Waffen-SS*, were declared to be war criminals. The *Waffen-SS* would take part in 12 major battles and were noted for their tough fighting qualities and aggressive leadership. The premier formation of the *Waffen-SS*, the *Leibstandarte-SS Adolf Hitler* – Adolf Hitler's Bodyguard – provided guards of honour for visiting VIPs before the war.

The *Waffen-SS* saw little action in Poland but fought in France, the Balkans and the Soviet Union. The *Waffen-SS* asserted that they were élite soldiers but their record in the fighting on the Eastern Front and in Western Europe shows that though their courage and skill cannot be disputed, they were also guilty of atrocities against civilians and prisoners.

At the beginning there were strict racial and physical standards for soldiers in the *Waffen-SS*; however, the search for manpower obliged Himmler's recruiters to look for ethnic Germans in Europe and later even Yugoslavs, Italians and Ukrainians. Most of the foreign formations were of little value in the field. The *Waffen-SS* practice of tattooing a soldier's blood group under his left armpit, while it made excellent sense for first aid, meant that members could not disguise themselves as *Wehrmacht* soldiers if they were captured. On the Eastern Front few *Waffen-SS* men survived capture.

punched through the Romanians, while the Fifth Tank Army crossed the Chir. Manstein's thrust was in danger of being enveloped itself.

The arrival of fresh forces in Stalingrad allowed the Soviet Sixty-Second Army to retake the *Krasny Oktyabr* Factory on 24 December. On the same day the Soviet XXIV Tank Corps under General Badanov reached the key *Luftwaffe* supply base at Tatsinskaya and after a brisk battle took the town and airfield. *Luftwaffe* losses were heavy as the base was hastily evacuated, 72 of the 180 transport aircraft being destroyed. Fighting would continue around Tatsinskaya for four days with the 11th and 6th Panzer Divisions surrounding and almost destroying the corps which Stalin had accorded the honorary title of 'Guards'. They broke out but were pursued

You and your soldiers should begin the new year with a strong faith that I and the German *Wehrmacht* will use all strength to relieve the defenders of Stalingrad and make their long wait the highest achievement of German war history.

Adolf Hitler's New Year message to General Paulus and Sixth Army, 1 January 1943

Below: Soldiers of the Italian Eighth Army retreat in the face of Operation Little Saturn in late 1942. The Soviet attack pushed the German front line further from Stalingrad and so made flights longer and more hazardous.

until they reached the Third Guards Army. The local success of the German ground forces during the last months of 1942 was in part because they were not sending Enigma coded reports and returns back to Berlin – their commanders were taking quick tactical decisions and acting on them.

Inside Stalingrad Wilhelm Hoffman's diary describes the optimism quickly followed by gloom and depression with the failure of *Wintergewitter*:

'18 December. The officers today told the soldiers to be prepared for action. General Manstein is approaching Stalingrad from the south with strong forces. This news brought hope to the soldiers' hearts. God, let it be!

'21 December. We are waiting for the order, but for some reason or other it has been a long time coming. Can it be that

it is not true about Manstein? This is worse than any torture.

'23 December. Still no orders. It was all a bluff with Manstein. Or has he been defeated at the approaches to Stalingrad?

'25 December. The Russian radio has announced the defeat of Manstein. Ahead of us is either our death or captivity.

'26 December. The horses have already been eaten. I would eat a cat; they say its meat is also tasty. The soldiers look like corpses or lunatics, looking for something to put in their mouths. They no longer take cover from Russian shells; they haven't the strength to walk, run away and hide. A curse on this war!'

CHRISTMAS IN STALINGRAD

On Christmas Day the German Propaganda Ministry in Berlin broadcast the 'Ring Broadcast', greetings from the crew of a U-boat in the Atlantic, men of the *Afrika Korps* in North Africa, the garrison of the Atlantic Wall and, over a crackling radio link, the men of Stalingrad, 'the front on the Volga'. Their voices then blended together in '*Stille Nacht, Heilige Nacht*', the classic German Christmas carol. It was dramatic and very moving – and faked up in radio studios in Berlin.

Within the pocket the Sixth Army had their Christmas meal – 170g (6oz) of bread, 85g (3oz) of meat paste, 28g (1oz) of butter, and 28g (1oz) of coffee. After a heavy bombardment beginning at 05:00, the 16th Panzer and 60th Motorized Divisions came under heavy attack until mid-afternoon. Despite heavy fighting they held their ground. Since the Sixth Army had been surrounded on 23 November it had suffered 28,000 casualties. For Boxing Day there was an extra treat for the men of the Sixth Army of two horsemeat rissoles per man. Paulus radioed Hitler to complain of the delivery of 71,120kg (70 tons) of supplies to the army on 26 December when it had been promised a daily minimum of 355,600kg (350 tons). Hitler's reply was that the Sixth Army was to fight to the last man. On 28 December he sanctioned a withdrawal by Army Groups Don and A to the

Every seven seconds a German soldier dies in Russia. Stalingrad is a mass grave. Every seven seconds a German soldier dies in Russia. Stalingrad is a mass grave. Every seven seconds a German soldier …

Soviet propaganda team loudspeaker broadcast, Stalingrad, December 1942

THE PRODUCTION BATTLE

Early in the war the Soviet Union had started dismantling their major armaments factories and moving them by rail hundreds of kilometres to the east beyond the Ural Mountains. Though this had caused considerable disruption it placed them out of range of the *Luftwaffe*. One of the biggest facilities in the Urals was the Ural-Kirov Tank Factory set up by the People's Commissariat for the Tank Industry in 1941 in Chelyabinsk. The city, commonly known as 'Tankograd', had engineers and workers of the Leningrad, Kharkov and Chelyabinsk plants. At first Tankograd supplied Klimenti Voroshilov heavy tanks, which participated in the crushing of German forces in the battle of Moscow in 1941–42. In the second year of the war the plant switched to the production of the T-34. In Tankograd there were eventually a total of nine large tank factories: six factories produced hulls and turrets, and three engines. Conditions in these factories were as grim as anything in the front line with workers putting in long hours on minimal rations. Berte Mendeleeva recalled of Tankograd: 'The machinists in the workshops were mainly women and even teenagers. Some were so young that they needed to stand on boxes to reach the work bench.' They worked in appalling conditions. At one tank factory 8000 female workers were housed in timber and earth bunkers. Tankograd was awarded the Order of the Red Star in 1944 and the Order of Kutusov 1st Class in 1945. In addition the test plant and the design bureau for diesels were rewarded with the Order of Lenin. Twelve members of the production staff became Heroes of Socialist Labour.

The Kharkov Locomotive Factory was moved to the *Uralmashzavod* (Ural Machine Building Plant) in the Urals and merged with the Nishni Tagil vehicle factory. During 1942 the Ural Heavy Machinery Company in Sverdlovsk started to produce T-34s. Tanks were also being built closer to the front at Gorki and Kirov. The weapons and vehicles they produced were by Western standards crudely finished, but they worked and were available in quantity. The USSR had won the production battle. The majority of the 6250 Soviet tanks that participated in the capture of Berlin in 1945 had been built in Tankograd. However, the huge size of the plant would eventually be its undoing after the end of the Cold War and in February 1998 the Chelyabinsk Tractor Plant, with a capacity for 60,000 tractors a year, was declared bankrupt.

line Konstantinovsk–Salsk–Armavir. This effectively doomed Stalingrad because the German front line was now 300km (186.4 miles) to the west. If the Sixth Army had been allowed to attempt a break-out during 'Winter Storm' they might have saved many lives.

On 31 December the Soviet Second Guards Army chief of staff, General Biryuzov, received an invitation to a New Year's Eve Party from General Pavel M. Rotmistrov, commanding the Soviet VII Tank Corps. Biryuzov was not sure whether it was appropriate to have a party in the middle of a critical campaign but when he arrived he found the Chief of the General Staff Alexander Vasilevsky was among the guests. There was a decorated fir tree in the room and the officers sat down to a meal that included cheese from Holland and France, butter and bacon from Denmark and tinned fish and jams from Norway. All these luxury foods were stamped 'For Germans Only'. Chuckling, Rotmistrov explained 'Not all my men can read German, so when they found this stuff they took it all. But we'll have to give the candles back to Hitler, so that he can light them in mourning for his Sixth Army.'

On 2 January the Soviet Third Guards Army captured Morozovskaia airfield, which meant that *Luftwaffe* supply missions now had to fly from the distant bases of Salsk and Novocherkessk. *Stavka* confirmed on 3 January that Operation Koltso, the reduction of the Sixth Army, would begin on 10 January. With *Stavka*'s approval Rokossovsky offered Paulus surrender terms on 8 January; he informed Hitler but was ordered to reject them.

OPERATION KOLTSO

Two days later a huge Soviet offensive rolled into action, squeezing the pocket from west to east. The Soviet forces deployed 281,000 men, 257 tanks and nearly 10,000 guns against the Sixth Army's 191,000 effectives, 7700 guns and mortars and 60 tanks. At the time of the attack the temperature was -35º C (-31° F).

The Sixty-Fifth Army advanced 10km (6.2 miles) on the first day against determined German resistance and counter-attacks. To the north and south only limited penetrations were achieved. Since 23 November Paulus had lost 40,000 killed or missing and suffered 29,000 wounded, while 7000 specialist troops had been flown out of the pocket. Now that he could not feed his own men adequately he ordered that all

Opposite: A train of flat cars loaded with T-70 and T-34 Model 1942 tanks moves westwards from new factories in the Urals. By 1943 Soviet production was outstripping the Germans and their weapons were more rugged and reliable.

PoWs should be sent back to the besieging Soviet forces. However, many of these men, fearing NKVD retribution, remained within German lines.

On the morning that the Soviet forces launched Operation Koltso, Colonel Herbert Selle, who commanded the Sixth Army Pioneers, encountered Paulus at his HQ.

The general noticed Selle and said:

'What do you say to all this?'

'I agree with what all the other older staff officers say, Sir.'

'And what is that?'

'The Herr General should have disobeyed orders, but the opportunity was let slip. As early as November the Herr General should have wirelessed, "I fight this battle with and for the Sixth Army. Until it is over, my head belongs to them. After the battle, my *Führer*, it belongs to you"'.

Paulus looked at Selle: 'I am aware that military history has already passed judgement on me'.

Selle was one of the fortunate specialist officers to be flown out of Stalingrad in January. However, his vocal opposition to the Nazi Party and association with men who were in the July 1944 plot to kill Hitler nearly cost him his life. He survived the war and settled in West Germany.

On 11 January the Marinovka sector of the Stalingrad pocket was crushed, Soviet forces herding the retreating Germans back to the Rossoshka. The last remnants of the 29th Motorized and 376th Infantry Divisions were destroyed in bitter fighting. With his army disintegrating, Paulus received an order from OKH stating that the Sixth Army was not to surrender without prior approval.

Signals from the Sixth Army teleprinter link at Gumrak conveyed the urgency of the rapidly changing situation:

'09:40. Enemy broke through on a wide portion of the front line ... Isolated strongholds are still intact. We are trying to rally and train last available parts of supply and construction units ... to set up a blocking line.

'19:00. Deep penetration east of Zybenko ... more than 6km [3.7 miles] wide. Enemy

Left: The T-34 Model 1943, built at Zavod Nr 183, which entered service in the spring of 1942 had a two-man hexagonal turret. Here tanks are topped up in the field from fuel drums stacked on a truck.

Opposite: Among the wreckage of the Krasny Oktyabr *(Red October) steel works, submachine gunners move in on the battered Sixth Army. As Soviet forces closed in, the Germans had been pounded by massive artillery fire as well as constant air attacks.*

had very heavy losses … Our own losses were considerable. Resistance of the troops diminishing quickly because of insufficient ammunition, extreme frost, and lack of cover from heaviest enemy fire.'

On 12 January the western salient of the pocket had been overrun. It had cost the Don Front 26,000 casualties and over 125 tanks. A day later Karpovka airfield in the south of the pocket was captured – there were now only six airfields available for supply or evacuation.

At Gumrak the Sixth Army signalled: 'Continuous bombardments since 07:00. Cannot reply … Since 08:00 heavy enemy attacks along all front lines with numerous

Opposite: The newly promoted Field Marshal Paulus accompanied by his Chief of Staff General Arthur Schmidt following the surrender of the 6th Army. Berlin would later suggest that Paulus could be exchanged for Stalin's son, captured in 1941. Stalin refused.

tanks … Army has ordered as a last means of resistance that every soldier has to fight to the last bullet at the place he is currently defending.'

Soviet forces continued their attacks, reaching the Rossoshka River on 13 January 1943. The Sixth Army signalled: 'Ammunition is almost exhausted. For the assistance of the completely worn-out … troops, no reserves

---

ULTIMATUM OF SOVIET HQ, 8 JANUARY 1943

To the Commander in Chief of the German Sixth Army, Colonel General Paulus, or his representative and to all the officers and men of the German units now besieged in Stalingrad [:]

The Sixth Army, formations of the Fourth Panzer Army, and those units sent to reinforce them have been completely encircled since 23 November 1942. The soldiers of the Red Army have sealed this German Army Group within an unbreakable ring. All hopes of the rescue of your troops by a German offensive from the south or southwest have proved vain. The German units hastening to your assistance were defeated by the Red Army, and the remnants are now withdrawing to Rostov.

The German air transport fleet, which brought you a starvation ration of food, munitions and fuel has been compelled by the Red Army's successful and rapid advance repeatedly to withdraw to airfields more distant from the encircled troops. It should be added that the German air transport fleet is suffering enormous losses in machines and crews at the hands of the Russian Air Force. The help they can bring to the besieged forces is rapidly becoming illusory. The situation of your troops is desperate. They are suffering from hunger, sickness and cold. The cruel Russian winter has scarcely yet begun. Hard frosts, cold winds and blizzards still lie ahead. Your soldiers are unprovided with winter clothing and are living in appalling sanitary conditions.

You, as Commander in Chief, and all the officers of the encircled forces know well that there is for you no real possibility of breaking out. Your situation is hopeless, and any further resistance senseless. In view of the desperate situation in which you are placed, and in order to save unnecessary bloodshed, we propose that you accept the following terms of surrender:

1) All the encircled German troops, headed by yourself and your staff, shall cease to resist.

2) You will hand over to such persons as shall be authorized by us, all members of your armed forces, all war materials and all army equipment in an undamaged condition. We guarantee the safety of all officers and men who cease to resist, and their return after the end of the war to Germany or to any other country to which these prisoners of war may wish to go. All personnel of units which surrender may retain their military uniforms, badges of rank, decorations, personal belongings and valuables and, in case of high ranking officers their swords. All officers, non-commissioned officers and men who surrender will immediately receive normal rations. All those who are wounded, sick or frost-bitten will be given medical treatment.

Your reply is to be given in writing by 10:00 Moscow time, 9 January 1943. It must be delivered by your personal representative, who is to travel in a car bearing a white flag along the road that leads to the Konniy siding at Kotluban station. Your representative will be met by fully authorized Russian officers in District B, 500m southeast of siding 564 at 10:00 on 9 January 1943. Should you refuse our offer that you lay down your arms, we hereby give you notice that the forces of the Red Army and the Red Airforce will be compelled to proceed with the eliminating of the encircled German troops. The responsibility for this will lie with you.

Representing Headquarters Red Army Supreme Command
– Colonel-General of the Artillery Voronov
The Commander in Chief of the Forces of the Don Front
– Lieutenant-General Rokossovsky

available in terms of men, tanks, anti-tank and heavy weapons.'

Incredibly among these grim messages there were routine administrative signals: 'Herr General Paulus gave permission to *Oberleutnant* Georg Reymann, Regiment 549 to marry *Fraulein* Lina Hauswald. Neustadt … Please forward.

'Recommendation for award by General Pfeiffer … *Oberleutnant* Boris received German Cross in Gold …'

On 14 January, Hitler ordered the highly capable Field Marshal Erhard Milch to take over the air resupply operations to Stalingrad. The daily delivery rate had dropped to 4064kg (40 tons) as aircraft struggled over longer

distances against increased Soviet ground and air opposition. On 16 January, the day that Milch moved to Manstein's HQ at Taganrog, the airfield of Pitomnik in the middle of the pocket fell to the Soviet Twenty-First Army. Panic spread in the Sixth Army since Pitomnik was the larger of the two airfields that had been supplying the Germans in Stalingrad and was the only airfield with a night flying capability. Now only the primitive airstrip at Gumrak remained; it could handle Ju 52s but the He 111s, which required a longer strip and had weaker landing gear, were unable to use it. Soviet forces kept up the pressure, advancing across the Chervlennaya and Rossoshka Rivers.

> On the tenth anniversary of your assumption of power the Sixth Army hails its *Führer*. A thousand years hence Germans will speak of this battle with reverence and awe. The Swatiska flag is still flying above Stalingrad. May our battle be an example to the present and future generations, that they must never capitulate even in a hopeless situation, for them Germany will emerge victorious.
>
> Heil mein Führer
> *Paulus, Generaloberst*
> *Last teleprinter message from Sixth Army HQ to Führer HQ,*
> *30 January 1943*

Above: The victors – officers and soldiers probably from the Soviet Twenty-First Army – dressed in winter warfare camouflage uniforms, stand in the smoking ruins of Stalingrad. They had been the hammer and the Sixty-Second Army the anvil that crushed the Sixth Army.

Incredibly, Milch now managed to increase deliveries to 60,960kg (60 tons) per day. He was a capable officer who had served in World War I. He collaborated with Göring, who chose to ignore the fact that Milch's mother was Jewish, in the establishment of the *Luftwaffe* in the 1930s. From 1941–44 he was the *Luftzeugmeister* – Air Inspector General.

THE END IN SIGHT

By 16 January the Germans held only 402 square kilometres (250 square miles) of territory, half what they held before the 10 January offensive was launched. However, the pace of operations was beginning to tell on the Soviet forces and their rudimentary logistic back-up, and Rokossovsky wanted to call a halt for two to three days. But Stalin urged that they continue as the exhausted and starving German soldiers were offering less resistance with each day. Now only Gumrak was still in German hands. From now on, air supply had to rely increasingly on parachuted containers because of the problems of landing at Gumrak.

Attempts to air-drop ammunition and rations foundered since the containers often sank into deep snow and the

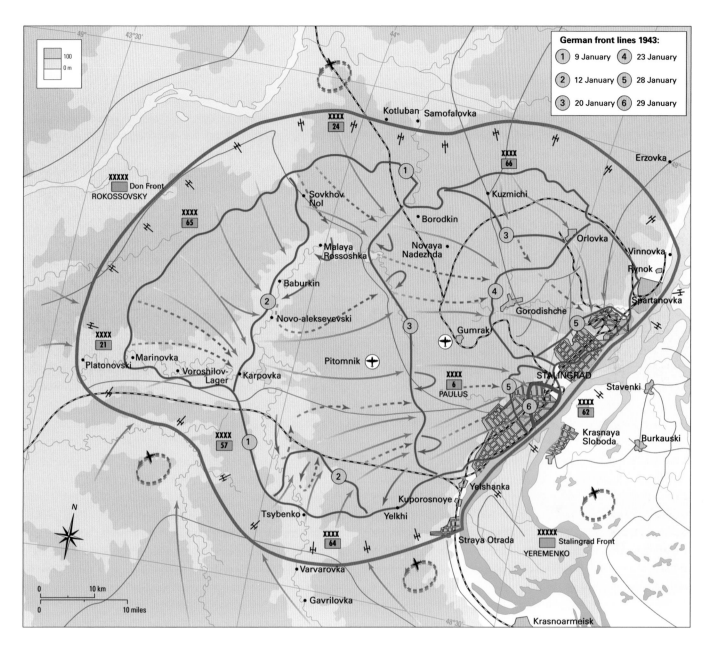

German front lines 1943:

①	9 January	④	23 January
②	12 January	⑤	28 January
③	20 January	⑥	29 January

Above: As airfields were lost and the Sixth Army was crushed into the wreckage of Stalingrad, defeat became inevitable. What was remarkable was how long the starved soldiers managed to resist, possibly inspired by the the harsh treatment they expected to receive as prisoners of war.

soldiers of the Sixth Army were now so exhausted and debilitated they lacked the strength and energy to recover them. One additional airstrip was hastily constructed within the pocket.

On 17 January Rokossovsky again offered the Sixth Army surrender terms and was again rejected. A day later artillery fire began falling on Gumrak as the Soviet Twenty-First Army was only 3.2km (2 miles) from the airfield. The airfield

fell on 22 January and Paulus signalled that rations and ammunition were now dangerously low and made an oblique plea to Hitler to be allowed to order his forces to surrender. His request was refused.

In darkness the Soviet Twenty-First Army linked up in the ruins of the city with the men of the Sixty-Second Army – the German Sixth Army was now split into two pockets in the north and south of Stalingrad. On the morning of 23 January a Soviet cameraman filmed a re-enactment of the link-up between the two armies.

The last German aircraft to make the flight to Stalingrad, a Heinkel He 111 carrying 19 wounded men and seven bags of mail, flew out of the pocket on 23 January. Some supplies

WOMEN IN THE RED AIR FORCE

Stalingrad was as much the turning point for the air force as it was for the Red Army, and Soviet flyers shot down approximately 900 German aircraft in the battle. They flew over 45,000 sorties over the area and dropped 15,240,000kg (15,000 tons) of bombs, and 10 Air Divisions of the Tenth Air Army were nominated as 'Guards Air Divisions', a distinction given to units who had excelled in battle.

One of the more remarkable features of the Stalingrad battle was the appearance of the 586th Fighter Air Regiment, equipped with the latest Yak-7B fighters, an all-female organization, from the CO to the mechanics. The women of this regiment claimed 20 enemy aircraft between them – the Soviet scoring system was the toughest of all, which only credited a 'kill' if the victim fell within Soviet lines and could be positively confirmed.

The 586th was part of the all-female 122nd Air Group that included the 587th Bomber and 588th Night Bomber Regiments. These units operated from 1942 until the end of the war and inflicted considerable losses on the Germans; by the end of the war 586th Fighter Regiment had flown 4419 sorties and had shot down 38 German aircraft. When back in October 1941 Marina Raskova, a vivacious 28-year-old pilot and navigator, who had won the Gold Star of the Soviet Union for her pioneering work in 1938, proposed that women should fly and service combat aircraft, large numbers of women came to Moscow. She took command of the all-female 125th Bomber Regiment but following her death was succeeded a man, Lieutenant-Colonel Valentin Markov.

Remembering Raskova, who he had encountered at Kamyshin airbase, Konstantin Simonov wrote in his diary: 'I had never seen her close to and I did not realize that she was so young and beautiful. Maybe I remember it so well because soon afterwards I heard that she was killed.' During the war 15 women were killed in action and five became Heroes of the Soviet Union. Women also flew with male formations. One of them, Senior Lieutenant Anna Timofeya-Yegorova, was the deputy commander of the 805th Ground Attack Regiment flying the heavily armoured Ilyushin Shturmovik.

---

were air-dropped in the last week. It is reported that the last letters from Stalingrad were never delivered but impounded on the orders of Goebbels who was fearful of the impact they would have on the German population. They were analyzed to assess the morale of the troops within the pocket. Some expressed belief in the ultimate victory of the Third Reich and the *Führer* Adolf Hitler, while others were bleak protests of anger and disillusionment.

The 'Stalingrad mood' was divided into five groups:
a) In favour of the way the war was being conducted – 21%.
b) Dubious – 4%.
c) Sceptical, deprecatory – 49%.
d) Actively against – 3%.
e) No opinion, indifferent – 23%.

In the southern pocket Paulus moved his HQ into the basement of the *Univermag* department store, from where the Swastika had flown triumphantly from the balcony in the early autumn. By now food was in such short supply that orders were issued that the 30,000 wounded in the pocket were not to receive rations. Many men had already died of starvation and the bitter cold.

On 24 January both Paulus and Manstein requested permission from Hitler for the Sixth Army to be allowed to surrender. Both were refused and the army told to fight to the last bullet. Four days later Soviet attacks split the VIII and LI Corps in the city from the XIV Panzer Corps and IV Corps around the ruins of the *Univermag* store. In a final superb gesture on 29/30 January some 124 *Luftwaffe* bombers and transport aircraft delivered rations and ammunition in a night drop. However, it was becoming increasingly hard to identify areas still under German control as the Sixth Army had been divided into three pockets.

THE SURRENDER

For the remnants of the XIV Panzer Corps, LI and VIII Corps the battle of Stalingrad ended when they were overrun by the Twenty-First and Sixty-Second Armies. Among the prisoners was General von Seydlitz-Kurzbach who would join the Soviet-controlled anti-Nazi *Nationalkomitee Freies Deutschland*, and make broadcasts against Hitler. In Germany his wife was ordered by the authorities to divorce her treacherous husband. After the war he settled in East

Opposite: I.V. Bocharova, a female armourer with the Soviet Air Force, checks the 12.7mm (0.5in) Berezin UB machine gun in the upper cowling of a Yakovlev Yak-9D fighter. Women served as pilots and ground crew in the USSR.

Above: Field Marshal Paulus (right) during his interrogation. He was exhausted and suffering from a nervous twitch and, as Hitler predicted, eventually cooperated with his captors with propaganda broadcasts to German soldiers serving on the Eastern Front.

Germany but when he finally returned to West Germany he was met by a grim silence from Stalingrad veterans.

At 06:15 on 31 January 1943 a radio operator at the Sixth Army HQ signalled that there were Russians outside the door. The last transmission came at 07:15, announcing to the OKH that they were destroying their equipment. At 07:45 Paulus surrendered his HQ in the basement of the *Univermag* building. Lieutenant Fyodor Mikhailovich Elchenko, a tank commander in the Sixty-Second Army, was approached by *Hauptmann* Boris von Neidhardt, a Russian-speaking officer who had worked as the main interpreter at the Sixth Army HQ.

The initial exchange seemed almost too banal:

'Our big chief wants to talk to your big chief.'

'Look here,' replied Elchenko, 'our big chief has other things to do. He isn't available. You'll just have to deal with me.'

Elchenko was the first to enter the basement of the *Univermag* immediately prior to the surrender. 'It was packed with soldiers – hundreds of them,' he recalled. 'You couldn't move a finger in such a crowd. It was worse than any

> The disaster of Stalingrad profoundly shocked the German people and armed forces alike ... Never before in Germany's history had so large a body of troops come to so dreadful an end.
>
> *General Siegfried von Westphal*

tramcar. They were dirty and hungry. And did they look scared! They had all fled down here, to get away from the mortar fire outside.' He went on to say that the surrender was negotiated by Major-General Raske and Paulus's dominant chief of staff, Lieutenant-General Schmidt. Of Paulus, Elchenko said 'He was lying on his bed here ... wearing his uniform ... he looked unshaven and miserable'.

Gaunt and exhausted, the recently promoted field marshal emerged with his staff to surrender. Hitler had stated that no German field marshal had ever surrendered and hoped that Paulus would commit suicide rather than capitulate.

Some officers did. General von Hartmann, commander of the 71st Division, chose a soldier's death. He walked out to a railway embankment in full view of the Soviet lines and began firing a carbine in their direction. A few minutes later his wish was granted as he was hit in the head by a sniper's bullet. Many of the starving wounded used pistols and grenades to end their lives rather than face death in captivity. Back in Germany at a luncheon conference when the subject of Stalingrad was raised Hitler snapped 'The duty of the men at Stalingrad is to be dead'.

On 1 February the XI Corps under General Strecker in the northern pocket surrendered. It had been reduced to a small area around the Tractor Factory and was subject to a final bombardment by Soviet artillery batteries so dense that each gun was only 3m (9ft) apart.

THE FINAL ACT

In the bombardment and subsequent fighting over 4000 Germans were killed. The Russians were enraged by this resistance and many Germans who attempted to surrender were shot or clubbed to death. Just before the Corps HQ was overrun Strecker signalled to Hitler: 'XI Corps and its divisions have fought to the last man against vastly superior forces. Long Live Germany.'

Below: High above Fallen Fighters Square a soldier of the Sixty-Second Army waves a red flag celebrating the Soviet victory. In the background partly hidden by the flag is the Univermag *store, in the basement of which Paulus had located his HQ.*

The Battle for Stalingrad has ended. True to its oath to fight to its last breath, Sixth Army, under the exemplary leadership of Field Marshal Paulus, has succumbed to the overwhelming strength of the enemy and to unfavourable circumstances. The enemy's two demands for capitulation were proudly rejected. The last battle was fought under a Swastika flag flying from the highest ruin in Stalingrad.

OKW communiqué, 1 February 1943

Paulus was taken from the *Univermag* to the HQ of General Shumilov, commanding the Sixty-Fourth Army. Here he was offered a buffet, but refused to eat until he had been assured that his men would receive rations and medical assistance. Then he and his senior staff picked nervously at the spread.

THE COST

Figures for the Russian victory at Stalingrad are hard to establish but German and Axis losses were in the region of 1.5 million men, 3500 tanks, 12,000 guns and mortars, 75,000 vehicles and 3000 aircraft. Of the prisoners, the last of the 5000 survivors returned to Germany in the mid-1950s. Many had died in grim labour camps from starvation, disease and overwork.

Many of the officers were the last to be repatriated, and those who had assisted their Soviet captors settled in East Germany. General Schmidt, who had dominated the increasingly ineffective Paulus, proved to be a stubborn prisoner. When the senior officers of the Sixth Army joined the *Nationalkomitee Freies Deutschland* and broadcast to German soldiers on the Eastern Front, Hitler dismissed Schmidt as an officer who 'would sign anything'. But Paulus's former chief of staff was made of sterner stuff; held in solitary confinement and physically abused, he refused to co-operate with his Soviet captors. Schmidt finally returned to Hamburg in 1955.

Above: Against the backdrop of a gutted factory, soldiers of the Sixty-Second Army are addressed by their officers and political officers – Politruks, or Commissars – following the capitulation of the German Sixth Army in February 1943.

On 23 August 1942 the city of Stalingrad had a total population of 400,000. On 24 February 1943, after Soviet Army medics had searched in the city's ruins in the Tractor Factory District, they found there were 150 people alive from a pre-war population of 75,000. In the *Barrikadi* District, 76 people were alive out of a population of 50,000 and in the *Ermanskiy* District 32 people were alive out of 45,000. Many of these survivors would only live for a short time after their liberation.

In all they found that at least 9976 civilians had lived through the fighting, surviving in the battlefield ruins. They included 994 children, of whom only nine were reunited with their parents. The vast majority were sent off to state orphanages or given work clearing the city. The report says nothing of their physical or mental state, witnessed by an

American aid worker, who arrived very soon after the fighting to distribute clothes. 'Most of the children', she wrote, 'had been living in the ground for four or five winter months. They were swollen with hunger. They cringed in corners, afraid to speak, to even look people in the face.'

Even in the twenty-first century the Stalingrad battlefield still claims children as new victims. Each spring, when the snow thaws, artefacts, skeletons, and unexploded ordnance are revealed by the change of season. The artefacts can be sold to Western tourists visiting the battlefield for hard currency, so children scour the old battlefields for treasure. About six are killed or wounded each year by the old shells – numbers to be added to the casualty list of millions killed at Stalingrad.

At Moscow in the winter of 1941–42 Nazi Germany was fated not to win World War II, but at Stalingrad a year later it was doomed to lose it. The defeat of the *Afrika Korps* and the loss of North Africa by the Axis to the combined Anglo-American armies was not a fatal blow to the Third Reich though it was great for morale in Britain and the USA. The year 1942 was significant not only for the battle that led to the victory at Stalingrad, it was the point at which Soviet war production overtook that of Germany.

The Soviet Union produced 24,446 tanks, 127,000 artillery pieces, 30,400 motor vehicles and 25,436 aircraft. In addition it received Lend-Lease Aid from the United States and Great Britain. In Germany in the same year armaments

Below: Captured soldiers of the Sixth Army, a force with which their commander General Paulus had been told he 'could storm the heavens'. Their threadbare and inadequate clothing contrasts with that of the Soviet soldiers.

factories produced 6180 tanks and assault guns, 23,200 artillery pieces, 58,049 motor vehicles and 15,556 aircraft. However, these weapons were destined for North Africa and Western Europe as well as the Eastern Front.

Had they known it, the front-line statistics at the end of 1942 looked grim for the Germans in Russia. Across the whole Eastern Front they had only 495 operational tanks and assault guns facing 8500 Soviet AFVs. The Italian and Romanian Armies had effectively disappeared with only the Hungarian Second Army intact, while the German forces were short of over half a million men.

In Germany, the nation, ignorant of these grim figures, was in shock from the huge losses at Stalingrad. Goebbels mobilized the press and radio to unite the nation in martial grief. Four days of mourning were ordered.

'THE LIVING AND THE DEAD'

Detailed instructions to the press told them that the enemy were to be called 'Bolsheviks' not 'Russians'. 'The whole of German propaganda must create a myth out of the heroism of Stalingrad,' Goebbels explained. It was 'to become one of the most treasured possessions in German history'.

On 18 February 1943 he made a speech at the *Sportpalastrede* (Sport Palace) in Berlin that set the new tone for the war. Under a huge banner that read *Totaler Krieg für Zester Krieg* – Total War for Shortest War, he carried his picked audience with him in a powerful speech in which they pledged themselves for combat and sacrifice.

The Reich Minister Albert Speer recalled: 'Except for Hitler's most successful public meetings, I had never seen an audience so effectively roused to fanaticism. Back in his home, Goebbels astonished me by analyzing what had seemed to be a purely emotional outburst in terms of its psychological effect – much as an experienced actor might have done. He was also satisfied with his audience that evening. "Did you notice? They reacted to the smallest nuance and applauded at just the right moments. It was the politically best-trained audience you can find in Germany".'

> The troops of the Don Front at 16:00 on 2 February 1943 completed the rout and destruction of the encircled group of enemy forces in Stalingrad. Twenty-two divisions have been destroyed or taken prisoner.
>
> *Lieutenant-General Rokossovsky, 2 February 1943*

DER TOTALER KRIEG – TOTAL WAR

The term 'Total War' was first used by the World War I general and post-war nationalist politician Erich von Ludendorff in his book published in 1935 entitled *Der Totaler Krieg* (translated into English as *The Nation at War*). His thesis was that Total War was a type of warfare that demanded 'the strength of the people'. The mobilization in the name of Total War that followed the defeat at Stalingrad included the drafting of women into the munitions industry and armed forces. Cultural life came to a halt, with the exception of entertainment that would help to boost the workers' morale.

It was a bravura performance, excerpts from which convey the power of the speech:

'The tragic battle of Stalingrad is a symbol of heroic, manly resistance to the revolt of the steppes. It has not only a military, but also an intellectual and spiritual significance for the German people. Here for the first time our eyes have been opened to the true nature of the war. We want no more false hopes and illusions. We want to look the facts in the face, however hard and dreadful they may be. The history of our party and our state has proven that a danger recognised is a danger defeated. Our coming hard battles in the East will be under the sign of this heroic resistance. It will require previously undreamed of efforts by our soldiers and our weapons. A merciless war is raging in the East. The *Führer* was right when he said that in the end there will not be winners and losers, but the living and the dead.'

Sweating and hoarse at the close of the speech Goebbels hurled 10 questions at the fanaticized crowd, each one demanding new sacrifices. Like a Greek chorus the audience responded to his demands:

'The English maintain that the German people has lost faith in victory,' he shouted.

'I ask you: Do you believe with the *Führer* and us in the final total victory of the German people?

'I ask you: Are you resolved to follow the *Führer* through thick and thin to victory, and are you willing to accept the heaviest personal burdens in the fight for victory?

Opposite: As the last day of 1942 flutters off the calendar a Soviet Krokodil (Crocodile) cartoon shows a still arrogant Hitler confronted with the stark reality, as his Italian ally Mussolini, in the shape of a candle, melts away.

Above: The survivors – an officer with a group of cheerful soldiers of the Sixty-Second Army near Stalingrad. At first sight they appear identical in their greatcoats and shapka-ushanka *caps; however, the soldiers' coats were secured with hooks, whereas officers' coats had buttons.*

'Second: The English say that the German people are tired of fighting.

'I ask you: Are you ready to follow the *Führer* as the phalanx of the homeland, standing behind the fighting army and to wage war with wild determination through all the turns of fate until victory is ours?

'Third: The English maintain that the German people have no desire any longer to accept the government's growing demands for war work.

'I ask you: Are you and the German people willing to work, if the *Führer* orders, 10, 12 and if necessary 14 hours a day and to give everything for victory?

'Fourth: The English maintain that the German people are resisting the government's total war measures. They do not want total war, but capitulation! (Shouts: Never! Never! Never!)

'I ask you: Do you want total war? If necessary, do you want a war more total and radical than anything that we can even imagine today?

'Fifth: The English maintain that the German people have lost faith in the *Führer*.

'I ask you: Is your confidence in the *Führer* greater, more faithful and unshakeable than ever before? Are you absolutely and completely ready to follow him wherever he goes and do all that is necessary to bring the war to a victorious end? (The crowd rose as one man and thousands of voices joined in shouting: '*Führer* command, we follow!' A wave of shouts of *Heil* flowed through the hall. As if by command flags and standards were raised as the crowd honoured the *Führer*.)

'Sixth, I ask you: Are you ready from now on to give your full strength to provide the Eastern Front with the men and munitions it needs to give Bolshevism the death blow?

'Seventh, I ask you: Do you take a holy oath to the front that the homeland stands firm behind them, and that you will give them everything then need to win the victory?

'Eighth, I ask you: Do you, especially you women, want the government to do all it can to encourage German women to put their full strength at work to support the war effort, and to release men for the front whenever possible, thereby helping the men at the front?

'Ninth, I ask you: Do you approve, if necessary, the most radical measures against a small group of shirkers and black marketeers who pretend there is peace in the middle of war and use the need of the nation for their own selfish purposes? Do you agree that those who harm the war effort should lose their heads?

'Tenth and lastly, I ask you: Do you agree that above all in war, according to the National Socialist Party platform, the same rights and duties should apply to all, that the homeland should bear the heavy burdens of the war together, and that the burdens should be shared equally between high and low and rich and poor?'

Ja! – Yes! the audience bellowed back to each of these questions. When this total affirmation had been roared back, Goebbels summed up the mood of the rally with the words of the great call to war from the Prussian War against Napoleon in 1812:

'Let our war-cry be: *Nun, Volk steh auf, und Sturm brich los!* (Now the People Rise Up and Storm Break Loose!)'

The storm would break – but over Nazi Germany, as following the victory at Stalingrad, Soviet forces began their remorseless drive westwards that would end on 2 May 1945 with the capture of the German capital, Berlin.

Below: The defeated German Sixth Army trudges away from Stalingrad in January 1943. The total cost of Stalingrad to the Germans and their Axis allies was about 1.5 million men, 3500 tanks, 12,000 guns and mortars, 75,000 vehicles and 3000 aircraft.

ORDER OF BATTLE, OCTOBER 1942

GERMAN FORCES

SIXTH ARMY (von Paulus)

VIII ARMY CORPS (Heitz)

113th Infantry Division (von Armin)

76th Infantry Division (Rodenburg)

XI ARMY CORPS (Strecker)

384th Infantry Division (von Gablenz)

44th Infantry Division (Deboi)

376th Infantry Division (von Daniels)

XXIV PANZER CORPS (Hube)

16th Panzer Division (Angern)

3rd Motorized Infantry Division (Schlömer)

60th Motorized Infantry Division
   (von Arenstorff-Oyle)

94th Infantry Division (Pfeiffer)

LI ARMY CORPS (von Seydlitz-Kurzbach)

71st Infantry Division (von Hartmann)

79th Infantry Division (von Schwerin)

295th Infantry Division (Korfes)

305th Infantry Division (Steinmetz)

389th Infantry Division (Magnus)

100th Jäger Division (Sanne)
   with Croatian Regiment 369

14th Panzer Division (Kuhn)

24th Panzer Division (von Lenski)

LUFTFLOTTE IV

SOVIET FORCES

SIXTY-SECOND ARMY (Chuikov)

10th NKVD Rifle Division

13th Guards Rifle Division

37th Guards Rifle Division

39th Guards Rifle Division

45th Rifle Division

95th Rifle Division

112th Rifle Division

138th Rifle Division

193rd Rifle Division

196th Rifle Division

244th Rifle Division

284th Rifle Division

308th Rifle Division

84th Tank Brigade

137th Tank Brigade

189th Tank Brigade

92nd Marine Infantry Brigade

42nd Special Brigade

115th Special Brigade

124th Special Brigade

140th Special Brigade

160th Special Brigade

EIGHTH AIR ARMY

ORDER NR. 4
TO THE FORCES OF THE STALINGRAD AND SOUTHWEST FRONTS

1 September 1942

The Army in the Field

Comrade fighters, commanders and political workers, heroic defenders of Stalingrad!

The bitter fighting for the city of Stalingrad has been raging for months. The Germans have lost hundreds of tanks and planes. Hitler's brutalised hordes are advancing towards Stalingrad and the Volga over mountains of dead bodies of their own men and officers.

Our Bolshevik Party, our nation, our great country, have given us the task not to let the enemy reach the Volga, to defend the city of Stalingrad. The defence of Stalingrad is of decisive importance for the whole Soviet front.

Without sparing our strength and with scorn for death, we shall defy the Germans the way to the Volga and not give up Stalingrad. Each one of us must bear in mind that the capture of Stalingrad by the Germans and their advance to the Volga will give our enemies new strength and weaken our own forces.

Not one step back!

The War Council expects unlimited courage, tenacity and heroism in the fight with the onrushing enemy from all the fighters, commanders and political workers, from all the defenders of Stalingrad. The enemy must and will be smashed on the approaches to Stalingrad. Forward against the enemy! Up into the unremitting battle, comrades, for Stalingrad, for our great country!

Death to the German invader!

Commander-in-Chief of Stalingrad and Southwest Front
Signed: Colonel-General A. Yeremenko
Member of the War Council of Stalingrad and Southwest
Front Signed: Lieutenant-General N. Khrushchev

ARMY ORDER FOR THE ATTACK ON STALINGRAD

SIXTH ARMY COMMAND
OPS. DEPT. NR. 3044/42. T.S.
ARMY HQ. 19 AUGUST 1942

1. The Russian enemy will defend the Stalingrad area stubbornly. He holds the high ground on the east bank of the Don and west of Stalingrad and has built defensive positions there in great depth.

It must be assumed that he has assembled forces, including armoured brigades, ready to counter-attack, both in the Stalingrad area and in the area north of the isthmus between Don and Volga.

Therefore in the advance across the Don towards Stalingrad the Army must reckon with enemy resistance in front and with heavy counter-attacks against the northern flank of our advance.

It is possible that the annihilating blows struck during the past few weeks will have destroyed the enemy's means for fighting a determined defensive action.

2. Sixth Army will occupy the isthmus between Don and Volga north of the railway line Kalatch-Stalingrad and will protect its own northern and eastern fronts.

With this intention the Army will cross the Don between Peskovatka and Ostrovskii. Point of main effort, on either side of Vertiatchi. With standing protection being provided along the northern flank, armoured and motorized formations will advance over the high ground between the Rossoshka and the sources of the Karennaia into the area immediately north of Stalingrad, and then to the bank of the Volga, while at this same time forces will be detached to fight their way into and occupy Stalingrad from the northwest.

This advance will be accompanied by a subsidiary advance on the southern flank by a detached force advancing along the central reaches of the Rossoshka. ...

Initially a weak covering force will hold a line facing southwest towards the area between the lower reaches of the Rossoshka and the Kartovka rivers and the

Don below Kalatch. This area will be mopped up from the northeast as soon as the forces advancing towards the Kartovka have arrived. With the progress of the advance on the east bank of the Don, the forces stationed along the west bank below Malyi will be reduced in strength, since their task will then be that of a security force. This force will later cross the river on both sides of Kalatch and participate in the destruction of the enemy forces in that area.

3. Objectives:
XIV Panzer Corps will hold the west bank of the Don from Army's right-hand boundary to Lutchinskoie (excl.) and, with the 71st Infantry Division, will prepare to leave a minimum security force to hold the Don while establishing a bridgehead on either side of Kalatch from which 71st Infantry Division will advance eastwards.

Release of this Corps headquarters for further employment elsewhere is to be prepared against. LI Army Corps will seize a further bridgehead across the Don on either side of Vertiatchi. ...

As soon as the XIV Panzer Corps shall have advanced eastwards from the bridgehead, LI Army Corps will become responsible for covering the right flank of the advance. With this intention, the LI Army Corps will attack across the Rossoshka between Nijni-Alexeievski and Bol. Rossoshka, will occupy the high ground west of Stalingrad. ...

The Corps will then capture and occupy the central and southern parts of Stalingrad.

Meanwhile weak forces will form a covering line between Peskovatka and Nijni-Alexeievski. A special Army order will decide when the time has come to annihilate the Russian forces located south of this line and north of the Karpovka.

XIV Panzer Corps, after the capture of the bridgehead by LI Army Corps, will push forward through the bridgehead, advancing eastwards over the high ground north of Malrossoshka and Hp. Konaia to the Volga north of Stalingrad. It will prevent all river traffic and cut all rail communications immediately to the north of the city.

Elements of the Corps will attack Stalingrad from the northwest and occupy the northern parts of the city. Tanks will not be used for this purpose. In the north a covering line will be established running along the high ground southwest of Yersovka and south of the Gratshevaia stream. While so doing closest contact will be maintained with the VIII Army Corps advancing from the west.

VIII Army Corps will cover the northern flank of the XIV Panzer Corps. It will launch a sharp attack in a southeasterly direction from the bridgehead captured between Nijni-Gerassirnov and Ostrovskii, and then, swinging steadily north, will form a line, which must so far as possible be proof against attack by armoured forces, between Kusmitchi and Katchalinskaia.

Close contact will be maintained with XIV Panzer Corps. XI and XVII Army Corps will cover the northern flank of the Army. XI Army Corps will hold the line of the Don. XI Army Corps will release 22nd Panzer Division, as soon as possible, to Army reserve. This division will be assembled ready for action in area Dalii-Perekovskoie-Orekhovskii-Selivanov.

4. D-Day and H-hour will be announced in a special order.

5. Boundaries as given on map attached.

6. VIII Air Corps will give air support, with point of main effort initially in LI Army Corp's sector, later switching to the advance of XIV Panzer Corps.

7. Army HQ as of 21 August: Ossinovskoie.

8. Contents of this order may only be communicated to subordinate commands, and only such parts as are relevant to the future operations may be communicated. This order is not to be carried by plane. Attention will be drawn to the secret nature of such parts of this order as are communicated to subordinate commands.

The Commander-in-Chief.
Signed: PAULUS.

BIBLIOGRAPHY

ABBOT, PETER AND NIGEL THOMAS. *Germany's Eastern Front Allies 1941–45*. Men-at-Arms 131. London: Osprey Publishing, 1982.

AXWORTHY, MARK AND HORIA SERBANESCU. *The Romanian Army of World War 2*. London: Osprey Publishing, 1991.

BEKKER, CAJUS. *The Luftwaffe War Diaries*. London: Macdonald, 1964.

CARELL, PAUL. *Hitler's War on Russia*. London: Harrap, 1964.

CHAMBERLAIN, PETER AND CHRIS ELLIS. *Soviet Combat Tanks*. London: Almark Publishing, 1970.

CRAIG, WILLIAM. *The Enemy at the Gates*. London: Hodder and Stoughton, 1973.

DEAR, I.C.B. *The Oxford Companion to the Second World War*. Oxford: Oxford University Press, 1995.

DORLING KINDERSLEY. *World War II Day by Day*. London: Dorling Kindersley, 1990.

DUNNIGAN, JAMES F. (EDITOR). *The Russian Front*. London: Arms and Armour Press, 1978.

EINSIEDEL, GRAF HEINRICH VON AND MAX HASTINGS. *The Onslaught*. London: Sidgwick & Jackson, 1984.

ELLIS, JOHN. *The World War II Databook*. London: BCA, 1993.

ERICKSON, JOHN. *The Road to Stalingrad*. London: Weidenfeld and Nicolson, 1975.

GRUNBERGER, RICHARD. *A Social History of the Third Reich*. London: Weidenfeld & Nicholson, 1971.

GUDERIAN, HEINZ. *Panzer Leader*. London: Michael Joseph, 1952.

HAUPT, WERNER. *Army Group South: The Wehrmacht in Russia 1941–1945*. Atglen, Pennsylvania: Schiffer Military History, 1998.

HOFFMAN, WILLIAM. *Diary of a German Soldier*. As reproduced in CHUIKOV, VASILI (EDITOR). *The Battle for Stalingrad*. New York: Holt, Rinehart and Winston, 1964.

HÖHNE, HEINZ. *The Order of the Death's Head*. London: Secker & Warburg, 1969.

HOYT, EDWIN P. *199 Days, The Battle for Stalingrad*. London: Robson Books, 1993.

Images of War. London: Marshall Cavendish Partworks, 1990.

JUKES, GEOFFREY. *Stalingrad the Turning Point*. London: Macdonald & Co, 1968.

KARPOV, VLADIMIR. *Russia at War 1941-45*. London: Century Hutchinson, 1987.

LUCAS, JAMES. *War on the Eastern Front*. London: Greenhill Books, 1979.

MANSTEIN, ERICH VON. *Lost Victories*. London: Methuen & Co, 1958.

MARSHALL, S.L.A. (EDITOR). *The Simon and Schuster Encyclopedia of World War II*. New York: Simon and Schuster, 1978.

MAYER, S.L. (EDITOR). *The Russian War Machine*. London: Bison Books, 1977.

PRICE, DR ALFRED. *The Luftwaffe Handbook*. London: Ian Allan, 1977.

SCHRÖTER, HEINZ. *Stalingrad*. London: Michael Joseph, 1958.

SEATON, ALBERT. *The Russo-German War 1941-45*. Novato, California: Presidio Press, 1971.

SHALITO, ANTON, ILYA SAVCHENKOV AND ANDREW MOLLO. *Red Army Uniforms of World War II*. London: Windrow and Greene, 1993.

TAYLOR, BRIAN. *Barbarossa to Berlin, Volume One*. Staplehurst: Spellmount, 2003.

TM.E 30.451. *Handbook on German Military Forces*. Washington DC: US War Department, 1945.

ZALOGA, STEVEN. *The Red Army of the Great Patriotic War 1941–5*. London: Osprey Publishing, 1989.

Websites

Encyclopedia of the Holocaust, http://motlc.wiesenthal.com

German Armed Forces 1919–1945 (The), http://www.feldgrau.com

Mannerheim Line, http://www.mannerheim-line.com

Russian Battlefield, http://www.battlefield.ru/

The Voice of Russia (The battle of Stalingrad), http://www.vor.ru/English/Stalingrad/stal_06.html

Third Reich Factbook, http://www.skalman.ru/third-reich/index.htm

World War II plus 55, http://www.usswashington.com/dl17oc42.htm

INDEX

PICTURE CREDITS

AKG Images: 22, 34, 37, 42–43, 46, 63, 66–67, 94–95, 97, 126–7, 134–5;

Art-Tech: 31, 122;

Art-Tech/Aerospace: 38, 58, 59t, 62, 83, 86, 98, 106t, 123, 142, 150, 162;

Bundesarchiv: 76, 87, 112–3, 137, 144, 158, 163;

Cody Images: 8, 9, 12, 14, 16–17, 19, 27, 29, 30, 49, 54, 59b, 68, 69, 84, 92, 93, 108, 111t, 115, 116, 117, 120, 129, 130, 139, 143, 148, 149, 153, 155, 166–7, 169, 171, 174, 178, 181;

E. W. W. Fowler: 6–7, 18, 23, 32–33, 35, 70–71, 85, 90–91, 136, 146–7, 173;

MARS: 96, 103;

Mary Evans Picture Library: 132, 183;

Nik Cornish at Stavka Military Image Research: 24, 25, 40, 44, 53, 61, 78, 82, 121, 128, 140;

Novosti: 73, 88, 106b, 125, 133, 145, 156–7;

Popperfoto: 13;

Robert Hunt Library: 57;

Ukrainian State Archive: 47, 48, 52, 64, 77, 81, 105, 111, 141, 152, 160, 161, 164 (both), 170, 177, 179, 180, 184, 158;

All maps by **Peter Harper** except for the following, courtesy of **Art-Tech**: 10, 15, 26, 175.